Eternity

INSPIRATIONS FROM HEAVENLY SOURCES

BY

SHAYKH NAZIM ADIL AL-HAQQANI

FOREWORD BY

SHAYKH MUHAMMAD HISHAM KABBANI

INSTITUTE FOR SPIRITUAL AND CULTURAL ADVANCEMENT

Library of Congress Cataloging-in-Publication Data

Published and Distributed by:
Institute for Spiritual and Cultural Advancement

17195 Silver Parkway, #401
Fenton, MI 48430 USA
Tel: (888) 278-6624
Fax:(810) 815-0518
Email: staff@naqshbandi.org
Web:
http://www.naqshbandi.org

First Edition June 2010
ISBN: 978-1-930409-83-5

Shaykh Nazim Adil al-Haqqani (right) with his disciple of fifty years, Shaykh Muhammad Hisham Kabbani. Head of the world's largest Naqshbandi Sufi spiritual order, Shaykh Nazim is known for his life-altering lessons in how to discipline the ego, reach a state of spiritual surrender, and achieve true liberation from the bondage of worldly distraction and pursuit. Shaykh Hisham Kabbani, Shaykh Nazim's deputy, has accompanied the venerable shaykh on his many visits to various regions of the world, where they have met with political and religious leaders, media, and throngs of common folk.

CONTENTS

FOREWORD..VI

INTRODUCTION...X

PUBLISHER'S NOTE..XIV

NOTES..XV

1 WERE YOU CREATED FOR THIS!?..2

2 PEACE BEGINS IN YOURSELF 10

3 GOLD CRISIS 18

4 IDLENESS: SATAN'S BEST FRIEND 24

5 TODAY'S GOLDEN COW...30

6 ETERNITY 34

7 BELIEVE IN THE UNSEEN 41

8 "LORDSHIP IS MINE!" 49

9 SATANIC ADVERTISING IS EVERYWHERE.............................57

10 ALL PROPHETS HAVE THE SAME MISSION 62

11 DON'T BE LIKE CROCODILES...68

12 GREAT SAINTS ARE OCEANS 75

13 MAN WAS CREATED WEAK 83

14 ADAM'S HONORED CREATION 92

15 THE POWER OF HOPE...98

16 SEEK THE HEAVENLY WAY 106

17 MANKIND HAS LEFT GOODNESS 112

18 THE MAIN MISSION OF GOD'S MESSENGERS............120

19 SEEK TO MOVE UPWARDS..128

20 THE SOUL IS OUR SULTAN..136

21 INDIA AND PAKISTAN: ONGOING TROUBLES.............142

22 THE UNIQUENESS OF EACH CREATION 146

23 UNSEEN FOUNDATIONS..153

24 SPARKLING LIGHTS IN ENDLESS DIVINE OCEANS 162

GLOSSARY 168

FOREWORD

Bismillahi-r-Rahmani-r-Rahim
In the Name of God, the Most Beneficent, the Most Merciful

All praise is due to God Almighty, Allah the Exalted and Boun-teous and the most fluent, abundant and sweet praise and blessings be upon His perfect servant, the mercy to all creation and exemplar of perfect character, ethics and morality Prophet Muhammad ﷺ,[1] and upon his family and Companions.

This book is a compendium of *sohbets* or spiritual discourses by our master—chief of saints and reviver of the Prophetic path to di-vine enlightenment, teacher of millions and worldwide leader of the Naqshbandi-Haqqani Sufi Order, Mawlana Shaykh Muhammad Nazim Adil al-Haqqani, may Allah grant him health and long life.

It is related that in the Last Days of this world—which, based upon the predicted indications is taking place even as I pen these words—those who adhere to the pure teachings of the prophets and saints will become rare. On the contrary, those who breach the Pro-phetic Tradition, the Sunnah, will be commonplace.

No prior prophet ever mentioned in such detail what Prophet Muhammad ﷺ foretold fourteen hundred years ago. In the seventh century, he gave a precise description with specific details which were not fully understood until their manifestation in the present age. The Prophet ﷺ explained what would transpire in the Last Days so that the people witnessing those events could recognize their

---

[1] ﷺ stands for *"Salla-Llahu 'alayhi wa sallam,"* meaning, "Allah's peace and blessings be upon him," the Islamic invocation for Prophet Muhammad ﷺ.

place in time. The Prophet ﷺ warned that when bedouin Arabs compete to construct lofty buildings in the desert the Hour of Judgment would be close. He predicted that in the Last Days, trustworthy people would be vilified regarded as traitors by the people.

In a Prophet Tradition[2] it is related that a bedouin came to Prophet Muhammad ﷺ and asked when Judgment Day would take place. He said, "When the trust (al-amana) is lost, then await Judgment Day." The bedouin asked, "How will it be lost?" The Prophet ﷺ replied, "When power and authority comes in the hands of unfit persons, then wait for the Judgment Day."[3] He also has said that "the trustworthy one will be called a traitor."

As the Prophet ﷺ predicted, the psychology of people in our time is the opposite of what is prescribed and it is nearly impossible to find a trustworthy person. At the same time, everywhere on earth, different groups are busy destroying what remains of faith and spirituality, each one following its own agenda. Even "spiritual" groups and individuals slander each other, and through their corrupt behavior, support falsehood—all the while claiming to be believers.

The words of the tradition, "The trustworthy, al-amin, one will be said to be a traitor," has an interpretation. Al-Amin is one of the names of Prophet Muhammad ﷺ, and one of the signs of the Last Days is that people will attack the Prophets of God, in particular the Last Messenger, Muhammad ﷺ, and the message he brought for mankind's felicity.

Alhamdulillah—praise God—we are fortunate to be students or disciples of Mawlana Shaykh Nazim. As long as he, and Sufi masters like him, continue to teach the ways of the the prophets and saints, hope remains for humankind. For his teachings, while outwardly

---

[2] Arabic: *hadith.*

[3] *Sahih Bukhari.*

plain, are endowed with a wisdom and grace seldom found today. The shaykh's words take you back to a simpler time, when people were straightforward, when they what they meant, and when they did what they said.

May God bless you as you pick up this volume and read some of the holy teachings he has brought. It is well known in the Naqshbandi Sufi tradition, that pure words of guidance are able to elevate the reader to the stations and states described simply through the blessed character, baraka, of one authorized to teach them. Futher, these teachings will remain with you and part of you in this life and on, into the hereafter.

I am only a student and I have been learning from my teacher Mawlana Shaykh Nazim, who, despite his 85 years of age is still incredibly active spreading the teachings that come to his heart from the spiritual "central headquarters." What I saw and learned from my master I cannot express because those fountains are always pouring forth, continuously flowing. The hearts of such saints are like waterfalls: giving always and they are not asking to take anything, asking only to give.

As the world around us seems to slide further into its darkest chapter, in a time when negativity and skepticism insistently challenge faith, the faithful of all beliefs seek a beacon that will lead them to a divine shelter of peace and protection. Presented in this volume are essential aspects of a spiritual discipline which dates back to the time when Prophet Muhammad delivered the divine message—a message preserved by Sufi masters over forty generations.

In these times when Islam is more and more visible on the world stage, it is hoped through this humble work that readers will come to better understand the true teachings of Islam, namely, the universal endorsement to practice moderation and follow the middle course, to hold patience, to uphold tolerance and respect for others, to approach conflict resolution in peaceful ways, to condemn all forms of terrorism, and above all, to love God, appreciate His Divine favors, and strive in His divine service. The greatest Islamic teaching is that there is no higher station than to serve the Lord Almighty.

Shaykh Muhammad Hisham Kabbani
Fenton, Michigan
October 28, 2007

INTRODUCTION

Endless praise and thanks be to God Most High, who guides His servants to His light by means of other servants of His whose hearts He illuminates with His divine love.

Since the beginning of human history, God Most High has conveyed His revealed guidance to mankind through His prophets and messengers, beginning with the first man, Adam ☙. The prophetic line includes such well-known names as Noah, Abraham, Ishmael, Isaac, Jacob, Joseph, Lot, Moses, David, Solomon, and Jesus, peace be upon them all, ending and culminating in Muhammad, the Seal of the Prophets ☙, a descendant of Abraham ☙, ☙who brought the final revelation from God to all mankind.

But although there are no longer prophets upon the earth, the Most Merciful Lord has not left His servants without inspired teachers and guides. *Awliya*—holy people or saints—are the inheritors of the prophets. Up to the Last Day, these "friends of God," the radiant beacons of truth, righteousness and the highest spirituality, will continue in the footsteps of the prophets, calling people to their Lord and guiding seekers to His glorious Divine Presence.

One such inspired teacher, a shaykh or *murshid* of the Naqshbandi Sufi Order, is Shaykh Nazim Adil al-Qubrusi al-Haqqani. A descendant not only of the Holy Prophet Muhammad ☙ but also of the great Sufi masters 'Abul Qadir Gilani and Jalaluddin Rumi, Shaykh Nazim was born in Larnaca, Cyprus, in 1922 during the period of British rule of the island. Gifted from earliest childhood with an extraordinarily spiritual personality, Shaykh Nazim received his spiritual training in Damascus at the hands of Maulana Shaykh 'Abdullah ad-Daghestani (fondly referred to as "Grandshaykh"), the mentor of such well-known figures as Gurjieff and J. G. Bennett, over a period of forty years.

Before leaving this life in 1973, Grandshaykh designated Shaykh Nazim as his successor. In 1974, Shaykh Nazim went to London for the first time, thus initiating what was to become a yearly practice during the month of Ramadan up to 1990s. A small circle of followers began to grow around him, eagerly taking their training in the ways of Islam and *tariqah* at his hands.

From this humble beginning, the circle has grown to include thousands of *murids* or disciples in various countries of the world, among whom are to be found many eminent individuals, both religious and secular. Shaykh Nazim is a luminous, tremendously impressive spiritual personality, radiating love, compassion and goodness. He is regarded by many of his *murids* as the *qutub* or chief saint of this time.

The shaykh teaches through a subtle interweaving of personal example and talks ("Associations" or *sohbets*), invariably delivered extempore according to the inspirations that are given to him. He does not lecture, but rather pours out from his heart into the hearts of his listeners such know-ledge and wisdoms as may change their innermost beings and bring them toward their Lord as His humble, willing, loving servants.

Shaykh Nazim's language and style are unique, so eloquent, moving and flavorful that not only do his teachings seem inspired but also his extraordinary use of words. His *sohbets* represent the teachings of a twentieth century Sufi master, firmly grounded in Islamic orthodoxy, speaking to the hearts of the seekers of God of any faith tradition from his own great, wide heart, in a tremendous outpouring of truth, wisdom and divine knowledge which is surely unparalleled in the English language, guiding the seeker toward the Divine Presence.

The sum total of Shaykh Nazim's message is that of hope, love, mercy and reassurance. In a troubled and uncertain world in which old, time-honored values have given place to new ones of confused origins and unclear prospects, in which a feeling heart and thinking mind is constantly troubled by a sense of things being terribly disordered and out of control, in which the future seems forebodingly dark and uncertain for humanity, he proclaims God's love and care for His servants, and invites them to give their hearts to Him.

Shaykh Nazim holds out to seekers the assurance that even their smallest steps toward their Lord will not go unnoticed and unresponded to. Rather than threatening sinners with the prospect of eternal Hell, he offers hope of salvation from the Most Merciful Lord, and heart-warming encouragement and incentive for inner change and growth. As one who has traversed every step of the seeker's path and reached its pinnacle, he offers both inner and practical guidelines for attaining the highest spiritual goals.

This book consists of Shaykh Nazim's talks from the February of 2002 through April. Each of these talks is entirely extempore, as Shaykh Nazim never prepares his words but invariably speaks according to inspirations coming to his heart.

In keeping with the shaykh's methodology—the methodology of the prophets, particularly of the Last Prophet, Muhammad, peace be upon him and upon them all, and of the Qur'an itself—of reinforcing vital lessons by repetition and reiteration, the same themes and anecdotes recur again and again. The talks seem to come in unannounced clusters, centering around a primary theme, which develops and evolves according to the spiritual state of the listeners. Thus, Shaykh Nazim may cite the same verse or *hadith*, or tell the same tale on different occasions, each time reinforcing a slightly different aspect of the eternal message of love and light which is Islam.

The shaykh's talks are interspersed with words and phrases from Arabic and other Islamic languages. These are translated either in the text itself, in footnotes the first time they occur, or, for general and recurrent terms, in the Glossary at the end of this volume. Qur'anic verses quoted in the text have been referenced for easy access.

Every attempt has been made to retain the shaykh's original language with minimal editing. However, since these talks were transcribed from audio tapes recorded on amateur equipment by listeners for their own personal use (or, in the case this volume, by a *murid* extremely familiar with the shaykh's language and ideas, by hand), some inadvertent errors may have found their way into the text. For these, we ask Allah's forgiveness and your kind indulgence. May He fill your heart with light and love as you read and reflect upon these inspired words, and guide you safely to His exalted Divine Presence.

PUBLISHER'S NOTE

Shaykh Nazim is fluent in Arabic, Turkish and Greek, and semi-fluent in Engish. Over three decades, his llectures have been transated into twenty or more languages, and to date have reached the furthest corners of the globe. We sincerely hope the reader will appreciate the author's unique language style, which has been painstakingly preserved in this work.

As some of the terms in this book may be foreign, to assist the reader we have provded transliterations, as well as a detailed glossary.

NOTES

The following symbols are universally recognized and have been respectfully included in this work:

The symbol ﷺ represents *sall-Allahu 'alayhi wa sallam* (Allah's blessings and greetings of peace be upon him), which is customarily recited after reading or pronouncing the holy name of Prophet Muhammad ﷺ.

The symbol عليه السلام represents *'alayhi 's-salam* (peace be upon him/her), which is customarily recited after reading or pronouncing the holy names of the other prophets, family members of Prophet Muhammad ﷺ, the pure and virtuous women in Islam, and the angels.

The symbol ﷜/﷞ represents *radi-Allahu 'anhu/ 'anha* (may Allah be pleased with him/her), which is customarily recited after reading or pronouncing the holy names of Companions of the Prophet ﷺ.

In the Name of Allah, The Beneficent and The Munificent

This, my English, is strange English. Not everyone can understand because, *subhanallah*, meanings are coming to my heart, and when running in my heart to give to you, I am using any means – from here, from there - bringing any word which may be useful.

I am like a person waiting for water to run out from the faucet. Then, when suddenly it comes, and he knows the water is going to be turned off, stop running, he may take any container – with a no-good shape, broken on one side, or anything he may find there – quickly bringing them to take that water and store it. Therefore, when meanings are coming to my heart, I am trying to explain with any word, which you may understand or not. But you must understand, because we have a saying, "Listeners must be more wise than speakers." Therefore, when inspiration comes, we must explain.

They are living words, not plastic – bananas, plastic; apples, plastic, and grapes. Even if the shapes are not much, they are living, real. When you are going to arrange them in measures, good system; when you are going to be engaged by outside forms, you are losing meanings. ▲

1

Were You Created for This!?

> This is a humble place, a "supermarket" where a seeker can find whatever he is seeking, a place tied to the earth. It is against nature to live in concrete houses, and to construct and use tall buildings, and whoever is not friendly with nature, nature will not be friendly with him. Humbleness is tied to the earth and is the sign of servanthood. The mission of the prophets and their inheritors is to call people to servanthood. The story of Sultan Ibraham Adham and the hunt. Nature serves those who keep their servanthood to their Creator, but those who do not keep it quickly go down. Those who follow Shaytan fall into troubles and sufferings, but those who keep servanthood to their Lord are protected.

Bismillahi-r-Rahmani-r-Rahim. This is an Association.[1] It is a market but not a supermarket—a flea market. All things, every kind, whatever you are asking for, you can find.

A person may go to a flea market, walking up and down. If there is anything interesting in it, he may ask, he may buy. No one is forcing him to buy something. If he is interested, he may buy; if not interested, he may go around, up and down, and he may leave, and people they are not fighting with him or quarreling. No—okay.

This is a market. You can find everything that belongs to your life, here and Hereafter. If you are interested in something, it may be

---

[1]Arabic, *suhbah,* Turkish, *sohbet,* meaning companionship, in a specific sense, to associate or keep company with a sheikh or spiritual guide.

good for you in this life or the next life. If you are not interested in anything, okay. You are going to be dust.

It is a humble place. It is not carefully prepared for people to take their full rest, no. We—when I am saying "We," that belongs to the Prophet, ﷺ, and whoever belongs to the Seal of the Prophets, they were never interested, during this life, in more than they were in need of, for building, for eating, for dressing, for whatever they needed. They were happy when they were at the lowest level of life here, because the lowest life is closest to the ground. To come from skyscrapers, these towers of Nimrods—it is not easy to come from high floors, upper floors, and to reach the bottom of earth; it is so difficult for our egos. But whoever is living, for example, in tents, they are living on the earth, or whoever is building a simple building of earth, not of concrete.

Concrete buildings are against mankind and are fighting mankind, giving trouble. Therefore, when people left off living in simple homes that are built of mud, of earth, and began to live in concrete buildings, first troubles began to increase for their physical beings because our structure is just the opposite of concrete materials. Man is not created from concrete elements, no. Our structure, physical being, is created from earth. Therefore, men are reaching familiarity when they live in earthen buildings, mud buildings, wooden buildings, not concrete. Our physical beings are never happy to live in concrete buildings.

That is one of the biggest problems for the life of man on earth. Concrete buildings are fighting mankind. It is a satanic invention that Shaytan brought to people, to live in concrete building, because it harms people's physical beings. And Shaytan is very happy to make people live in concrete buildings because their sufferings are beginning when they enter; when first stepping into them, their sufferings are beginning. And we are looking and seeing the biggest advertising on cement and concrete buildings.[2] Everywhere—people are so heedless; they are destroying their healthy buildings that they were living in and building in their place concrete buildings.[3] In the summertime they are like ovens, in wintertime they are like frigidaires. I am fighting but no one is listening; no one is listening. And troubles are becoming more and more.

Everywhere, no more old villages, no more old towns, no more old cities are remaining. They are carrying them away and building concrete buildings, such ugly buildings. And they are putting so many floors, one after another, trying to reach higher than others as much as possible, and it is mentioned in Holy Prophet's miraculous news about Last Days that people are going to be occupied by which of them is going to build higher buildings than others.[4]

And you heard about one of highest buildings on earth, what happened for it. In two minutes, what took perhaps ten years to build was just finished, and everyone that was in it, also, because angels are cursing those people who want to be higher. After two floors, the angels are saying, "O 'adduwullah, enemy of Allah, what are you asking to do? You are asking to do the same thing that Nimrod did!" (he was asking to reach the Heavens and fight the Lord of the Heavens, and he built that huge building in Babylon). "Where are you going? Not enough space for you on earth? Is space on earth finished that you are doing like this?"

And what happened in Turkey three years ago—such high buildings, falling down like cartons and killing people through earth-

---

[2]Referring to the plethora of advertisements in Turkey for cement and concrete.

[3]In Turkey and many places in the Muslim world, people live in apartments in concrete buildings.

[4]Mentioned in Muslim, 001, and in a number of *ahadith* in Bukhari.

quake. Mud buildings, wooden buildings are never affected by earthquake, no. And after two floors there is danger.

Allah likes His servants to be humble. Those people, with their high buildings, are becoming such proud ones. I am sorry that Arabs are reading the hadith of the Holy Prophet, ﷺ, that the angels are cursing whoever makes high buildings, and yet they are building against the Prophet's warning, blaming those people who were going to build high buildings and giving their description, that they were going to be shepherds of camels or other animals, coming to the holy land of Hijaz,[5] and they should be in competition for buildings, which ones were going to be made higher. This it is written. They know it through the holy books of hadith and they are against the *wasiyah*, the advice of Rasul, ﷺ, his warning.

We are saying that all prophets were advising that people must be close to nature, and when a person comes close to nature, nature is going to be friendly to him, no harm coming to him. When they are living in high buildings, they not friendly with nature, they are escaping from nature, because when they are in huge cities, nature has just disappeared; only concrete, concrete, concrete buildings, towers of Nimrods—full of them. They are fighting nature and nature is fighting them.

All prophets were making man to be humble, to be close to nature. Whoever is close to nature is going to be humble, and servanthood needs humbleness. Those people, they are not humble. Humble people may put their foreheads on the earth, moving to Allah Almighty easily, and nature protects them, no harm coming to them. But those people who are living in Nimrod's towers, they can't live without pills—pills, tablets, countless kinds of medicine they are using for eating, for drinking, for sleeping, for resting. For

---

[5] *Bukhari*, 1:47, 6:300, and *Muslim*, 1.

everything that they want to use their physical body for, they can't move, can't work, without using those artificial, harmful medicines.

Therefore, Shaytan is urging people to build higher and higher buildings so that they should fall into troubles and sufferings, and they should be in need of medicines. Therefore, they are going and coming, Shaytan arranging for mankind, for foolish mankind, for heedless mankind, for unbelieving mankind, doing for them what it is worst for them, and their punishment is beginning on earth without going to the graveyard.

This is a humble place. And you are coming from different countries, huge cities, huge buildings; you are living modern life. Here perhaps it is going to be strange or funny for people, how they are sitting in such a place, like a stable for horses. (I am not saying a stable of donkeys, no; a stable of horses. I am not saying camels. Camels are never coming in this stable, no. They are always free, outside; they are very proud.). And *alhamdulillah*, we are happy. So many people are coming with a handful of pills and here they are leaving them, saying, "No need, no need here—finished." We are trying to be friendly to nature and nature is ready to accept our friendship because we have honor, and it is honor for nature that we are walking on it. But these high-building people, they are never walking walk on nature—in their high buildings, and when they are coming down, they are quickly getting in their cars, never stepping on the earth, escaping from nature.

Servanthood begins with humbleness. Therefore, all prophets were calling people to be humble ones. And that invitation, that calling people to servanthood, never stops. From the first man, they just began to call people to servanthood.

So many centuries have passed but still people are being called to servanthood, nothing else. Don't think that high buildings are preventing ourselves from calling people to servanthood. Those

6

proud ones must be called to be servants. I am calling everyone to servanthood. That is the mission of all prophets and whoever is following them, following their steps, and it is not going to finish. Some people among mankind, even though they are just falling into Heedless-ness Oceans, some people around those oceans are calling them, "O people, come to servanthood! You have been created for servanthood, not anything else."

It is an old story, a historical story, that is written in traditional books: One of the famous *sultans* who was one of most respectful toward *Shari'ah*, the heavenly rules in the Holy Qur'an, was Ibrahim Adham Sultan—Ibrahim, Allah bless him, the *sultan* of Balkh in Afghanistan, Baluchistan, 'Ajamistan. He was a magnificent *sultan*, a powerful *sultan*.

He was respecting Allah Almighty's orders, Allah Almighty giving him more honor, and he was magnificent among states, among people. And he had a hobby, hunting; he liked hunting too much.

Once he was chasing a game on his horse. From the right hand, he heard a sound that was clear to understand, and it was saying in Arabic, "*Ya Ibrahim, a-li hadha khuliqta?*" (saying, "*Ya Ibrahim*," not saying "*Sultan*"). "Do you think you have been created for that purpose?"

"*A-li hadha khuliqta?*" Then, from the other side, another sound came to him, saying, "*Au bi-hadha umirta?*" The first was saying, "Do you think that you have been created for hunting?" and the second was saying to him, "Or have you been ordered to do this?"

Taking reins of his horse, stopping, turning back, leaving that game and coming—these two words were enough for him for awakening. He just woke up and came, because he understood that he had not been created or had not been ordered except for servanthood—finished. He came to himself through these words, just making him to understand what was his mission, our mission—

servanthood. And our mission is to call people to servanthood, nothing else.

As long as we are running away, we are falling into many more crises and troubles and sufferings and miseries, till we come back to ourselves. People are thinking that when they are running to reach something, there is going to be much more benefit and rest and a comfortable life for them. Can't be! But those who are leaving such things and coming to servanthood, nature has just been ordered to carry the burden of servants. Never are servants carrying any heavy burden on their shoulders; nature is carrying. Not any *hem*[6]—they do not have any care about anything because nature is under their service, nature is serving them.

Now people are not keeping servanthood to Allah but they are serving nature for living, and they are not living properly—so difficult. Everything they are eating is becoming like poison, everything they are drinking is becoming like poison, everything they are looking at is poisoned, everything they are turning towards is becoming poisoned, poisoned winds coming to them, poisoned winds making their physical beings quickly to lose the brightness of their faces, of their bodies, inside and outside, blowing on them a kind of poisoned air.

Therefore, men and women, quickly their faces are becoming ugly; from everywhere are coming those windy poisons, making them ugly. But for those who are keeping servanthood, the winds of Paradise are coming to them. They are coming for servanthood after midnight, and winds from Paradise are coming to them, that wind coming.

O people, try to keep servanthood to Allah Almighty. You should be happy here and Hereafter, no trouble for you. Don't fol-

---

[6]Care, anxiety, trouble.

low the first-class troublemaker, Shaytan; don't follow him. Anyone following Shaytan will fall into troubles, but those who are not following Shaytan will never fall into troubles—finished.

May Allah forgive me and bless you. For the honor of the most honored servant of Allah Almighty, Sayyidina Muhammad: *Fatehah.*[7] ▲

---

[7] And the good outcome is with Allah. For the honor of [*Surat al-*] *Fatehah.*

2

PEACE BEGINS IN YOURSELF

"Bismillahi-r-Rahmani-r-Rahim" is the key to all things. Western nations are competing in technology, supposing that it gives them authority, while at the same time heedless Muslims imagine that by adopting the Western principles which produce Western technology, they will reach high civilization. But this technology inevitably predisposes to violence, destructiveness and eventually nuclear war. Despite this, people are not interested in spirituality and consequently are becoming more and more violent. People are asking for power but the more power they have, the more problems are increasing. The leaders of Muslims do not accept the saying of *"Bismillahi-r-Rahmani-r-Rahim"* but instead invoke the name of their leaders, living or deceased, to control people. But Muslims who do not use *"Bismillahi-r-Rahmani-r-Rahim"* will never attain anything in this world or the Hereafter.

A'udhu bil-Lahi min ash-Shaytani-r-rajim, bismillahi-r-Rahmani-r-Rahim. Bismillahi-r-Rahmani-r-Rahim. Meded, ya sultan al-awliya.

"Bismillahi-r-Rahmani-r-Rahim, In the name of Allah, the Merciful, the Beneficent" that is the key of the holy land. *"Bismillahi-r-Rahmani-r-Rahim,"* that is crown of Islam on the heads of Muslims— the crown, the crown. You must try to keep it. Every closed door opens through *"Bismillahi-r-Rahmani-r-Rahim."* Every treasure from the earth and in the Heavens is going to be opened through *"Bismillahi-r-Rahmani-r-Rahim,"* and that is the sign of sincerity, of obedience.

An obedient person, his sign is to say *"Bismillahi-r-Rahmani-r-Rahim,"* but Shaytan is trying to make Muslims, also, not to say *"Bismillahi-r-Rahmani-r-Rahim"*. If for every occasion, for every work, that he wants to do, a Muslim says continually *"Bismillahi-r Rahmani-r-Rahim,"* Muslims blame him. And Muslims are heedless. The most heedless people on earth now are Muslims.

Christians, they are on their way, claiming that they are Christians. It is well-known that from the beginning they lost their way and their heedlessness just began from their childhood and continued. Muslims, they are on right path, but in their heedlessness they are blaming Islam and its principles, and trying to change Islamic principles into non-Islamic principles that are all artificial.

The whole non-Muslim world is using imitation mind-products instead of the true principles that were sent from the Heavens to mankind, and they are insisting and saying, "We can find or we can bring better principles than Muslims are using." No! And they are making a big, big advertising on that point, and our heedless Muslims, they have been cheated and they are saying, "Western civilization, it has reached a high technology. Through that technology they are now going up in space; they are traveling, they are looking around," and their measure of civilization or to be at the highest level of mankind is to reach more technological authority.

For whichever country has reached more authority from technology, they are saying, "They are Number One." For example, they are saying, "Americans' technology is much more powerful than Russians' technology. Russians, they are not reaching the level of Americans' technology." And European, euro-countries, among themselves each one is claiming that they are at the top level of technology.

German people are saying, "M-mm, you can't reach! Where we are now, you can't reach." French people are saying, "No. We are making Mirages, Phantoms, going like this and coming like that," and there is competition between French and Germans. Russia is saying, "I don't care, my technology is best," and they are fifty years behind new technology but they are saying, "We are first-class." Italians are saying, "Ah-h, we don't care too much about that. Let them to fight each other," and several European, Western countries are fighting about which one's technology is higher, and they are thinking that the balance of civilization depends on their technology levels.

No! That is their heedlessness, and our Muslim leaders and our communities who have been cheated with wrong thinking, believe that whoever has that nuclear power is on top. "Ah!! Ah!! We must acquire nuclear bombs, nuclear power. Our principles have not given a chance for us up to today. We must change our principles into Western principles. We must throw them away and we must take Western principles to reach to their level."

And I am asking, "To where are they reaching through their weapons?" Do you think that it is a civilization? Nuclear weapons do not make people live happily and peacefully in communities; nuclear weapons are intended to destroy cities, towns, farms, men, women, children, animals, forests—everything. That is their understanding of civilization.

If to kill and destroy is the measure of civilization, may Allah curse them! If that is their measure of civilization, to make as many people die as possible and to destroy their cities and towns and villages—if we can say that is civilization, Allah curse them and their technology. But they are making such wrong advertising. There is never going to be any principle for humanity among technological principles.

Technology is just occupied or used by the material world, and you can't find good characteristics in it because technology belongs to the material world and the material world is nothing apart from our five senses. Therefore, technology can't be a measure of civilization. But what shall we do? Our heedless leaders leading Islamic countries are thinking that technology is the first means for reaching civilization, and they are cheating people and they are liars.

Now the whole world is on the line of technology, making a competition about which is going to be the first one, and for that purpose they are quarreling and fighting, and the final result is going to be against themselves because technology should destroy everything, first their civilization. Western civilization is going to die or to be destroyed.

To be destroyed means to die, but no thinking about it, neither Europeans, Western countries, or no-mind people from Muslims, heedless Muslims, asking for the principles of Western countries that we call a *wahshi* civilization.[1] European civilization or Western civilization represents wildness, violence.

For animals it is normal to be wild because they are not educated; no universities or elementary schools or secondary schools or academies for animals. But you, mankind—it is a blame for mankind who are being educated through so many schools, higher educational institutions, and still you are graduating as a violent person. A violent one is worse than a wild animal. No blame for animals to be wild, but for man to be violent, it is the biggest blame on them, although they are educated and graduated.

That violence is coming through technology. People are not educated in spiritual values; no spirituality for mankind now. Do you think that spirituality is for animals in jungles—we are going to teach them spirituality? If you are not interested in spirituality, spirituality

---

[1] Savage, brutish, untamed, wild, uncivilized.

is for *whom*—for mountains, for jungles, or for the inhabitants of mountains, of jungles?

It is not for them. Spirituality it is for ourselves. But the twenty-first century's people are only interested in technology, never interested in spiritual values, to learn them, and materialism is leading them to violence. Everywhere you are looking, ninety-nine per cent of the news is about violence among people, among communities, among nations, among races, among continents, through oceans. And look, through their TVs, only advertising and wanting to teach youngsters violence, nothing else—to kill, to destroy, to burn, nothing else.

That is their civilization. They must be blamed and they must be ashamed of saying that they are civilized people. And as long as people are not taking care of their spiritual beings, they should be much more violent.

Now people are running through the streets, thousands of people. They are saying, "We are not asking for war, we are asking for peace." I am asking, "Did you bring peace to yourself first of all? If you have brought peace to yourself and everyone brings peace to themselves, then that community is going to be in peace." But if you find among them someone that is not reaching to peace, that person is making the whole community unhappy and no peace for that community.

People are lying now and their leaders are lying, because every country is governed by politicians, and the capital of politicians is to cheat people and to tell lies. That is politicians' importance, nothing else, and they want through that to reach power according to their minds, according to their knowledge.

If a person reaches power, a power-point, they should be happy during this life—and they are not saying "The next life"; they should be so happy to reach one point of power. In the nineteenth century up to the twentieth century, the power-point was only one, one person; he had the power-point. But now, countless people are coming and sitting on power-points and they are asking to do everything, through that power that has been given, that is honor and peace for themselves.

The more people are getting to a power-point, the more troubles and sufferings are increasing. As much as they are making it less, less, less, troubles are coming down, coming to the point of zero. But the biggest satanic teachings are through democracy, making a possibility for everyone to reach a power-station or a power-point and to do as he likes. And they are never reaching pleasure through their powers because any time our authority for reaching a power-station, power-point, becomes more and more, our troubles and sufferings are going to increase more and more.

Therefore, we are speaking now about saying *"Bismillahi-r-Rahmani-r-Rahim."* That is our honor, the honor of servanthood, to say *"Bismillahi-r-Rahmani-r-Rahim."* But those heedless people, ignorant people, no-honor people who are not using the Holy Names of Allah Almighty but they are asking *their* names to be said, as in our countries, they are not making people to say the name of Allah Almighty, but for every occasion they are saying someone's name: "He said like this, he orders like this, he advised like this." They are trying to put a person that has disappeared in place of the Lord of the Heavens, and they are so proud to mention his name and his principles, that have no value. And if you are saying *"Bismillahi-r-Rahmani-r-Rahim,"* they are preparing to fight to you, saying, "For what? For what are you saying *'Bismillahi-r-Rahmani-r-Rahim'*? Only in your mosques you can say *'Bismillahi-r-Rahmani-r-Rahim,'* not anywhere else—no! In community functions you can't use it. For community functions you must say, 'Our leader was saying this.'"

You can't say *"Bismillahi-r-Rahmani-r-Rahim,"* according to Allah Almighty's order, saying, "No! You must not be in our time and you must not be in our countries, you must not be among ourselves. Your principles are not suitable for our community's purposes."

For community functions, they are preventing to be said or to begin, "By the name of Allah Almighty, All-Merciful, Most Beneficent and Most Munificent. We are working for His honor." They are not saying this, and they are taking away the saying of this word, "We are working for the honor of our Lord." They are not saying this; they are saying, "Because our leader once upon a time said like this, like that, and we are following him."

I am asking, "Your leaders that are doing everything against heavenly principles—from where did they graduate?"

They are surprised. "We don't know."

What is that? "Graduated from where, from which university, and who gave them these diplomas?"

Heh, they are surprised! I am saying, "From Shaytan—they were all of them graduated by, through Shaytan." Therefore they are saying for community functions, "Our leader was saying like this." Your leader was like yourself, and if he passed away, go and open his grave and look at what is lying there. Look!

Still you are saying this, ordering us? What is this? All of them were graduated by Shaytan, Shaytan giving to them a Ph.D. to make them lose the right path and come to the wrong, wrong way.

When you are saying *"Bismillahi-r-Rahmani-r-Rahim,"* Allah Almighty sends to you angels to keep you on His true way, towards His direct pleasure. Therefore Shaytan very angry if a person says *"Bismillahi-r-Rahmani-r-Rahim."*

No way to the land of blessings except for those whom they are saying *"Bismillahi-r-Rahmani-r-Rahim."* Whoever is saying *"Bismilahi-r-Rahmani-r-Rahim,"* they may reach the holy land, the land of Paradise, or they will never, never, never even smell its good scent, not to mention coming into it. The good, beautiful scents of Paradise are coming from a distance of five years'; from a five years' distance, a *mu'min*, a believer may smell the beautiful scents of Paradise. But those people who are objecting to *"Bismillahi-r-Rahmani-r-Rahim,"* they are not even going to smell the scent of Paradise from such a distance.

May Allah bless you and forgive me. For the honor of the Seal of the Prophets, the most honored servant of Allah Almighty, Sayyidina Muhammad, ﷺ: *Fatehah.* ▲

3

GOLD CRISIS

> It is from the divine ordering that creatures sleep during nighttime, and man too is programmed to sleep at night. However, since the invention of electricity, the rhythm of days and nights has been disrupted in our lives, and in our time night life has reached its peak. This is from Satan's handiwork. The huge sums on nighttime enjoyments play a major role in current economic conditions, and if night life were banned, the current "economic crisis," which is rather a crisis of wastage, would soon be resolved. This crisis is inextricably connected to the replacement of gold currency with paper money, against all historical precedent, resulting in careless and lavish spending which would not occur with gold, which has an intrinsic value. Until nations restore gold as the basis of their economic structure, the global economy will not be able to attain stability.

Meded, ya sayyidi. Allahumma, la takilna ila anfusina tarfata 'ayn. A'da l-'aduw nafsika-l-lati bayna jambayk.[1]

It is an Association. This is not a schoolyard, this is not a lecture. It is an Association for the sake of Allah Almighty and for the honor of His most honored servant, the Seal of the Prophets, the Honor of Creation, Sayyidina Muhammad, ﷺ. May Allah bless him and peace be upon him from pre-eternity up to eternity, and may

---

[1]"The worst of enemies is your *nafs*,lower self, which is between your two sides." (Hadith)

18

Allah keep us to be his followers here and to be his neighbors in Paradise.

Days are running. Weeks are following one after another, months running one after another, years also running one after the other, and centuries also running, and another one running after it and asking to join it, as a river runs, runs, and reaches an ocean, and there it settles. Running rivers, running waters, springs, are asking to reach to somewhere, and the final point, the final goal for rivers, it is to reach to an ocean.

Perhaps they know or not, but they are running, and finally they are reaching an ocean and seeing that its waters can't be measured. They are coming with a handful of water, but they are seeing that that ocean is not a handful of water. When they are reaching and finding an unlimited ocean, according to their knowledge, they are going to be in peace through reaching that ocean and their running is just finishing. And their waters are joining oceans and oceans' waters are trying to rush on a continent. The ocean is trying to come out, its waves coming and trying to reach *qarrahs*, continents, running; the ocean is trying to come, to cover everything. The same waters, some of them are running to reach oceans and some waters that belong to oceans are trying to come to cover continents.

And we are running, every day running. From morning we are awakening and we are finding ourselves running up to evening. At evening we are settling, sitting down, no more distance for us to run on, night preventing it, saying, "No more running now for you. You have reached an ocean, the ocean of nights. You must rest. No more running."

Daytime, like rivers, everyone is running, but at nighttime, when darkness comes and people are reaching the ocean, oceans of darkness, they are coming down, sitting down. *Wa ja'alna nawmakum subatan*,[2] He made nighttime for resting—for resting. You can't stop yourself from resting. Therefore, night work is forbidden for people. If not obligatory, everyone must rest, and though for some reasons some people must be awake, for all of mankind who are reaching the ocean of darkness, they must take their rest.

Now mankind they are never listening and hearing and obeying heavenly orders; they have left them. But also on earth there are some obligatory laws that we must obey—natural orders, we may say, natural harmony. Nature is asleep at nighttime because nighttime's darkness carries an atmosphere that is full of fear, and through fear there is *haybat*, awe.

Nighttime has too much of that. In the daytime at the same place you do not feel that, but when the curtains of the oceans of darkness come down, you feel fear within yourself. Therefore, people, if they are far away from their homes, want to quickly reach home before that curtain of darkness comes down fully. That is the ordering of the Creator, Allah Almighty's divine wisdoms, making that manifestation for mankind.

Everything, everyone must take their correct positions for night. Before this century, beginning from the nineteenth and twentieth century, people wanted to cut off the curtains of Darkness Oceans and to make artificial light. Then they found through electricity a secret power that gives lights and illuminates darkness. Before, they were using lamps or candles, such things, and it was not powerful enough to take away the curtains of darkness, but when electricity was granted to mankind, they began to use that power as light to make artificial day during night.

That is the will of Satan, satanic will. It is not the divine Will but it is satanic will, to make people be unrested, and when people

---

[2]*"And We made your sleep [a means of] rest."* (78:9)

are unrested at nighttime, in the daytime they are never going to be rested. They should be tired and more tired, wanting to occupy themselves day and night.

Therefore, night life began to appear through electricity and it spread everywhere, everywhere, and now we are at the top point for night life. People are not obeying the holy commands that the Lord of Heavens, our Creator, put, saying, "O people, I made daytime for your work, to run and to look after your sustenance,[3] and I made nighttime a rest time for you."

That is a holy order and holy manifestation, holy arrangement, for the life of mankind. But Shaytan is doing the opposite, saying, "No. I am making for you artificial day with so many kinds of lights," and bringing to their service neon lamps, so many kinds, making such an appearance at nighttime that people are running to it. Even though they are finished, they are saying, "We must look, we must go, we must sit, we must eat, we must drink, we must dance, we must play. Oh! It is our holy time, nighttime. We must not sleep; no! Allah is saying 'Sleep' but we are saying 'No—look!'"

Allah is saying, "Take your rest." They are saying, "No. We are young people, we are not in need of rest. Daytime, nighttime, we can work. Daytime, like donkeys, we may work and at nighttime, also, we are going to enjoy ourselves." And every problem is coming after this, people following Shaytan.

No economic crisis! They are liars, they are liars. If those people that are living on earth—perhaps they are six billion people—if six billion people did not come out one night, no more crisis; finished. What are they spending every night, six billion people—how much, can you think? Trillions of dollars, not millions—trillions of dollars they are wasting for one night. If for one night everything were

---

[3] *"And We made the day for livelihood."* (78:11)

made to run in its original path, no more crisis. Yes! It is not a financial, economic crisis, no. It is a crisis of wasting.

They are not saying, *never* saying "wasting crisis," not "economic". Why is the economy coming down? For what? The world is the same world, people are the same people. You can reach so many. How can it be a economic crisis? Why are you not saying the true name for this crisis? Why are you not saying "It is crisis of foolishly wasting, abnormally wasting"?

Why are they not saying this? *Why?* If you prevent night life, three days will make the whole world go up. If you say, "Three days is so short," I may say "Thirty days." If this is not enough, forty days is okay for everything on earth. But Shaytan is not letting them say "Wasting crisis," saying "Economic crisis, the dollar coming up, Turkish money coming down, and finally we must cover this foolish wasting, we must have marks, francs, liras, pesos all together in one currency—the euro!"

However many names you are changing on that paper, it has no value. Look! [He takes out euros.] How much must I give? Before, it was okay to give coins, not like this. When a person used gold coins, he thought about it, when he was asked, saying, "I am giving so much gold." He couldn't give gold but this may easily be given because it is paper. [He makes a loud ejaculation.] Five, five; take, take—yes. So easy. But gold—can you give?

Satanic directions are cheating all mankind, Shaytan directing people, saying, "Don't use gold, use paper," because paper is so easy to be given but when you are giving gold, you are saying, "How can I give this?"

COMMENT: Checkbook is easier.

SHAYKH: Checkbook is easier than this, writing by numbers—finished. A million, doesn't matter. That is the real reason that no sociologists or philosophers or economists are able to speak on this point. You can't find either in the East or the West what we are saying now. Heh—it is paper, so easy to be given, but gold, no. Gold belongs to you. You feel gold like your soul and want to keep it. You can't waste gold.

Therefore, in our days, we are in a wasting economy. They invented paper money for what? To be easy to waste because no one is taking any care of it, but gold—never! Therefore, it is wanted that people use paper money because it is easy to give, no value. But gold—you are looking and keeping it in your hands. "Give it to me." "No, no."

Therefore, I am always saying, "Do you think that by your rules, on a paper foundation, the economy can stand up?" And people are surprised.

The economy must use real value, the real value that Allah Almighty sent to man to keep his values stable, sending to them gold and silver. That is a heavenly order, and until you are coming to real values, no hope for your economy to stand up because it is finished. No more, no more can cardboard and paper carry this heavy building—finished. World economy needs a strong base to be built on. Anything other than gold and silver can't be a foundation for your building. Come to real values; you should reach the solution. All others are satanic works.

No one can make any objection to my words now throughout East and West, throughout the whole world—finished. May Allah forgive me and bless you. It is enough, it is enough. I am asking for more honor for the Honor of Mankind, for the Honor of the Universes, Sayyidina Muhammad, ﷺ—for his honor to be sent to us real guides who have good understanding, to save humanity on earth soon. ▲

4

IDLENESS: SATAN'S BEST FRIEND

Human beings are a composite of earthly and heavenly parts. We belong to the earth through our physical beings and egos, and to the Heavens through our souls. It is critical to keep our ego occupied. Load work on it. Don't leave it idle because when it is idle, unoccupied, it always goes after harmful, destructive things under the tutelage of Shaytan, destroying mankind.

All of you, I am asking unemployed people or no-mind people or heedless people or depressed people or mental-house people—what do you think? You understand? You have time, unoccupied people.

Dastur, ya sayyidi, meded. A'udhu bil-Lahi min ash-Shaytani-r-rajim, bismillahi-r-Rahmani-r-Rahim. This is the most important point, that we must look at it too much. *Meded, ya sultan al-awliya.* After that problem, if you bring a solution to it, the life of mankind on earth is going to be arranged and people will get to be in satisfaction, getting to be in peace, getting to be in rest, getting to be in comfort, getting to be a blest community. If it is not solved, never-ending troubles, never-ending sufferings, never-ending wars, fightings, never-ending enmities, never-ending envy and hatred.

There is one point. What is that important point? *Hadha kalam: 'Ash-sharra-l-nafsik, lammatu sharra-l-nafsik, yusharr ilayk"*—*hadha ma'na.*[1] I am saying one word in Arabic to make it understood that I am bringing this from real knowledge, our traditional knowledge, that everything just turns on.

Now, we have been created and settled on earth, coming and going. Our creation is a different creation from heavenly beings and earthly beings. Heavenly beings that belong to the Heavens, angels, their creation is different. Allah Almighty just granted to them to be in existence, and their importance is to glorify Allah Almighty.

The world of angels—they are only for glorifying; no need of what we are in need of. From divine Light Oceans they have been created, and their creation is going on, never finishing. No material in their creation that we have; no *nafs*, no ego for them. They are in the Divine Presence, glorifying, and they are at the last point of happiness and peace and enjoyment, never getting to say, "Enough, our glorifying." Every glorifying gives more love towards Allah Almighty, and they are increasing, through their glorifying, in enjoyment, and increasing in lights and coming into the Love Oceans of Allah Almighty. Never-ending; they are going, a new creation coming. Love Oceans are oceans, countless oceans. In their oceans, countless creations, angels, they are so full of love and glory for their Lord, Almighty Allah.

And there is another world that is our world, earth. On it, there are countless kinds of creatures. That is animals' world, and in animals' world there are countless kinds of animals. Their creation is different from the creation of heavenly beings and mankind. They are only interested in their material aspects. They were created for

---

[1] This saying: "The calamity of your *nafs* is that if you don't occupy it, it will occupy you"—this sort of a meaning.

another kind of creation—that is, for mankind, for human beings. They were created for ourselves because we are in need of them.

We have material from the earth as well as from heavenly beings, our souls, coming together. When coming together, another creature just came into existence and Allah Almighty created man. We are now on earth, our level above the level of animals, under the level of the Heavens. Because of our ego, we belong to the earth; for the reason of our souls, we belong to the Heavens. Then a struggle is going on between the two opposite and different kinds of creation.

Our material being that represents that one is our ego, fighting against our souls that are our heavenly representatives in ourselves. One of them is asking to go up, to rise to the Heavens because their pleasure is to rise to the Heavens; they are asking to reach endless Oceans of the Divine Presence. But our material being and its representative, ego, is always asking to be closer to nature because their happiness is with nature, with earth.

Now we are coming to that point, that if we do not occupy our ego and leave it, we will lose, perhaps finally losing everything. Therefore the Prophet was saying, "You must take care of your ego, not to leave it without being occupied." When you are sitting unoccupied, Shaytan is coming and saying to ego, "Do this, do that," advising ego to make our bodies to be occupied with something that is not good for our souls, as a donkey, if its owner does not drive it, tries to drive a person.

You must be very careful on that point. You must not leave your ego to be unoccupied; quickly riding on you, making you its donkey—no! Therefore, all troubles are coming through our ego. We are heedless, leaving it unoccupied, and our ego is quickly riding on ourselves and making us run as it likes. Always it is running on harmful things, bad things, violent animals' characteristics, going to dress on people.

Now in the whole world, people are dressed in violence and they are violent. What is the reason? Because they are representing their egos, not representing their heavenly beings; no, dressing people in violence. Everywhere, fighting, quarreling, destroying, doing bad things—everywhere. That is the whole world, representing their egos.

When they are dressed in the dress of egos, cursing is coming on them and no mercy. When mercy goes up, violence is coming and dressing on people, and people are asking to kill each other, to harm each other, to destroy, to burn, to do everything that is satanic work because cursing brings those bad works, satanic works, living through cursing, and mercy and blessings are going up.

Therefore the Prophet was saying that the best treatment for everyone, if you are asking to save yourself from cursing, is not to leave your ego free. Put on it always, put on it always some responsibility. *Asta'idhu bil-Lah.* "*Fa idha faraghta fan-sab*"[2] [94:7]. What we said about Prophet's advice, Allah Almighty just made it as a judgment, never changing: "*Fa idha faraghta fan-sab*, O people."

Allah is not saying, "*Fa idha faraghta wan-sab*,"[3] but, "Don't leave any space." He is saying, "*Fa idha faraghta*—if you are going to finish a good thing, a heavenly order, quickly run to another. Don't leave your ego unoccupied! Load on it another load; don't leave it without a load.

That is one letter [*fa*], giving like an ocean of meaning. "*Fa idha faraghta fan-sab*. O My servants, if you are finishing one kind of servanthood, don't leave your ego free. Quickly put on it another

---

[2] I seek refuge with Allah. "*Then, when you have finished [your duties], stand up/get up [to continue your efforts].*" (94:7)

[3] "Then, when you have finished [your duties] *and* are standing up/getting up [to continue your efforts]."

load!" One verse, and in one verse one letter may save all mankind—the greatness of Holy Qur'an. You should be happy, you should be happy!

Eh! People are fighting now. They are saying, "Weekly we can work thirty-six hours ." One week, how many hours? Seven times twenty-four, how many hours? Seven days, twenty-four hours. *Yüz altmış sekiz*, one sixty-eight hours, seven days.

They are quarreling to make their work hours thirty-six hours, yes? Take thirty-six hours from one sixty-eight—what remains? One hundred thirty-two hours. What are they doing? Ask!

What are they doing? Unoccupied; they are leaving their egos to do everything. How can these people be saved, how is the crisis going to finish? To think about it, it is foolishness. People are working, during one week, thirty-six hours and doing nothing one hundred thirty-two hours. How are these people going to save themselves? That is foolishness! No one knows *hisab*, no one knows arithmetic? What is that?

They are coming under the command of Shaytan one hundred thirty-two hours, under the command of Shaytan and devils. What is that? This is our *dunya*, this is our world—all, everywhere; one hundred thirty-two hours, what are they doing? And they are saying, "Economic crisis, economic crisis! People are suffering." Allah should make them suffer much more. If doing nothing for one hundred thirty-two hours, they are under the control of Shaytan and devils.

This is so clear. Even if they may work one hundred thirty-two hours and thirty-six hours are free, that thirty-six hours is destroying one hundred thirty-two hours, also. Leave it! If you give one hour to your ego, it may finish the whole week's efforts that we are making; *every-thing*—one hour is enough for ego to destroy everything.

Therefore the Prophet was saying, "O Allah, O my Lord, don't leave me in the hands of my ego even for the blink of an eye."

Therefore I am asking, "O Allah Almighty, *ya Rabbi*, send us someone to awaken people." We are in need of heavenly involvement. Without heavenly involvement, we are in the hands of devils and Shaytan. And everyone is *gönüllü*, a volunteer for Satan and satanic works; all people are volunteers.

"How do you see the coming days? What is your opinion?" people are asking me. What shall I say? How I can say anything that gives you hope for the coming days if we are in such a situation?

May Allah bless you and forgive me. It is enough. I must prepare myself for tomorrow, *insha'Allah*.

Keep it. Don't take the ropes off the horse. When you are pulling a cart, putting the horse and tying it; always the cart must be behind the horse or mule or donkey, ready for service. Your ego must be ready for service up to the last moment, and you have seen that the *arabacı*, driver of the cart, is keeping a whip in his hand, also, the whip, *kırbaç*, going like this, like that. Then you should be happy! If taking it back to make it rest, don't give rest to that ego.

Shaytan is unhappy with me, too much [laughter]. My ego, also, is so. I am saying, "I am finished. I am saying to young people to keep themselves." Shaytan is hopeless from me but very angry when I am warning you.

Eh! Allah gives much more honor to the most honored prophet and most beloved servant of Allah Almighty, Sayyidina Muhammad, ﷺ. *Fatehah*. ▲

29

5

TODAY'S GOLDEN COW

The world is covered by deep darkness. Allah's divine vengeance is to be feared because people are saying, either by their tongues or by their actions, that they do not believe in God. This is reminiscent of the time when the Children of Israel, under the direction of al-Samiri, worshipped the Golden Calf, drawing upon themselves Allah's wrath, and thick darkness descended, during which, by the divine order, the innocent killed the guilty among them. Now, in a similar situation, Allah's vengeance is expected because people do not believe.

A'udhu bil-Lahi min ash-Shatani-r-rajim, bismillahi-r-Rahmani-r-Rahim. Allah! Keep us, put all of us under Your protection from devils and evil.

The whole world is just covered with deep darkness, no lights in it, darkness covering lights. That means that good ones just disappeared or they are *gizlendi*, hiding themselves. Bad ones have just covered all our world. We are fearing Allah Almighty's vengeance because the earth wants to throw away from itself into space all people who are saying "No God."

Some people, they are saying with their tongues "No God." Another group, they are not saying "No God" with their tongues, but by their actions, by their dealings, the meaning of their actions and dealings is the same as those people who are saying "No God" with their tongues, the other group proclaiming "No God" by their actions, by their dealings.

If a person is taking no care for the holy command of Allah, what does it mean? The *adhan*, the *muedhdhin*, is calling to pray. On behalf of Allah Almighty the divine order came to Rasul-Allah, ﷺ, and he was ordering his nation, "Five times you must call them to obedience, to servanthood, to pray to their Lord, Almighty Allah. Call them to pray! Call them to listen! Call them to hear, call them to keep My orders." Then people who are never interested, never taking any care, the meaning of their actions is that we do not accept that order or any orders to call the *adhan*. That is denying the existence of Allah Almighty through their actions.

Holy command, "Don't drink." People are saying, "We are drinking, we must enjoy our-selves." If you are saying, "The Lord of the Heavens is making that *haram*," he says, "He may. Who is that One? I am enjoying myself by drinking; I don't care about any order." His action is an evidence that he does not believe in the existence of Allah Almighty. Therefore, now the whole world is running into a deep darkness.

When the Children of Israel made a cow, the Golden Cow, making *sajdah*, saying this is our God, and also they were saying that Moses, pbuh, lost his God and went to look after him, Samiri was saying, "Here your God, this Golden Cow."

When they made a cow as their god, *astaghfirullah*, because it was a shining golden cow, so shining, it was mooing—"*Oh-h-h!!*" only saying, "*Oh-h-h!*" And Samiri was saying, "Look at your Lord here, mooing at you," saying, "This your God. Moses has lost Him and has gone to look for him."[1]

---

[1] This is mentioned in the hadith of the Trials of Moses, reported by Ibn 'Abbas (R).

And the Lord of the Heavens, He was angry with Children of Israel, and when Moses came,[2] He ordered to Moses that all those who had worshipped that cow must be killed. That is a heavenly order that is going on up to the end of the world. Whoever worships gold, money, they should be killed, they should be destroyed. That is my fear now, because all people they are worshipping money. They should be killed.

And when the divine order came to Moses, those who had not followed Samiri, not obeying and not answering his call, were ordered to kill everyone who had obeyed Samiri and accepted the Golden Cow as their god.[3] But it was so difficult for the killers to kill those people because some of them were their children, their fathers, their mothers, their sisters, their uncles, their brothers, their fathers—it was so difficult. And when they hesitated about how they could do this, Moses asked Allah Almighty to show a way that they could do that without hesitating.

Then there came a black cloud, such darkness in the daytime that that day was like night—only one day, like night. Through that darkness they were killing, not seeing who they were. When the number of those people who should be killed was complete, Moses and Aaron, *'alayhima as-salam*, peace be upon them and upon our Rasul-Allah, ﷺ, fell into *sajdah* and said, "O our Lord, pardon! The Children of Israel are just going to be killed, all of them. Asking Your pardon, your mercy, on the Children of Israel!" And at that time, that cloud, darkness, went up and everything stopped. That was at the time that the last one was killed, and their number was 70,000, just complete.

---

[2]That is, when he returned to his people from his meeting with Allah on Mount Sinai.

[3]*"And [recall] when Moses said to his people, 'O my people, indeed you have wronged yourselves by your taking of the Calf [for worship]. So repent to your Maker and kill yourselves. That is best for you in the sight of your Creator.'"* (2:54)

Now I am fearing. I am fearing that a big, huge, terrible killing of mankind, that never happened before, should be now. Out of seven, one is going to remain and six are going to finish, or out of six, one will remain and five must be killed. That is what we are calling *Malhamatan Kubra*, the biggest war, that in other holy books is mentioned as Armageddon, that never happened before and never going to happen after. Whoever is with Allah is going to be protected. Whoever is not taking any care and saying, "No God" through their tongues or "No God" through their actions should be taken away—finished.

May Allah forgive us and bless His servants. Even though we are bad servants, we are asking forgiveness, we are saying "Pardon" to Allah Almighty. For the sake of the most honored prophet, Sayyidina Muhammad, ﷺ, *bi hurmati-l-Fatehah*. ▲

6

ETERNITY

| Contains very deep matters concerning the value of man. |

["Where have you been?"]

"In Cyprus."

"You went for what? You have been there for what?

"There was an international mental house. I went for treatment. A famous place for the mental house chief, famous in East and West."

"What did he say, the chief guardian of mental house?"

"He said something but I never understood."

The Prophet was saying, pbuh, that some people who are present in such a meeting, such an Association, are listening and then reaching people, and that some of those who were present in that meeting and carried that news to others are less understanding than those people whom it reached.[1] Perhaps you do not understand, but through these cassettes that you may take to your countries, homelands, the people listening may understand more than you. That is Prophet's holy words. Yes. Perhaps they will take much more bene-

---

[1] In his last sermon, the Holy Prophet ﷺ said, "Those who are present should inform the absent. Perhaps some of those to whom it is conveyed will be more attentive to it than some of those who heard it." (Bukhari, 5:688)

fit, much more understanding, much more training themselves. Therefore, it is important.

A'udhu bil-Lahi min ash-Shaytani-r-Rajim, Bismillahi-r-Rahmani-r-Rahim. Meded, ya sayyidi, meded. We are such small ones, such weak ones—such weak ones, weaker than an ant. An ant is very weak in front of ourselves and we are weaker than ants in creation. Our material is so weak, but our value it is not with our material. Therefore, man likes to see himself big and great.

If he is looking at his material, that is nothing. Through our material we can't claim greatness for ourselves, but in such small material, the Lord of the Heavens just granted us—new page—granted us something that we are calling *"dharra,"* the smallest particle of matter (you may say atom or electron or protons or neutrons; you may say very small particles), and you are reaching a point among those particles, small pieces, that you can't cut it. It is last cut of matter. If you are cutting it after that, there should be zero.

Understand? After that particle of matter that we are calling *"juzu la yatajazza,"*[2] the last, smallest particle of matter that we can divide into two, we are reaching—not practically reaching to cut it, but we may reach a point that, through our intellect, we are saying that it is impossible for that particle to be divided into two because after that dividing, nothing remains. One-line-under-it is infinity;[3] it is a *taqsim*, equal to zero. If you are continuing to make one into two, into four, into ten and then you are putting infinity, it is going to be equal to zero. That means that one, if you are dividing it and continuing to divide, finally there is going to remain only zero.

---

[2] An indivisible particle.

[3] I.e., one over infinity or one divided by infinity.

That means that all creation, it is from nothing. Zero means *nothing*. Understand? Zero means finishing—nothing. If you are saying zero, nothing there—finished.

The Lord of the Heavens is gathering zeros and bringing this appearance into existence. People are saying, "We are here." We are not here. All universes with their *ihtisham*, magnificence—all of them, they are only an appearance. They are all zero, coming to zero, gathering zeros and coming into existence. Therefore, *La mawjuda illa-Llah. Anta tifham?*[4]

MURID: Everything is zero and He is the One.

SHAYKH: Oh-h! Congratulations to you! How did it happen? [Laughter.]

MURID: Everything is zero and He is the One. *Allahu akbar, la ilaha illa-Llah!*

SHAYKH: *La mawjuda illa-Llah, al-mawjud bi-Allah.*[5] Don't say I am here. Therefore, the biggest sin is to say "I—I am here."

You are not here. You are nothing. Don't claim for yourself this and that; no. In existence there is only Allah Almighty's existence, not anyone else's existence because His existence never leaves any room for anything else to be there. "*La sharika lahu*"—that is the meaning. No partner for Allah, for His existence. How are you saying "I am here"?

If you were not just a one-and-a-half meter tall person but every man was like this universe, still you are nothing, you are in the line of zero. But zeros, after one on the right hand, they are taking value. After one zero. it is going to be ten, two zeros going to hundred,

---

[4] There is no existent except Allah. Understand?
[5] There is no existent except Allah, existing through Allah.

three zeros going to be thousand, six zeros going to be million, nine zeros going to be billion, twelve going to be quadrillion zeros. As much as it is going, still you are zero. *Allahu akbar, Allahu akbar!*

But people, they are occupying their heads only with economic crises. There is not any idea or thought except sleeping with crisis, economic crisis, awakening with bankruptcy, the whole day at this stock market. People are square-headed, enclosed in a millimeter square, never letting their heads think about the Lord of the Heavens, the Lord of existence. Therefore men are *kisir*,[6] bringing nothing in their heads except money, money, money; stock money, stock money, stock money. These three or four ideas, they have been imprisoned in them; they are like mongoloid children, nothing else. They are not thinking anything; the whole day and the whole night, their *dhikr* is this stock money, to where reaching, from where coming. "Dollar, dollar, dollar, dollar, dollar . . ." [He imitates counting money in different currencies.] "Euro, euro, euro . . ." If they were saying, instead of "Euro, euro, euro, euro," "Allah, Allah, Allah, Allah," Allah should fill the whole world, in one night, raining on them gold.

Therefore I am saying that although we are only one-and-half or two meter tall people, still Allah Almighty is giving such a value for a man, only one man, that includes the whole universe in himself. He is doing the whole universe in yourself, putting it into yourself. *Wa ma dhalika 'ala Allah bi-'aziz,*[7] it is not difficult for Allah Almighty to make this huge universe in yourself, and His endless *iqtidar*, ability, puts this huge universe, without making it smaller and without making you bigger, into yourself.

---

[6]Barren, sterile, unproductive.

[7]*"And that is not difficult for Allah."* (14:20)

Understand what I mean to say? The Lord of creation, Allah Almighty—I am saying now that the whole universe is in yourself, and He is able, even though in this universe there are countless distances, so big, and you, in front of this huge universe, are nothing, you are less than a electron—He is able to put this huge universe into that atom, and He is not in need to make the atom big and to make the universe small and to put it in it *because He is Allah.*

Don't use your balance, your scale, for Allah! Your scale, your intellect, is saying to you, "If we are going to put this universe into one person, that person must be bigger than this universe so that we may find room in a man to put it into him." That is your scale.

Don't think that Allah is like you—no. Allah is not a man. Allah, He is the Creator, He is not a creature. A creature's scale is just different. You can't put a scale for Allah Almighty. Therefore, we are saying, "*Wa Huwa 'ala kulli shayin qadir.*[8]" That is His ability for everything.

He may put this huge universe into an atom as it is without difficulty. That is an opening for *m'arifatullah.* We are asking to reach an understanding about the Lord of the Heavens because we have been created to know about Him, and this is, as a first step, knowledge that we can know.

Then, then, then, then, then—coming, coming, coming, coming . . . up to eternity. *Eternity*—that word, even though it is from your language, European, English language, but there is a kind of attraction in it, with love and with greatness that belongs to Allah. Eternity, eternity. You must make your goal e-ter-ni-ty—e-ter-ni-ty, *abadi, abadi, sarmadi, daymumi,* Allah-Allah, Allah-Allah, Allah. Eternity—endless oceans, endless oceans. *'Alam al-ghuyub,*[9] O Allah.

---

[8]*"And Allah is powerful over all things."* (2:20 and thirty-five other verses)
[9]Knower of the Unseen.

Allah-Allah. '*Alam al-ghuyub—ghuyub,* the unseen, oceans, unseen worlds, unseen creation.

That is for our level, but for Allah, for Allah—'*alam al-ghuyub,* '*alam*[10] meaning that no one can reach to knowing anything in front of Him Almighty. *Ghuyub,*[11] that is a plural of hidden oceans— hidden oceans, countless and endless from pre-eternity through eternity. Oh-h, oh-h! People are thinking that Allah is only for this world. *Allahu akbar, allahu akbar, allahu akbar!* That is a real *dhikr,* giving satisfaction and pleasure through the hearts of mankind. Allah-Allah, Allah-Allah, Allah-Allah.

This was closed to Adam in Paradise. If not coming on earth, it would have remained closed. Then, when Adam asked to reach these closed, hidden oceans, it was said to him, "Here, as long as you are in Paradise, you can't reach. You must go, you must come down and you must reach from earth to those Oceans, endless Oceans, hidden Oceans, hidden Oceans." *Allahu akbar!* Countless, countless!

O people, *bushra lana*—good tidings for you, endless good tidings. Take, take something from this life for an opening. When you are going to die, an opening will come to you.

May Allah bless you and forgive me. It is a very deep ocean. We can't reach even . . . ; countless distances we must look. But it is a preparation for mankind because they have been created to be deputies of Allah Almighty, and for a deputy it is necessary, it is obligatory, to know his Lord who granted to him to be His deputy.

You must give your correct value to yourself and to every one of mankind—that the Lord of the Heavens, the Lord of creation, the Lord of eternity granted to mankind to be His deputies, and for eve-

---

[10]Knower.

[11]The plural of "*al-Ghayb,*" the unseen realms that are hidden, invisible or concealed from mankind.

ryone to try to know who granted to him to be deputy—who is that One. And we are trying to open—to open such a small, such a little knowledge about the actions of the Lord of the Heavens. We are not even approaching His Holy Names' Oceans, and after His Holy Names' Oceans, His Divine Attributes Oceans—never reaching. And then Essence—impossible! No possibility, finished.

May Allah give an understanding; it is important. *Ya Allah, ya Rabbi*, send us, from Your Divine Presence, some lions, to take away wolves and foxes and dragons, and to teach us, to open for us an understanding of Your actions, and through Your actions to know something about Your greatness and about Your Hidden Oceans. *Amin.* For the honor [of] the most honored servant of Allah Almighty: *Fatehah.* ▲

7

BELIEVE IN THE UNSEEN

Allah Almighty created all human beings as different, unique. Each one has a *qiblah* or goal to which he directs himself. Up to the age of maturity, children are protected. Then the opening comes to them and they search for a direction. Instead of keeping to the main road, many exit to the right or left, following Shaytan, and thus lose their way. People accuse believers of being backward or deluded, of believing in imaginary ideas, and demand proofs of God's existence, but we have been asked to believe in heavenly books and what they contain without discussion—simply to believe because we can't grasp such spiritual realities with our minds. Allah gives high honor to those who keep to beliefs in this time. As for others, death is waiting for them, slowly or suddenly, whether young or old, rich or poor. Therefore, beware of Shaytan, whom the twenty-first century's people have taken as their friend.

Meded, ya sultan al-awliya, meded, ya sultan al-awliya. Allah Almighty keeps ourselves on His right path. Oh-h! So many, so many exits. The main road is the safe way for reaching the real goal. If a person goes like this, right or left, leaving the main road, he can't reach his real goal. He may reach other goals but he may lose main goal.

Allah Almighty created man. You can't find two persons similar, the same; must be a difference between two. Can't be hundred per cent same because Allah Almighty He is not making copies, no, giving to everyone an independent *shakhsiyah*, personality.

Look! Here are so many people. Each one, with his different personality, is appearing in existence, and in our inner existence—that is, our spiritual being—also, we are not the same, and really our outward appearance is coming from our spiritual being's manifestation. So everyone is independent and unique in his own being; you can't find another the same, no. And we are saying, "*Subhana man awha 'ala kulla qalbin ma yushghilah.*" That is a reality that means "Glory be to Allah Almighty who granted to each one of mankind, men or women, to make their hearts occupied with something."

Everyone is thinking something, everyone is asking for something, everyone is making for himself a *qiblah*, a goal that he is asking to reach—*awla qiblah*[1] that we are moving towards. If your heart does not bow, your praying is really only a physical body's movement. If your heart does not bow to *qiblah*, it only belongs to your physical being; it is not real praying. Therefore, everyone also has such a different *qiblah* that his heart bows towards and asks for his desire or his will to reach that point.

Everyone is just occupied with so many things. Up to our maturity-age, we have been protected on the true way, but when you are passing that limit from childhood to the age of maturity, an opening comes. Those little ones are closed; when they reach the age of maturity, they are opening. Heh, sometimes I am opening the chickens' stable. Ooh-h—coming like this [makes wild noises], so different that you can't reach them, some running, some doing like this, some jumping, but as long as they are in that stable they are very quiet. When the opening comes, you can't reach them.

Therefore, childhood goes on up to the age of maturity; then comes an opening. When the opening comes, so many different desires begin to appear that are urging them to reach there. When they

---

[1] The main, chief or most important direction or goal to which one directs oneself.

look at the open motorway and there is nothing on it, they take the right hand or left hand, and seeing something that they are very interested in, they begin to run this way or that way. So many exits they are finding, and if they lose one, they are reaching a second one, entering. Very few people are remaining on the main road, the majority of the people running to the right hand or left hand.

The main road leads to Allah, and the separate exits lead to their egoistical goals. Whoever leaves the main road, they are running after their egoistical desires, and after a while that finishes and they are falling down. Whoever goes straight, they are using their will power and also using their minds, but those who are leaving the straight, right path, the straight road, all of them are following satanic ways and their egoistical desires, and it is going to finish after a short while. Some of them, a few of them, may come slowly to right path but mostly they are going to lose the right path.

And that is the general view of mankind now in the twenty-first century. Very few people you can find on straight path, very, very few, and those who are leaving the straight path, going to the right hand or left hand, they are also swearing at those people who are not joining them, saying, "They are *muta'akhir*, retarded people, no-mind people, foolish people, crazy ones, living in imagination. They are leaving what is now in front of them and running after imagination." They are saying even for the existence of their Lord, "It is man-made imagination," *astaghfirullah*.

They are not accepting the Creator although they are creatures; they know that they did not create themselves but yet they insist on saying, "No Creator." There is creation and creatures; must be a Creator. That is intellect, forcing people to say "Yes," but they are not using it. They have lost their intellect; they are not saying that. They know, but they are drunk people, they are finished. And they are swearing at those believing people, saying, "Look, running after imagina-tion! They are saying that they should find, at the end of this long way, something that should be for them forever, and they are carrying a heavy burden in walking towards that imaginary goal. *We* are just putting one step and finding what we are asking for. We are reaching pleasure, we are reaching our goals so quickly. How we can leave this and continue on a dry way? Everything is here!"

That is the twenty-first century's people's mentality and their judgment about themselves, and accusing believers of being crazy ones, no-mind people, funny people, and they are also claiming, "Those people never believe in science or such things. They believe in something that they can't bring any proof for us."

Yes, mostly those, such foolish people, were coming in front of prophets and they were objecting to prophets' invitations, and when the Prophet said, "O people, you have a responsibility. You should be asked on the Last Day, Judgment Day, what you did throughout your whole life," they were saying, "How can it be?"

The Prophet was saying, "After your death, that should be."

They were saying, "How can it be? After death, when our bodies are going to be dust, how are you saying that we will come back as before and that we will come to Judgment Day for judgment on ourselves? We can't understand, we can't reach any satisfaction with what you are saying. Give us a proof!"

Always, up to today, they are saying, "Bring those who passed away so that we can see them. Then we may believe." But everything it is not going to be within our sight, to be seen.

If we are asking, "Do you believe in atoms?" he should say, "Yes." Then he may ask me, "Do you believe in the existence of atoms?" and I may say, "No, because when we are saying that there is a Creator, you are saying, 'Show me so that I may believe.' Now you are asking me and saying you believe in existence of atoms, and I am saying 'No.'"

"Why?"

"Show me so that I may believe." Same mentality.

If he says, "Because they are so small, they can't be in our sight because they are atoms, such small ones," I may say, "Our God is also so great that it is impossible for Him to come into our sight." But yet they are insisting on saying "No." And when they are saying, "No," they are remaining in the darkness of their physical beings, and the material world is going to grind them and to finish them.

Yes. So many things we are accepting only through our minds and intellect. Physically we cannot reach everything but through knowledge we can understand, and we are not asking how it happened, how it was before, how it can be—no. And heavenly knowledge that is coming to us through prophets, don't discuss it. No one can make any discussion concerning holy books; holy books, they are above our level, never belonging to earth. They are coming from the Heavens, and the Lord of the Heavens is only asking for you to believe without any discussion.

Therefore, "Muslim" means someone who accepts without any discussion of their realities because our level of understanding is so low for reaching that level. If we use our spiritual power, we may reach the first level of understanding. Under it, you must say "Yes," as a small child, beginning to recite the Holy Qur'an, must say, "Bismillahi-r-Rahmani-r-Rahim. Alif-ba-ta-tha-jim-ha-kha,"[2] must believe that this is *alif* without knowing if it is real or not. When he reaches to joining letters together and meanings of words come, then he understands that that was really *alif*, that was *ba*, that was *kaf*, that was *lam*, that was *mim*.

---

[2] The first letters of the Arabic alphabet.

Therefore, the principles of beliefs have come from the Heavens for people. You must say, "I believe in God, His existence and unity; in the existence of angels; the existence of holy books, the existence of prophets; the existence of Hells and Paradise, and the coming of the Last Day, Judgment Day," without any bargaining on it. No discussion, because your intellect can't reach that point.

But people now they are the same as at the time of the Prophet, whose tribe was objecting to the Prophet and saying, "We do not believe your prophethood. If the Lord of the Heavens had wanted to send us a prophet, He would have sent us an angel. You are just like ourselves." And the Prophet he is not like an ordinary person. Outwardly he was a man, but his inner, real being belonged to the Heavens; only outwardly he had been dressed as a man. An angel wouldn't be able to do anything with mankind and therefore Allah Almighty sent prophets from among men for understanding. We understand men, not understanding angels, and angels do not understand the real position of men because they are a different creation.

Therefore, we are in difficult days. From the beginning of life on earth with Adam and Eve, that separation between believers and unbelievers just began, and from time to time, believers took power in their hands and defeated unbelievers. Now it is a pity for believers that we are living in a time when the whole world is against believers, and they think that their technology is powerful, much more powerful than our belief in God, and because of the weakness in ourselves we are fearing their weapons. It is a big test for believers.

Therefore, now in our days, to believe in God and in the principles of Islam gives us big honor on Judgment Day because we are keeping the Prophet's and heavenly principles of faith, and Allah is granting us such a high honor that was not granted to people of past times. Therefore, you must be thankful to Allah Almighty that you believe. And so many believers also, now, they are running to the mentality of Western people and they are asking to be modern Muslims or westernized Muslims.

Can't be westernized Muslims, no; it is *batil*, false. "Westernized Islam" means to be Christian, and Christians they are on falsehood, *batil*. If you would like to be in safety here and Hereafter, keep to that main road. If you are not asking and you are happy to follow your ego, to be a servant for your ego, you are free. But death is searching for you; death never leaves unbelievers, not at any time. Death, they are saying as an example, death is like a dog following a man, a *gharib*, unknown person. Some dogs, if they know that someone is not from their people, they bark. But some of them don't bark; they follow them and suddenly bite. But you can't know. Following, yes—mostly barking, not biting, but some of them they are silent, following you and at any time they may bite you. And death is running after, following after everyone silently. You can't know at which time it may catch you.

No safety for young people. Young people are saying, "Old people must look out for death. We are so young." Or rich people—they can't say that we are rich; death may come to poor people. Learned people, they can't say, "We have no fear for ourselves because we are learned people. There may be fear for illiterate people." Generals can't say, "We have so many stars or swords or eagles or crowns on ourselves, and here also is full of medals. If the Angel of Death looks at us, he may be afraid of us because we are commanders-in-chief. Under our command hundreds, thousands or millions of soldiers may march, we are so powerful." No, no! No safety for anyone. Any time he may catch them.

Beware of Shaytan. People are writing "Beware of the dog." They are not writing "Beware of Shaytan," no, because Shaytan is their friend. Hah-hah—very friendly! The twenty-first century's people are very friendly with Shaytan, saying, "Oh-h, my friend, my *holy* friend!" Shaytan is not a girl friend or a boy friend, Shaytan is a *holy* friend for the twenty-first century's people. They are saying, "Oh-h, you are so holy—to be with you. We are tasting the sweetness of *hayat*, of life, with you. Oh, my holy friend! If you were not in existence, what could we do? Nothing! Holy friend!"

True or not? Every nation is making Shaytan a holy one. The twenty-first century's people, they are saying only, "There is one holy one, not any other holy one on earth; only Shaytan, only one. Shaytan is the holy one," like a poem. "The holy one for the twenty-first century is Iblis, our holy friend. We are proud to be with you."

Eh! *Wa min Allah al-tawfiq.* It is okay now; I am tired. And he is happy when I am saying, "Shaykh is tired"—oh-h! Heh! "Now is the time for me," Shaytan is saying. *Astaghfullah, ya Rabbi, ya Allah. Nas'aluka, Allahumma, al-hifdhu wa-l-aman min sharri-sh-Shaytan wa sharakihi, min an-nafs wa sharakihi, ya Allah, wa la takilna ila anfusina tarfata 'aynin,*[3] because Shaytan is the partner of our ego or our ego is from Shaytan.

We are asking forgiveness from Allah Almighty, and blessings, also. For the honor of the most honored servant of Allah Almighty, Sayyidina Muhammad, ﷺ, *Fatehah.* ▲

---

[3] I ask forgiveness, O my Lord. We ask, our Lord, the safety of protection from the evil of Shaytan and his associates, from our egos and their associates, O Allah, and do not leave us in the hands of our egos for even the blink of an eye.

8

"LORDSHIP IS MINE!"

People are in darkness. Everything concerning the past, present and future is to be found in the Qur'an, whether in summary and in detail. The darkness of the present era is mentioned in the verse, *Idha akhraja yadahu, lam yaqad yarāha* (24:40). No one has the power to lift this darkness except Mahdi, as, when he comes with the light of prophethood.

Bismillahi-r-Rahmani-r-Rahim. A'udhu bil-Llahi min ash-Shaytani-r-rajim. By the name of Allah, All-Mighty, All-Merciful, Most Beneficent and Most Munificent. We are in need daily, daily, of sustenance. And as we are in need for our physical being, our spiritual being is asking daily for sustenance.

Every day a new manifestation is coming. If you can catch that manifestation through your spiritual being, you are lucky. If you are sleeping, perhaps the river may be running, but if you are not opening it to your land, it goes away and your land remains dry. Therefore, you must be awake. And glory be to Allah Almighty, it is difficult now! On our island you can't find another gathering, sitting freely as we are sitting here, because people have just sunken into Darkness Oceans, looking and seeing nothing.

49

People they are in darkness. *"Lam yaqad yaraha"*[1]—Allah Almighty is saying that there should be a darkness. The Holy Qur'an is showing coming days, also, as well as informing about past times, from the beginning up to the time of Rasul-Allah, ﷺ. That is its specialty, Holy Qur'an. It is not an ordinary book—*hasha*![2] It is *umm ul-kitab*.[3] All knowledge that has been recorded or written in books comes from that Book, from that holy Book.

Millions of books, all of them are taking their materials, their essence, from the Holy Qur'an—seeds of knowledge, countless seeds of knowledge. If anyone may plant it, it is grow-ing, growing, growing, and that plant of knowledge is never falling down. It is not like our plants. Knowledge-plants are forever; you can take, you can take. And the Holy Qur'an is giving those countless seeds of knowledge to people. Can't be like an ordinary book; *hasha, astagh-firullah!* It is an endless ocean. You can take from it countless pearls, countless jewels.

Therefore, its specialty is showing, from the beginning up to the time of Sayyidina Rasul-Allah, ﷺ, what happened. You can take all knowledge both as a summary and with details, *mukha-saran wa mu-fasalan*. You can reach details, perhaps the deepest details, of what happened from the first time, when Allah Almighty said, "I am going to make (*'ja'al'*; it is not like 'create') on the earth a *khalifah*."

Asta'idhu bil-Lahi, "*Idh qala Rabbuka lil-malaikati, 'Inni ja'ilun fi-l-ardi khalifah*,'"[4] so that the creation of Adam was *musabbaq*;[5] it was in

---

[1] *"[When one takes out his hand (therefrom)], he can scarcely see it."* (24:40)

[2] God forbid, never!

[3] The mother of the book, the source of all knowledge.

[4] *"When your Lord said to the angels, 'Indeed, I will place a deputy [khalifah] upon the earth.'"* (2:30) The story of Adam is told in 2:30-38, 4:117-120, 7:11-27, 15:26-43, 17:61-65, 18:50, 20:115-126, 38:71-85.

[5] [Known] in advance.

the divine knowledge. His creation was ready, but about the title that Allah Almighty gave to Sayyidina Adam—the divine Will that signaled the time of the appearance of Adam and his being dressed as a *khalifah*, as His deputy on earth—Allah Almighty was *then* informing the angels.

Therefore, the angels they were saying, "O our Lord, we are ready for that mission, for that *mansab*, position. We are more suitable for that purpose, to be caliphs. You are going to make that new creature and they are going to fight each other."

They knew about the children of Adam. Therefore they were saying, "We are doing as You say, as You order; we are not going beyond what You order. Why are You not making a *khalifah* from ourselves, and You are going to bring a new one into existence and dressing him to be Your *khalifah*?" That means they knew, before Adam's appearance in existence—they knew about the children of Adam and his children, and therefore they were saying that.

The Holy Qur'an, you can take from it every detail, from the time that no sun was shining or moon turning or earth moving. And then, from Adam's creation and his coming to be titled as His *khalifah*, every detail you can take from the Holy Qur'an. Then, every time, every century, every year, what happened between East and West, and between men, the caliphs of Allah Almighty—what they did, what they are doing and what they are going to do in the future—up to the end, also, you can find.

Therefore, the Holy Qur'an is informing about everything that we are in now and everything about the coming days, and it is a great ignorance to object to *anbiya* or *awliya* when they are saying something concerning news of the future. So many *jahil*, ignorant, people, they are objecting; they are saying, "No one knows about news." Those people are no-mind people, never understanding, and Rasul-Allah was saying as well, "*Fihi, Qur'an al-Karim, khabar ma qablakum wa naba' ma b'adakum.*"[6] And *naba'* is something like "news," but in Arabic it has a different meaning.

It is enough; if anyone has any *fiqh,*[7] any understanding with himself, that he must not make any objection if a *wali* speaks about coming days' events, saying, "No one knows what is coming for the coming days." That is ignorance, because the Prophet was saying, "You can find in it everything that belongs to the past time. If you are asking, you can find it as a summary and you can find it with details."

Nubuwwah, naba', prophethood—those ignorant people are asking to make prophets like ordinary people; they are saying, "They also don't know anything." Prophethood gives them authority to look, to know, what is on the Preserved Table for coming days and about those events, and they must warn their nations. How you are saying, "Even the Prophet did not know"?

Why did he not know? How was he the Prophet? If he was like me, like you, what would be the difference between an ordinary person and a prophet? But those Wahhabi people are mixing up the beliefs of *mumins*, believers. *Khazahumullah*, may Allah defeat them.

We believe that the Prophet knew because he took from the Holy Qur'an. Whatever he was saying, he took it from the Holy Qur'an. For *ashratu-s-sa'at*, the signs of Last Day and up to Last Day—for everything, Allah was giving the meanings.

Allah was teaching Rasul; no teacher for Rasul-Allah, ﷺ. *Asta'idhu bi-Allah. "Ar-Rahmanu 'allama-l-Qur'an";*[8] Allah Almighty just taught the Qur'an to His most honored Prophet, Sayyidina Muham-

---

[6]"In it, the Noble Qur'an, is information about what preceded you and news of what is after you," Hadith.

[7]Understanding, comprehension.

[8]*"The Most Merciful taught the Qur'an"* (55:1-2).

mad, ☙. What Allah taught him, Jibril couldn't know, was never going to know. When he said, "*Bismillahi-r-Rahmani-r-Rahim. Alif lam mim*,"[9] only the Prophet knew, Jibril did not know.[10] The archangel Gabriel was saying, "*Alif lam mim*," and Rasul-Allah was saying, "I understand." That was like a code between Allah Almighty and His most beloved servant.

Therefore, now we are looking at, *asta'idhu bil-Lah,* "*Idha akhraja yadahu, lam yaqad yaraha.*"[11] This *ayat al-karimah*, this verse, signals the view of coming days, coming days' pano-rama: that there should come a time that, if a person puts his hand in front of him, he won't be able to see it because of darkness. That is also a kind of sign that *dukhan*, smoke, should come on earth, covering it for forty days. One person won't be able to see another. And so many people are going to die; they won't be able to breathe—so many people, millions of people, and after forty days there will be an opening. And this also signals the death of the materials of people. But that darkness—"*Idha akhraja yadahu, lam yaqad yaraha*"—if a person puts his hand in front of himself and wants to see it, he will not be able to see even his hand from the deep darkness.

Now we are in it. People they are not seeing anything in the deep darkness. Therefore I am saying now that you can't find even a small group like ours in East or West. You can find perhaps very few groups but not such a group, and the majority of people they are heedless. They are in darkness; they can't see what is reality, where they are going, where they are moving, what they are doing—they can't know it. And therefore *awliya* are asking from Allah Almighty to send Mahdi, as, with the lights of prophethood—to be opened

---

[9] "*In the name of Allah, the Beneficent, the Merciful. Alif lam mim*" (the first three letters of the Arabic alphabet at the beginning of the second *surah* of the Qur'an) (2:1).

[10] That is, although Jibril (Gabriel) brought the verses of the Qur'an to the Prophet, ☙, Jibril did not know their meanings. But the Prophet, taught by Allah, did.

[11] Same as footnote 31.

once again the lights of prophet-hood on earth. If he is not going to bring those lights of *nubuwwah*, there can't be any *taqaddum*, progress, for him—no. He would be like other people, who may carry a candle in their hand. But a candle can't give enough light for all people. They are in need of the sun.

A torch,[12] it is not enough; a torch only a little light when you are walking. But this huge world can't be in light with torches, no, and not millions, even billions of candles can't give one- millionth of what the sun is giving to the earth. Therefore, all *awliya* are now expecting and asking this to be granted to Mahdi, as, when he comes, opening it. Therefore, *awliya* can't do anything with their candles, to take them from *dhulumat ila nur*.[13] "*Huwa al-ladhi yusalli 'alaykum wa malaikatuhu, li yukhrijakum mina-dh-dhulumati ila an-nur.*"[14] If Allah Almighty gives to only one person, that is enough to take the whole world from darkness to light, and everyone is going to look, saying, "Oh! What am I in?"

Heh! One person, one *murid*, was coming and saying to his shaykh, "Every night I am sitting on the *'Arsh*, the holy Throne [of God], and I am speaking with the Lord of the Heavens."

His shaykh was saying, "O my son, take this knife and tonight, when sitting and speaking with that one whom you are calling the Lord of the Heavens, cut off his ear."

"Yes, sir, I can do it."

The second night, also, he was saying it. Eh! The same film, movie, was going on, and he took that one's ear, cut it and put it in a paper or cloth, and brought it quickly to his shaykh.

---

[12]British for "flashlight".

[13]"*[From] darknesses to light.*" (33:43)

[14]"*It is He who confers blessing upon you, and His angels, that He may bring you forth from darknesses into the light.*" (33:43)

"You cut it?"

"Yes, sir. Last night I was speaking, also," and he opened it and looked. It was the ear of a donkey, Shaytan bringing him and making him sit in a stable where they put straw and barley, and animals were coming and eating there. And Shaytan brought that *murid* and made him sit in this place, and in front of him was a donkey, eating, and Shaytan was saying, "This is your Lord. Speak to him. You are now sitting on the holy Throne."

Now people they are so heedless, Shaytan making them. "Oh-h! You are such, such civilized people, no one has reached where you have reached now."

And everyone is saying, "Ye-s! The twenty-first century's people, we are the most civilized people. Oh-h! With blue jeans, men and women." [Laughter.] Heh-heh! All of them are sitting in sewage, like big rats, jumping.

When Mahdi, as, comes, he will open and show them where they are sitting, what is their civilization. Till Mahdi, as, comes and those lights come on people, they are looking, "Oh-oh-oh! Where are we?" Now they do not know. Like that *murid*, they think that they are sitting with the Lord of the Heavens on the holy Throne because such darkness now—so dark. When the lights of *nubuwwah* come, the lights of prophethood, sunshine, everyone will look there.

All *'ulama'* [Islamic scholars] are all just in dirtiness. Therefore, we are looking now only for a few people; we can use our torch and show people but we can't do more than this because it is nighttime. All *awliyas'* power can't reach; if coming all together, can't show to all nations, to all mankind, where they are sitting, what they are doing, what they are eating, what they are drinking, after what they are running. But then Mahdi, as, will come. Therefore *awliya* are asking for Mahdi, as, to come, with the lights of prophethood, *anwar nubuwwat*.

Eh! "Use your power, *awliya*!" Some square-headed people are saying, "You are a *wali*, you are a *qutb*,[15] you are *awliya*—why are you not stopping these things?"

It is not enough power; our power is not reaching to all people. We are only, They are saying, like an oasis in a huge desert—a limited place with a little bit of water, giving life around it, but all deserts must spring up from rains, making deserts to be green fields, with everything. Therefore, we are asking from Allah Almighty, because when Mahdi, as, comes, our power, They are saying, must be more and more.

May Allah bless you and forgive me. For the honor of most honored servant of Allah Almighty, Sayyidina Rasul-Allah: *Fatehah.*

Shukur, ya Rabbi, shukur, ya Rabbi, shukur alhamdulillah, every day they are sending new sustenance for the honor of Rasul-Allah, ﷺ. *Fatehah.* ▲

---

[15]The 'pole' or chief of the *awliya.*

9

SATANIC ADVERTISING IS EVERYWHERE

> Advertising for Shaytan is everywhere, in everything, and most people are under his command. Allah is very angry with two kinds of people: those who make Shaytan a partner to Him and those who take Shaytan as their God, even though they may claim to believe in Him. Everyone must look to himself to see whether he is following Shaytan and his ego, and whether his actions are for the sake of his ego or for the sake of his Lord.

Everything that Allah Almighty is doing is perfect and His judgment for everyone is perfect judgment. What He is preparing for us, that is best. What we are preparing for ourselves, it is so useless, harmful and giving a bad result.

If we are able to accept His will without our putting our wills above His will, that is perfection for ourselves. But always our egos are asking to put their wills first and asking to take away the will of Allah, and all trouble in the world, throughout East and West, from North to South, has only one reason—that people are trying to put their wills over the will of their Creator or the will of the Lord of the Heavens, the will of the Creator of all the universes.

That is real. It must be, because people are not getting introduced to their Lord. People they are mostly knowing nothing about their Lord, and all mankind they are getting an introduction only to Shaytan. Everywhere, every advertising—for what? It is only to make people to understand or to know about Shaytan, and satanic works are now running between East and West, from North to South. And people mostly they are under his command, the command of Shaytan, and Shaytan wants to be well-known by all mankind.

Therefore, people, through their egos, they are only accepting the existence of someone, and they do not see that one but they are following his way so easily, so strongly, so speedily. People are following Shaytan in twenty-first century because there is countless advertising about him everywhere. Everything is for his honor, the honor of Shaytan, and really there is no honor for him but people are exalting him. They do not know anyone exalted over Shaytan. They are making him their Lord and they are obeying to him, not making any objection.

The twenty-first century's people, their general view is this. People are following Shaytan but they are not saying "Shaytan". They are thinking that he is their *sultan*, they are thinking that he is the highest supporter for them, and beyond Shaytan, people are never accepting anything or anyone. They are saying, "Our best friend and the most exalted one in our sight is only that one." Beyond that, they are not proclaiming anyone's existence. They are followers of Satan as their king without any objection to his treatment, to his activities. Every activity that Satan gives to people, they are seeing as, oh, so perfect.

As we are saying now, for every new fashion in the lives of mankind now, among women and men, the founder of new fashions is Shaytan. It may be so ugly, but they are accepting it and saying, "So perfect," because satanic advertising is covering every place and if anyone says that fashion is so bad, they may attack you and say, "You are bringing dishonor to our chief, to our king, and we are moving through his inspirations that he is giving us. How you are

refusing, not accepting? Why are you saying this is ugly? It is perfect!"

Allah Almighty forgives every sin except making a partner for
Him, not forgiving that, and the partner that is coming under that
description, it is Shaytan. Don't think that if I am doing my hand
like this, [wiping] on a holy place, I am going to be a *mushrik*.[1]
These things are nonsense from Wahhabi people, but *shirk*, partnership—that is to make Shaytan partner, or even not partner but no
one *except* Shaytan.

Most people they are not believing in God Almighty. If they
are believing and also following Shaytan, that means they are making
Shaytan partner to their God. But now people are wholly denying
the existence of God Almighty and they are only reaching to Shaytan, and beyond Shaytan they are not accepting anything, so that
Shaytan, for some believers, is a partner to God.

Whoever believes in God and follows Shaytan, they are going to
be accused of keeping a partner. A lot of people they are saying,
"No God but Allah," but they are following Shaytan. Then that is
partnership with Allah, and Allah is getting very angry with those
who are saying, "We are believers in Allah," but not following Him,
and saying, "We are not accepting Shaytan," but following him. That
makes Allah Almighty to be angry with them.

But now most people they do not believe in the existence of
God and they have no partners for Him because Shaytan is their
Lord, and they are saying, "Only Shaytan. No God but Iblis, but
Shaytan." And Allah Almighty is very angry with those people who
are saying, "*La ilaha illa Shaytan*"—those who are moving with their

---

[1] For example, wiping one's hand on the walls of the K'abah out of love for its sanc-
tity. *Mushrik* is one who attributes partners to God; *shirk* is polytheism—attributing
partners to God or associating others with God's divinity.

egos, and either Shaytan is a partner for them to God Almighty or they are saying, "No God but Shaytan, but Iblis."

Now we are seeing that all people they are believing in Shaytan, in nothing but Shaytan. Therefore, it is such a difficult time now to carry away from the minds of people the partnership of Shaytan. Because of this, Allah is very angry. But even more than this, He is angry with people whom they are not only making Shaytan partner but they are saying "No God but Iblis."

The majority of people is following Shaytan, some of them saying "He is our Lord," some of them saying, "We believe in God but we are following Shaytan." They are making Shaytan partner for Allah, hearing and obeying Shaytan, not hearing and obeying Allah. And our egos belong to Shaytan. Therefore, Allah Almighty is never going to forgive those people who are either making Shaytan His partner or making him Lord.

Therefore, mankind now they are in a very dangerous position. From both ways, they must be taken away because they are between two groups of mankind, one of them calling Shaytan "Partner," another group calling him "the Lord of the Heavens." As long as they are on that way, they must be defeated, must be destroyed, must be taken away.

You look, what you are, whom you are following, after whom you are going. You must look. If it is satanic work, quickly, quickly you must leave and come back. That means you have lost your way; you are on the wrong way. You must come to the correct way. Therefore it is a very dangerous time coming on people, and very few people are going to be saved because the majority they are keeping Shaytan as their Lord and a group of them they are keeping Shaytan as partner for their Lord. Both sides are equally bad.

For every activity, you must ask, "Is this for my ego or for Allah? Who is going to be happy with this activity?" If you know that your ego is going to be happy, that means that you are keeping a partner and that is your ego. "I am your Lord. On behalf of my Lord, I am your Lord, O man," our ego, *nafs*, is saying. "I am your Lord. You must obey me." But what our physical being is tasting, it is very brief and has a very little amount of enjoyment, cheating people, and they are asking to follow Shaytan. That is the reason.

Then as we were beginning our Association, our aim is to save people from false beliefs, to save people from false activities, to save people from bad movements. If catching you from one side, Shaytan may carry you. Don't give a chance to Shaytan to carry you away from the right path, because he is so quick to run after people and to catch them, to carry them to follow him. That is the dangerous situation that people are getting into now, day by day darkness and danger mounting and people fearing, and they do not have taste for their physical life because heaviness is coming on them from their souls, and they are escaping from their souls, from good-dealing ones, and falling through the darkness of falsehood, *batil*.

Everyone must take care of this because it is so important. A wing of mankind is saying that Shaytan is a partner and the other group is saying, "No, he is Lord." You must try to save your ego from the hands from both mistaken ways. If not, you should be carried with others to a bad result, a very bad result.

May Allah forgive me and bless you. For the honor of the most honored prophet, Sayyidina Muhammad, ﷺ. *Fatehah.*

Mühim olan, important subject. [After some words in Turkish, he adds:] Lifting children from their school, children's school, bad schools, all advertising Shaytan and his ways, nothing else, and children are growing up full of love for Shaytan and satanic works. May Allah protect them and save them from the hands of devils. *Fatehah.*

▲

10

ALL PROPHETS HAVE THE SAME MISSION

> From the first to the last, the mission of all prophets was the same: to prepare people to take the jewels that Allah Almighty sent down to earth with Adam, symbolizing man's return to the Divine Presence in Paradise. All the prophets brought the divine invitation to mankind, reminding them that this is their real goal. But Shaytan is trying to divert people from this goal, and if one loses the chance that is offered to him, there will be no second chance.

Dastur, ya sayyidi, meded. Meded, ya sultan al-awliya, meded. Dastur, ya şeyh. La hawla wa la quwatta illa bil-Lah, la hawla wa la quwatta illa bil-Lah, la hawla wa la quwatta illa bil-Lah. A'udhu bil-Lahi min ash-Shaytani-r-rajim, bismillahi-r-Rahmani-r-Rahim. By the name of Allah, All-Mighty, All-Merciful, Most Beneficent and Most Munificent.

We are asking: *Dastur, ya sayyidi, ya sultan al-awliya.* That is our line to the Heavens through my Grandshaykh. What it is necessary for you know, They know well. Therefore, I am asking humbly that They may open that line for this gathering to be prepared to be obedient servants to our Lord, Allah Almighty.

All prophets they tried, and the Seal of Prophets just tried—for what? What were their missions? For which purpose had they been sent?

That was common message up to the Seal of the Prophets. What were those precious stones?

Allah Almighty, when He was forgiving Adam, when He was saying, "O Adam, tell, inform about My invitation to your children, that I am inviting them to come to enter into the Paradise that I have prepared for My servants.

"When I sent you out, Paradise was empty, and I am not in need of Paradise. I did not create Paradise for Myself; I am not in need. Countless universes and countless paradises I created and am creating, and My creation is going on. Don't think that I have, that I created only eight paradises. They are for you and for your descendants, and you are just a handful of servants. I have countless universes, countless servants, countless paradises. It is only *one* that you are on.

"When I sent you out, I asked you and your descendants to come back. I just sent you out by My divine wisdoms. If you had been there, you would not have given real value to Paradise—no. It is a grant to you. I sent you on earth, and I am putting Hells in front of Paradise so that, from fear of the Fire and hope of reaching My Paradises, you should try to come back.

"When you come back, it should be valuable to you. After passing so many exams, trials, tests, you will come, saying 'Oh-h!' but if I had given it to you free, you would say, 'Eh-h-h!' Every free thing is cheap, but because you have bought it, it is valuable." (Therefore I am saying, don't give to people anything without payment. No. Let them pay and take; then it should be valuable for them. "We paid." If writing even one page, charge some money for it. Then they should keep it; otherwise they may break it and throw it away.)

Now believers, they are running towards Paradise and they are in fear of the Fire, and they are fearful, also, that they will be at that time without a bridge. They have been in Paradise, but now Allah Almighty is putting a bridge—so long, so thin, so difficult to walk on for reaching Paradise, from one side to the other side, so difficult a bridge. Therefore, they are fearing how they can pass on it. When they are passing, they should say, "*Alhamdulillah* that we passed." Are you understanding?

And the most valuable jewel for Adam and his children that was thrown on earth, to take it and bring it, all prophets came to guide people to where it is, that most valuable jewel. That is prophets' mission—guidance for people to those jewels, and when they were following them, common people following prophets, they were teaching them something that was their main goal for all people.

The mission of prophets—that is preparation for the Divine Presence, to come back to His Divine Presence, and the missions of prophets are never going to be changed, neither Adam nor Noah nor Abraham nor Ishmael nor Isaac nor Zechariah, or Jesus Christ, Moses, David, Solomon. Everyone's never-changing mission, it is to prepare people for the Divine Presence. They are guiding people and saying, "Look, in that direction you can find some jewels. Go and take them, and as much as you can bring of jewels, you may be closer to Allah Almighty's Divine Presence."

Therefore, the mission of all prophets is preparation for the divine invitation. They are trying to prepare all people for the divine invitation in Paradise. People are thinking that when they are saying, "We are Christians," their direction of movement is opposite the direction of Muslims. But they are ignorant people. No; Christians, Muslims, Jewish people—all of them are under the umbrella of humanity, of mankind, and all of them they have been invited to be in Paradise for the divine invitation. And all prophets just came to prepare people for that divine invitation.

But people they have lost their ways. They are following Shaytan, and when Adam followed Shaytan, he was thrown out of Paradise. And Shaytan was asking to cut off the ways of mankind, not to be in the Divine Presence and to be granted endless favors in the Eternal Life. Therefore, beware of Shaytan!

What we are saying, it is a common wisdom for all nations from the beginning up to today. As a summary, if you keep it, you should reach every good aim, the best goals. If you are not listening, you are going to lose, and if a person loses once and asks to come to prepare himself a second time, it is going to be the same—no way. Therefore, there is only one chance for all nations, for all mankind, to know what is the divine goal for nations, for what He created and for what He sent His prophets to them. They must know it. ▲

11

DON'T BE LIKE CROCODILES

Generally people work out of necessity and as little as possible, occupying much of their time with satanic, useless or nonsensical activities. A real human being must have the characteristics of humanity, not the base characteristics of animals. Shaytan, the eternal enemy of the children of Adam, is making human beings violent and wilder than any wild beast. People are not interested in learning or obeying heavenly teachings, and hence they have no future except to perish in the final conflict between good and evil.

I heard it said that when Allah Almighty was giving everyone's shares of the material *dunya*, no one was looking at what he had been given or no one was saying that I have been granted the best share from my Lord, but always looking—"Oh! Such-and-such has been given much more than me." Everyone was thinking that others were just granted good shares except himself. Then it became like a habit among the children of Adam, this always looking at people, not looking what he himself had been granted.

Then Allah Almighty granted the shares of their minds to people, and everyone was coming, taking their shares and, without any discussion, without any looking at others, taking and going away. They were saying, "Oh-h! My mind—a big mind I have been granted. No one can be like me. I know everything! The one who has been granted the best mind, I am *that* one. People must ask *me*. I am not in need to consult with anyone. He doesn't know, that doesn't know, this doesn't know."

This is a characteristic of our egos, *nafs*. *I* am claiming, also, that I know much more than everyone, I am a much more clever person, and I am saying, "If it is true, every day so many people are coming to me and I am giving a little bit, a little bit. Then my mind is becoming less and I am afraid that one day it may finish"—yes, empty like a football, with nothing in it. And particularly in our days, people's heads they are like footballs, never seeing anything.

A'udhu bil-Lahi min ash-Shaytani-r-rajim. People are running and following satanic teachings, and Satan is occupying people with nonsensical things, useless activities. If you are looking, individually or generally, at people, they are giving much more of the time of their lives for nonsense and useless works and activities. If they did not fear for their provision, no one would work, doing something that could be useful for himself and for others, but they are seeing that if they do not work, they may be hungry and through hunger they may die.

Therefore, the fear of hunger is making people to work, and also they are asking to work as little as possible. They are trying to give, out of twenty-four hours for their provisions, for their work, the least time, and the majority or a big part of their day, of their time, to be free for useless works and for harmful works and for nonsensical works. If they could reach, even in one hour, to their provision, they would keep twenty-three hours for their egos, to make their egos happy and in pleasure, running after Shaytan and satanic works.

Therefore, all religions, all beliefs, are fighting against Shaytan, and Shaytan is fighting against all prophets. It is something that has never changed from the beginning up to today, up to the Day of Judgment. Shaytan is asking people to follow him, and people they like to follow satanic activities, satanic works and satanic pleasures, asking for the pleasure of Shaytan and nothing else.

Therefore, it is the first step for every believer to know who is their enemy, who is their most dangerous enemy. They must know him. Therefore, Allah Almighty is making clear through so many holy verses that Shaytan is the worst and most dangerous enemy for the children of Adam, and warning, also, all mankind, through His messengers, not to follow Satan and his works. But people they are happy to follow satanic activities, and now they are crying, shouting.

The twenty-first century's people, perhaps six billion people, they are unhappy, they are not feeling peace on earth, and if people individually are not reaching peace in themselves, they can't reach a common peace in East and West. As long as East is fighting West, West fighting East, northern countries fighting southern countries, no peace. So many tribes are fighting each other for nothing; they can't reach peace. Nations, throughout centuries, they are fighting each other for nothing, and they know this. Therefore they are not reaching peace.

Therefore, it is the most important point for a person who is asking to reach peace in himself—he must know who is the worst and most dangerous enemy that is giving trouble to people individually and generally. And Allah Almighty is saying, *asta'idhu bil-Lah*, "*Inna ash-Shaytana lakum 'aduwun, fat-takhiduhu 'aduwa.*[1] The most dangerous enemy for you, no doubt—that is Shaytan. I am declaring to you, I am informing you," He is saying, "and I am warning you of Shaytan because he is the most terrible and dangerous enemy to you, and his mission, from the beginning up to the end, is to destroy mankind, first beginning to destroy human nature."

Human nature—that is a high level of being. A human being must carry good characteristics. Those among common people who have been trained and taught and practiced and accepted good char-

---

[1]"Indeed, Satan is an enemy to you, so take him as an enemy." (35:6)

acteristics, they are coming up and they are going to have such good human nature that anyone who reaches that point is going to be like angels. Angels they are not harming anyone, and that person is not going to harm anyone through his tongue or through his organs. "*Al-Muslimu man salima-l-Muslimuna min lisanihi wa yadihi.*"[2] Therefore, this Prophet's *hadith*, holy saying of Rasul-Allah, 🌸, is bringing a full description of human nature, of humanity. When a person reaches humanity, no one is going to be harmed by him through his hand and tongue.

That is the perfection of mankind. All mankind, originally their egos, in the hands of Shaytan, represent violence on earth, and there can't be any other creature more violent than mankind. A wild animal may kill one animal for eating what is necessary; what it is in need of to continue its life, it must eat, hunting and eating. Wild animals they are not killing without a reason, but mankind, they are trying to find dangerous weapons that you are calling nuclear weapons; if they are throwing one, killing one million people. They are much more wild than wild animals.

That is the level of mankind. When they are going to be a prepared or treated or just taught through heavenly teachings, they will reach their real level of being from human nature.

Now people mostly they are on the level of mankind. Very few are reaching real humanity. Therefore, we are looking and seeing and reading and hearing that states, governments, they are saying, "Human rights," not saying "Mankind's rights." At that level, they will never know rights. Therefore, now the whole world has just fallen into cruelty because at their level they do not know the real position of being a perfect man through humanity. On that level they are wild people, wild creatures, more than any other creatures.

---

[2] "The Muslim is one from whose hands and tongue the Muslim is safe." (Bukhari, 1:9)

Therefore, every wild animal is in fear of mankind. Even though mankind are weak ones, they may harm the biggest animal. They may kill lions and tigers and snakes and elephants and such huge animals—weak man may kill them.

That warning from Allah Almighty was to all mankind from the beginning of our life on earth, Allah, the Exalted One, saying and ordering and warning His servants not to follow Shaytan because satanic teachings are making mankind to be the most wild creatures on earth. Therefore we are saying *"A'udhu bil-Lahi min ash-Shaytani-r-rajim."*

If you put one hundred guardians around our place, our *dergah,* they can't defend you from Shaytan. If bringing one thousand guardians, they can't guard you from Shaytan; Shaytan may come through them, also. But when you are saying *"A'udhu bil-Lahi min ash-Shaytani-r-rajim.* O my Lord I am running to you from Shaytan. Protect me, keep me, shelter me, from the arrows of Shaytan," because he is always shooting and asking to reach people through his poisoned arrows, [you may be in safety from him].

Therefore, people they are in endless troubles now in our days because they are not taking any care of warnings to them from Allah Almighty and they are saying, "We are not taking care about Shaytan or such things. They are like fairy tales, these things." For everything that belongs to the Heavens, these bad-characteristic people are saying "Fairy tales, fairy tales."

When they are saying "Fairy tales," that means they are giving no value to anything that is coming from the Heavens, and they should eat each other now. As long as they have such bad thoughts, they should kill each other, they should eat each other, they should destroy each other, and this world should be in ruins and there are going to be cemeteries everywhere because millions of people should be killed now in Armageddon, the biggest war that should finally be on earth.

Every day a person must try to say at least forty times, "*A'udhu bil-Lahi min ash-Shaytani-r-rajim.* O my Lord I am running to you from Shaytan and satanic works. Shelter me and keep me away from his tricks and from falling into his traps."

Almost all the world now is just falling into the big trap of Shaytan. Everything they are doing, it is satanic teaching. They are never accepting heavenly teachings. They are saying, "Positive knowledge. Beyond this, no knowledge."

That means they are denying and they are throwing away wisdoms because wisdoms are not from positive knowledge, never giving value to wisdoms that are coming from the Heavens to some chosen people, because not everyone can reach the level of wisdoms or it is not easy to reach the Ocean of Wisdoms. It is so difficult. If you are reaching it, you should find the realities of everything there.

Here, you can't see, you can't hear, you can't reach because it is the material world, but behind the material world there are unseen Wisdom Oceans, oceans from which prophets and *awliya*, saints, are taking wisdoms, and to reach to those oceans you must be very light, you must save yourself from the attraction of the material world.

When you should be free from material aspects, you should reach. You may go up, you may rise and reach heavenly Wisdom Oceans. Otherwise, you should be here like lizards—you know lizard, running on earth?—or crocodiles. People like to be crocodiles or lizards or snakes, some of them running under the earth, some of them on the earth; they are never interested in heavenly worlds, heavenly aspects. They are happy to be a lizard or crocodile. Yeh, you are happy?

May Allah protect you from falling in front of a crocodile. One second, inside, and then opening its mouth and birds are coming to take what remains of that man in its teeth. May Allah forgive us and bless you. For the honor of the Seal of the Prophets: *bi-hurmati-l-Fatehah.* ▲

12

GREAT SAINTS ARE OCEANS

> Grandshaykh Shah Bahauddin Naqshband's advice to man-kind concerning the importance of *sohbet* or Association with the shaykh of *tariqah*. Allah's support is with the con-gregation as long as their hearts are together, but if there is opposition among them that support is withdrawn. Since the French Revolution, with the demise of monarchies, na-tions have lost the cream of their societies, their royal fami-lies. In our time, there is so much advertising for democ-racy, but it does not hold solutions to the problems of peo-ple. The alternative to democracy is rule by the law of God. As long as economies are based on paper currency, there will be crises. The only alternative is to return to gold and silver as the medium of exchange.

Oh-h! *Dastur, ya sayyidi, ya mawlay. Meded, ya sultan al-awliya; meded, ya sultan al-awliya, meded, ya sultan al-awliya.* Support, support our believers. *A'udhu bil-Lahi min ash-Shaytani-r-rajim, bismillahi-r-Rahmani-r-Rahim.*

"*At-tariqatu-s-sohbet wa 'l-khayru fi l jami'ah.*"[1] That is Grand-shaykh Shah Naqshband's advice to all people.

Small lakes may belong to some territories, but no one is going to say that the Pacific Ocean, that is only for me, or the Atlantic Ocean, it is only for me, or the Indian Ocean, it belongs to me only. But small seas, so many people are fighting each other that this is for

---

[1]"*Tariqah* is Association and the greatest good is in the gathering."

me, this is not for you. And the great ones of the *ummah*, they are like oceans. Great saints like Shah Naqshband, he is an ocean and anyone with a boat or vessel may sail in his ocean. Therefore, when we are saying Shahu Naqshband, he is addressing all nations as well as all *awliya*.

Awliya also may sail through his ocean, and his words are just stamped by Rasul-Allah, ﷺ, because the Seal of the Prophets, he was opening an ocean for his big inheritors from his Knowledge Oceans.

It is impossible for a small boat to travel on an ocean. Must be a tonnage to be able to sail on an ocean because the sailing conditions of oceans are not same as the conditions of small seas or lakes; there must be a special structure for vessels to be able to sail on oceans. And through the Oceans of Knowledge and Wisdoms of Rasul-Allah, ﷺ, only those big ones may enter, may look, may take pearls and jewels from the Oceans of Wisdom, Oceans of Knowledge of Rasul-Allah, ﷺ.

The Prophet was saying, "*Yadullahi m'a al-jam'ah.*"[2] Rasul-Allah, pbuh, he was saying, "Allah Almighty protects under His divine Hand a gathering if the hearts of that gathering are on the same direction." If there is opposition, not all of them on the same direction, then Allah Almighty's support leaves them. Therefore, opposition, it is a big hindrance, perhaps the biggest hindrance, for people to reach their real goals in this life.

Therefore, the democratic system it is *batil*, false, because there is a group of them that are governing a country and another group that are against them. But opposition makes weakness for nations. Therefore it is *batil* and there is no democracy in Islam.

---

[2] "Allah's hand is with the congregation."

No. People or governments of people must all of them be on the same direction. If some people are saying, "We do not agree with you," don't keep them inside. Throw them out; they are trouble-makers. Therefore Shaytan is making democracy with different parties, groups of people under different names, to make people's coming days not to be successful, and always there must be troubles among people because some are saying this, some others saying "No."

Therefore, from the time that Adam landed on this planet, up to the twentieth century, throughout all historical periods, nations have been governed by one person, no opposition. But that opposition just began in 1789 with the big, dirtiest revolution, the French Revolution, which opened the doors of dirtiness to people, and people were running in it, running in it, and they were asking to take more and more of dirtiness.

By that, they just took away the cream of the milk, throwing it away and leaving only the water part of the milk. The cream of people, it is the noble people, royal people. They killed them, all of them, killing them and throwing them out, and only the water of the milk remained. And everything that they did up to today, with no value, no taste, is only growing through democratic systems, troubles growing, sufferings mounting, and many more miseries among people.

The democratic system looks like Nero's palace's garden system. Nero, he was keeping wild animals in his gardens but not feeding them, letting them to go around everywhere, and also slaves were working, going-coming. Then if any of the wild animals was hungry, it would attack him or her, and slash them and eat, and Nero was looking and he was becoming so happy.

The democratic system never, never takes any care against bad people, giving a chance for them more than for good ones. In each country that you can see, power is in the hand of violent ones, wild ones, ignorant ones, dishonorable ones, non-religious ones or no believers with them. They are denying everything except what they are eating and enjoying themselves with.

And it is impossible for a heavenly revelation to accept to say to people, "You must chose your governing people"; no. Allah is saying in His Holy Qur'an that you must have kings and *sultans*. When the Children of Israel were in a very difficult situation, they were coming to their prophet and saying, "O our prophet, ask from Allah Almighty to send us a *malik*, a king, a *sultan*," not saying, "We are going to choose someone from among ourselves to be our king"; no. "Let Allah send us." And the heavenly command and order came to that prophet and informed the Children of Israel that that one, Talut [Saul], should be your king, even though some people said, "We don't like him to be our king because he is only a poor one and we have such big wealth with ourselves. Why He is sending us such a person?"

And their prophet answered them by Allah Almighty's order, "Allah chose that one because he was granted by his Lord power in his physical being as well as knowledge beyond your knowledge—*fi-l-'ilmi wal-jism*[3] more than any one of you."

"Allah *chose*." That means that choosing the governing body it is from Allah, not from people, people choosing their governing bodies. No; it is *batil*. Therefore, since that trick of Shaytan, it is going to be accepted by people, because Shaytan was cheating people, saying, "Why are you not going to reach power? Why are you leaving power only in the hands of one family, royal people? You must have it also."

---

[3]*"Indeed, Allah has chosen him [Saul] over you and has increased him abundantly in knowledge and stature."* [2:247]

That is cheating, and Shaytan cheated people and people they said, "Yes, we must also reach that power-station, power-point, to do as we want to do, as kings were doing before." But it is *batil*, and therefore after the big French Revolution, countless troubles came, everywhere trouble-makers increasing and noble people killed, and never any cream remaining, only water. Everything was just taken, as people, when they are milking their cows, are taking this cream and then they may make, from that remaining milk, cheese or something else, and finally there remains, also, water, and that water either they are throwing on the ground or making food for chickens or for some other animals.

Now people they have lost the cream. Every nation has just lost the cream part of their nations, that earlier each nation had a royal family as their cream. When democracy came, it was fighting against kingdoms, and they are carrying the flag of the kingdom of Satan. And now we are looking and seeing where we have reached.

Through the democratic system we have reached to that point that people they are in *hayret*, in wonder. They do not know how they can save themselves because of the democratic system that has brought them to a most dangerous position. Now they are trying to save themselves but there is no room in that democratic system, and they are now in wonder because if they want to come and bring a solution for people's situation, they must come back to royal families. But they are too proud to do that, and if they are doing it, first of all *their* heads should be gone. Dangerous! Therefore, they are insisting and saying, "Democratic, democratic." If anything is advertised too much, that means that there is a trick in it, cheating people.

Now no one is advertising for kingdoms because a kingdom has no need. Pearls have no need to be advertised, or rubies or emeralds or diamonds; no need to make advertising on big boards—no, no need. But for washing powders, you can find big advertising, and this *nane şekeri*, mints, *polo*. *Polo*!!! Oh-h, oh-h-h! Everywhere *polo*;

must be something in it for cheating people. *Polo* you can find advertised everywhere. You can open the TV. It is also *polo* or washing powders, Tide or Ariel or Persil, so many, saying, "This it was so dirty. Look, going to be so nice. Every day little ones are making these white clothes black, and look, this washing powder is doing it first class." Have you seen anyone doing advertising for diamonds? No.

Therefore, for hiding the bad sides of democracy, they are making *so-o* much advertising about it, to hide its real face.[4] Therefore, now people they are thinking that there is not any alternative; they are never asking to say that there is an alternative for democracy. Yes, there is. The alternative democracy is theocracy.

Theocracy. "*Demos*" in old Greek language is "fool." Fool; it means crazy, stupid. But they are hiding this meaning. Yes. A French professor said to me, "Do you know, shaykh, what is '*demos*'? *Demos* [has] two meanings. One means "people". Another meaning, the real meaning of *demos*, is foolish people; mental-house people, they are saying. Really, mental-house people are governing the whole world.

Therefore, they are making advertising twenty-four hours a day, saying "Democracy, democracy." I am putting cotton. [Laughter]. Cheating, cheating, and people are just falling into crisis now.

[Takes out money.] Paper can be money? This is money? Where is gold? Through all historical periods people were buying and selling with gold and silver. Now democracy is taking gold and silver from people and giving paper.

That is democracy, the biggest cheating system on earth from the beginning up to today, and they are falling down now because

---

[4]Perhaps here and elsewhere he is reflecting on the political phenomenon of Turkey or Europe rather than America.

this paper can't give support to the world. You can't build an economic system on it; on this paper; finished. Gold must come so that
the economy may get up and crisis leaves them.

If it is gold, you will think about using this easily; you will think.
You can't give gold, if a coin, so easily. People keep it, and when
keeping it, the economy will come to its real level. But this paper
money, no one takes any care.

And more than this, there are credit cards. Credit cards, if you
give a billion, you will think, "Write it down." If gold, you can do
this? With paper money, you may do it so easily, so easily. (If our
money is used for one day, it is going to be suitable for the dustbin;
you can't take in your hand, it is becoming so dirty, and I do not like
to put in my pocket, I like to spend it. But gold, gold—never.)

That is such a strange cheating method, from satanic teachings.
And no way now. It is impossible for their economic situation ever
to be arranged with these paper monies. No, finished. No paper
money, and the whole world must come to that point now. And my
heart is working among the hearts of economists to understand and
to come to this point. *They must come.*

May Allah forgive me and bless you, and give us good understanding. For the honor of the most honored prophet, Rasul-Allah,
☙: *bi hurmati-l-Fatehah.*

Grandshaykh he had some money from the time of the Russian
emperors. They were banknotes like this [very large], so many things
on it, not like this. And in one night up to the morning, it was just
finished, those papers becoming of no value.

They are cheating, big cheating. Now they are wondering how
they should save themselves because they have built their economical
system on paper. Now they are thinking how we can change it. I
am saying, change democracy to theocracy, change paper money to

gold coins and silver; you should be happy. Take away banks and the money market, stock markets, and finish. As long as you have banks, as long as you have paper monies, as long as you have shares in stock markets, you are never going to be saved from crisis. You should die, you should finish. They are thinking about it now. ▲

13

MAN WAS CREATED WEAK

> Man is weak, but by human standards, according to his wealth he is powerful and strong. Men think that their wealth is the source of their power and strength, and if it leaves them they are nothing. Economy based on paper money has no substance nor ability to survive crises because its foundation is valueless. Governments must bring back gold and silver as a monetary base in order to escape from crises. Allah has endless Treasure Oceans but He is not in need of them nor of anything from any of His creations. We should ask Him not for the treasures of this life but for the eternal treasures of the Eternal Life.

A'udhu bil-Lahi min ash-Shaytani-r-Rajim, bismillahi-r-Rahmani-r-Rahim. May Allah bless our gathering and grant us from His endless favors.

He has endless Favor Oceans. This life that we are living is such a short period, very short, and His Favors Oceans are unlimited oceans. Do you think that He is in need of endless Favor Oceans or endless favor treasures?

Meded, ya sultan al-awliya. Allah, the Exalted, His attributes are never going to be like creatures' attributes or characteristics. If anything is like creatures' attributes, then He is going to be a creature. The Creator can't be like a creature. Impossible; can't be.

You may think that for a king, for a *sultan*, for an emperor, their power is according to their treasures and according to their territories. A king may have so many treasures. If he has only one treasure, he is not a big one. If he has ten treasures, compared to a hundred treasures he is still a small one. If he has one hundred treasures, a king or emperor, according to someone who has one thousand treasures, he is still a small one. I mean to say that people, now and before, their power-measure or their greatness-measure or balance was according to their gold and treasures and the bigness of their treasures. Yes? Wealth—their value is through their wealth.

Now in our time, also, people are respected according to their financial power. If they have a big amount of wealth, they are going to be respected among the community according to their financial power or ability to do something. And those people, they are in need of their wealth, and their wealth—we may say treasures—if it is taken from them, they are going to be nothing. They are supported by material pillars. If no material pillars, they are going to fall down; they can't stand up.

Every time this, what we are saying, it is just true—an *ifade*,[1] description, full explanation for them of the position of mankind from the beginning up to the end and in our times, in our days, never changing because man is created weak, and their weakness is going away through wealth. People are thinking that wealth may take weakness from them. Through their material aspects, the material pillars that are supporting them, they are feeling that they are powerful. But it is not true, it is not true. Any time, if that wealth leaves them, they will fall into an endless weakness, not as they were at the beginning. Everyone is just created weak but if a person is supported by material pillars and he loses them, he falls down from the level of weakness, also, not coming back to the level that he was first at and then rising up.

---

[1] Expression, statement, expounding.

Now the whole world is just falling into a much worse situation. Perhaps, from the beginning of historical periods up today, mankind has never fallen into such weakness and inability to do anything as in our days, in our time now. Everywhere, everywhere that people were trusting in a material base and pillars, it has just been taken from them, and the whole world now has fallen down. And they are saying, "It is a crisis."

What "crisis"? They are not telling the truth. It is not a crisis, but that is their falsehood, bringing them to that point, because they left real, correct values and truth, and then they tried to bring some theories or ideas, and they were thinking that their ideas and new concepts should bring them much more. And it is only one world. However you are using it [claps hands to show that this is the limit], it is not going to be more than this.

What you are doing, it is like a bakery, making *'ajin*, dough. Dough is not going to be more if you put more water into it; no. You put only one kilogram of flour and you begin to make bread. If you think that this one pound or two pounds of flour, when you put more water into it, will give you more than three or four breads or such a thing—no, it is impossible.

Theories that are based on *batil*, falsehood—they think that if we are using our theories we can reach more richness than from a small amount. And they have lost everything now, saying, "Oof! What we put into it of flour just disappeared; also so much water, just disappeared. Oof! What we shall do? How are we going to bring that back again?" Impossible. That is the reason of crisis.

Finished. Again and again, they tried to cheat people with paper money. This is not money, this is not valuable. But their theories are making this "money". This is not money. You can't buy anything with this, you can't sell. But through their theories they are saying, "This is one million pounds. You must accept this, even though your intellect is saying. 'Can't be. One million pounds, this can't be. How I am accepting it?' *You must accept!*"

Therefore, they are now very depressed from this and they are thinking, "What must we do? We must take away all monies like peso, like lira, mark, and we may put another money, euro. They are thinking that if they are doing this, something is going to be changed. Never changing!

Those headquarters of *dunya* (they are saying "Ee-Me-Te," International Monetary Fund), they are thinking that they may do something new, and when they are doing this they may be able to control everything under their hands, but it is impossible. It is impossible, because you must accept that that is a paper. Paper money was *never*, never used before, even among more *ibtida'i*, primitive, people. They were using golden and silver.

The twenty-first century's people, officially they are cheating people and saying "This is like that." Can't be! They want to take more control into their hands and they are joining so many countries' monies to make it into one. No! The whole world may join gold without putting anything. No! If the German government is making coins with the Kaiser's stamp on it, England also has golden coins, and Italy. It goes everywhere. But they are asking to cheat people, never asking to give back what they are stealing from people, all the gold, taking it under their control, those people who are saying, "We are controlling all the economy on earth," cheating people.

They are insisting, "Do not bring values of everything, gold and silver, for the economy," and it is impossible now for the crisis to be taken away till gold and silver comes to the market. Finished! [Claps hands together.]

We are saying this for some point; I am going to speak on it. Before, people they were keeping their gold and they were feeling that we are powerful people. Now no one can keep gold in their homes; so many bad conditions. They don't like it. If anyone has some gold, he must give it to banks, to markets.

Now we are coming to people's power. They were thinking that material aspects are giving them power, but they passed away. Now people who have only paper in their pockets, they are understanding that papers can't carry, can't support them.

So many people are asking me, "O shaykh, what we shall do in the crisis? We are getting Turkish money and we may buy American dollars or euros or pounds."

When I am saying, "Buy gold," they are saying, "But gold never brings any interest." They are not happy when I am saying to them to buy gold. They are saying, "Why? American dollars bring every month such-and-such amount of interest." And I am saying, "But you must not be heedless. Maybe in one night up to morning all that paper will be nothing, but whatever you are keeping in your safes of gold and silver, that is for you. Don't trust in paper, even if there is written on it, 'In God we trust.'" In reality, they are not trusting in God but they are ashamed to write, "In Shaytan we trust." Actually it is that, but they are ashamed to say this, saying, "In God we trust." Like this, you are trusting in God—*on paper?* What is this foolishness?

This is a panorama of the whole situation, through East and West and from North to South, on continents, on oceans. Yes. Men, their power is with their wealth. We are discussing wealth because it is important, so many people coming to me, asking me, "What is the way that we can get out of this crisis?"

You can't. It is not just one person; individual activities can't take nations out of crisis. Governments must say, "After today, after this, we will bring gold and silver to our markets."

Then we are coming to the point that Allah Almighty, He has endless Treasure Oceans, endless treasures, endless Favors Oceans. Do you think that He is asking support from His treasures? You must be foolish. Therefore we are bringing this—that in the sight of people, a person is powerful according to his wealth, his financial capacity or ability.

Men are in need of that support. Without it man is weak, but Allah—endless Power Oceans for Him. He is not in need of those endless Treasure Oceans. Eh! He is not like His creatures, *no*! He is, from pre-eternity up to eternity, the King of Kings—Allah Almighty, the Lord of all creation, the Lord of the Heavens from pre-eternity up to eternity, and eternal sultanate, hegemony and power are only for Him. That power is in Him, not coming from outside. We are asking from the endless Favor Oceans of Allah Almighty.

Once Sayyidina Musa, Moses, pbuh, he was going to Tur Sina, Mount Sinai. He met a person; he was using only one piece of cloth for covering the underside of his body, another piece of cloth on his shoulders, and he was saying, "O Moses, please ask from your Lord to give me something."

Sayyidina Musa was saying, "Yes, I will." And he was on Mount Sinai and Allah Almighty was addressing him.

He was saying, "Anything, O Moses?" He knew everything. "You remember?"

"Yes, my Lord. One servant, very, very poor, nothing for him, only two pieces of old cloth, rags, is asking for something."

Then Allah Almighty was saying to Moses, "*Min al-qalil aw min al-kathir*—from the small side or from the big side? I have so many treasures, counted treasures and countless treasures. Counted treasures are for *dunya*, countless treasures for the Hereafter."

"According to your generosity, O my Lord, give to him much."

"Granted." And Moses ran to give good tidings to that person; he thought that he was waiting at the same place. He reached there and found him just passed away, and he came and said. "Oof, I just came to give good tidings to this servant and he died. O my Lord, what is this? What happened? You gave to him, but he never reached it and passed away."

And Allah Almighty addressed him, saying: "O Moses, I asked you, 'I am giving from big amount or from small amount?' You said, 'It is not for You, according to Your generosity, to give a small thing. No—give!'

"I just gave to him, because as much as I may give during this life, it is only a small amount, just going to finish after a while. Even if he lives a hundred years, two hundred years, a thousand years, it is going to finish. But for eternity—I gave to him from eternal treasures. Therefore, when I gave to him, I sent 'Azra'il[2] to take him and to put those treasures."

Therefore, Allah Almighty may give everything here but it is nothing. Yes, during this life His favors are making people to stand up, to run, to work, to reach something, to be happy, but it is only in very brief limits, going to finish. Therefore, Allah Almighty is urging people to ask for His endless Favor Oceans, that they should be for the Eternal Life.

His servants may ask and He may give unexpected amounts. If they are asking for one, He is granting unexpected numbers of treasures. It is another measure for *akhirah*, for after death, for the Eternal Life.

O people, we are all heedless. We are running after nothing, after dirty aspects. No; it is not correct for true servants to run after

---

[2] The Angel of Death.

something that finally it is going to melt and finish. You must run after real life's aspects, to ask from your Lord's never-ending treasures, to be in His Divine Presence, to enjoy yourself with endless pleasures in the Divine Presence of your Lord, Almighty Allah.

May Allah bless you and forgive me. For the honor of the Seal of the Prophets, Sayyinina Muhammad, ﷺ: *bi hurmati-l-Fatehah*.

[Exchange in Turkish.] He may use it for reaching to endless treasures. It is a bridge for you. If you can't use it, it is against you. You may fall down, never reaching. *Alhamdulillah, alhamdulillah, wa-sh-shukru lil-Lah. Astaghfirullah, astaghfirullah, astaghfirullah.*

You must know that you are alone; you must know that you are alone. Don't think that these people are around yourself and you are not alone. You are alone, you are alone.

Anything that is coming on you is coming to you only. If illness comes, you are alone; if death comes, you are alone. Don't think that these people are with you—no. Everyone will leave you and go away. Think that you are alone.

People are very heedless. They are thinking that "Oh, we are all together." People will never carry what comes on you, no. Everyone will leave you and go away, and finally they will put you alone in a coffin and put you there. You are alone, coming alone and going alone. Don't think that this crowd of people is making you not to be alone. Loneliness it is written for everyone. *Astahgfirullah, astaghfirullah!*

When you are putting your head on your pillow and your wife is sleeping there, your children sleeping there and you are on your pillow, you must feel that you are alone. If anything comes from above to you, no one will be able to reach you. You are alone; loneliness is just written for everyone. Allah-Allah, *Allahu akbar! Fatehah.*

Oh-ho-ho-ho! King George the Sixth—you know him? You are not from London? Father of the Queen, King George the Sixth. I was remembering his father's time, the time of King George the Fifth. I reached his silver jubilee and I was granted a medal, also for that ceremony. I was twelve years old at that time.

Then his son was coming, Edward the Eighth, but he was not accepting to leave a common woman, and he left the crown and the throne for a woman. He was thinking that he was doing the best. He left, and then his younger brother, King George the Sixth, was on throne and he had a coronation, also. I was given also another medal for the coronation ceremony.

Now I am saying that finally, because according to their traditions, the king and queen can't sleep together. You understand? From old times, some bad things happened, perhaps a queen cheated to kill a king or a king to kill a queen. Therefore, they were sleeping in *ayrı odaları*, separate rooms, the king in his room, the queen in her room. And he died, passed away alone in his room. In the morning they found King George the Sixth dead in his bed. The Emperor of the British Empire, the empire on which the sun never sets—that person, the King of England and Emperor of India, he passed away alone in his room. ▲

14

ADAM'S HONORED CREATION

This talk was given on 1 Muharram, the new year of 1424. The summary of it is that this year is coming with tremendous spiritual power. All those whose hearts are not with Allah will be taken away. Beware of the divine punishment that is coming upon mankind by Allah's decree, and shelter yourself under the castle of *"La ilaha illa-Llah, Muhammadu Rasul-Allah,"* ﷺ.

A'udhu bil-Lahi min ash-Shaytani-r-rajim, bismillahi-r-Rahmani-r-Rahim, bismillahi-r-Rahmani-r-Rahim, bismillahi-r-Rahmani-r-Rahim. Bismillah miftahu. Ya mufateha-l-abwab, ifta lana khayr al-abwab. Bismillah ifta tahtu, wa 'ala Allahi tawwakalt. Wa man yatawakal 'ala Allah, fa Huwa hasbuh, Subhanahu wa Ta'ala.

Dastur, ya sayyidi, ya sultan al-awliya. New page—new page, new face; new view, new news.

New page,

new face,

new view,

new news,

like a poem, saying now. Yah, good? My English is open, like Shakespeare's. If Shakespeare was present, he would laugh too much. He was never thinking of such a thing--

New page,

new face,

new view,

Q News.[1] [Laughter.]

MURID: *Muazzam!*

SHAYKH: *Eh—nau khabar.*[2] *Ah, ya Allah, ya Allah, ya Allah!
Haqiq! Wa'dak al-Haqq, innaka la tukhlifu ul-miyad.* Allah, what He
said must come, must happen, must appear. I hope that preparation
for that big change on the whole planet is beginning from tonight
and going on.

The number of years of the Islamic calendar that is just going to
begin tonight is 1424, and it is coming with greatness, with power.
Awliya are seeing that this moon of Muharram, and also the new
year, is coming with *heybet*, greatness—greatness that is giving to
hearts a kind of fear that you can't bring a description of. It is not an
ordinary fear.

Ordinary fear may be for some time, but now the whole world
is going to fall into a Fear Ocean, beginning from this night's sunset.
Particularly the leaders and heads of all countries, they are going to
feel that fear deeply in their hearts, civil people or military. All headquarters that are against divine laws, heavenly rules, are beginning to
fear deeply a fear, but they can't give any description for what this
fear is coming, and then fear is going to increase, day by day, week
by week, month by month going to grow and to cover them wholly.
Either they are going to resign or they should be in a mental house

---

[1] The name of a well-known British Muslim magazine.
[2] New information, tidings.

93

or they should be killed, either killing their own selves or finally going to be killed.

This year is coming with such a powerful manifestation; a very powerful sight is coming now. Oh-h-h-h! Beware, mankind! Those who are trying to climb to the level of humanity, they should be supported and they should be saved, also, and they should be under heavenly protection. Those who are not asking to climb, to reach the level of humanity, will remain down, a storm coming and taking them away, a storm of fire, a flood of blood coming now.

Therefore, it is a warning now today, coming to me, warning the whole world that everyone *must* think about their final end, either to be on the level of humanity or remaining on the level of violence, with violent ones, and violence is going to be finished now, beginning from tonight.

Allah Almighty never looks at your outside but Allah Almighty looks at your hearts, what is there. If your hearts belong to Him, you should be saved; if your hearts are not with Him Almighty, you should be taken away, destroyed. Everything that they did up to today is going to be destroyed; every building that was just built on falsehood, *batil*, should be taken away, finished.

That is *farman, faraman ilahi. Farman* is the proclamation of the *sultan*. There must be one word in the English dictionary that they are using for kings and emperors, and for this we are not saying "announcement from the Heavens" or "declaration from the Heavens," but we are saying that what belongs to Allah Almighty must give more fear, full of greatness, to the hearts of people. It is not an ordinary declaration, anyone's declaration; no—heavenly.

Decree; yes. It is not only a person, a *sultan* or king—no, with power, so that people who hear it must fear. That is coming now, tonight, for all headquarters of mighty people among *awliya* who are keeping heavenly might in their hands. Now the command is coming: "Go on, go on *kufr*,[3] go on falsehood, go on to destroy the satanic kingdom on earth." Finished!

May Allah forgive me and protect ourselves. Believers should be protected. Therefore Allah Almighty is looking at people's hearts now. Whoever is with Him, whoever is for Him, should be sheltered, should be saved. Whoever is not with Him Almighty or not for Him Almighty should be taken away, destroyed. Big destruction is coming now on earth.

A new view. Today this just arrived, because my heart is also getting very angry; from last night, too much power is coming to my heart, also. I am nothing, but when this divine power line is open, I may destroy all *kufr*. I am the weakest one, now the weakest one. Tomorrow, I don't know.

Ey, ya Rabbi, ya Allah, ya Allah, ya Allah, ya Allah, ya Allah! Beware for your name, beware for your names. Two tables or lists— names should be written on them: "To be saved" and "To be destroyed"; "To be sheltered" and "To be taken away"; in one, the names of people who should be sheltered, should be protected, and in another table, those on whom that heavenly revenge will come.

Keep yourself. Beware not to have your names written on second table, the list of those who should be taken away. No one can save them, and there is no protection now for people except heavenly protection.

This is a holy month. Throughout the centuries, from the beginning of the life of man on earth, this month has been such a sacred month, a holy month, a very holy month, a very powerful month, that Allah Almighty's heavenly and divine power, when He wants to take revenge on disobedient people, has come during this

---

[3]Unbelief.

month. Don't put your head under the guillotine. Whoever puts it under it must be cut; it is impossible to prevent it. And the warning is coming, "Take your heads out or the guillotine will come on you."

How many millions are putting their heads, in one moment going to be taken away—not like the French guillotine, one after another, one after another, no? Beware of the heavenly 'guillotine.' Don't say, "I am this one, I am that one. I am not afraid."

Beware, O people, beware! These feelings are now coming through the pure-hearted people, who should ask for a shelter from the Heavens. And the only shelter that is granted is the shelter of Sayyidina Muhammad, pbuh. People must be told, "Go and shelter yourself under the shelter of the most honored one. Don't be outside. If you do not enter, you should be taken away."

La ilaha illa-Lah hasni, wa man dakhala hasni ay mina-l-adhabi. The Unity of Allah Almighty, Oneness of Allah Almighty, "*La ilaha illa-Lah,*"[4] is not going to be accepted without saying *"Muhammadu Rasul Allah,*[5] ﷺ." That means that the castle, the divine castle on earth, whoever may enter it is going to be in safety, the castle of *"La ilaha illa-Llah, Muhammadu Rasul-Allah,* ﷺ," and that flag on the towers of that castle now can be seen from the far East to the far West, from the far North to the far South, everywhere now should be seen.

May Allah forgive me and let us enter the divine castle. The castle, that is the castle of the Lord of the Heavens, to say *"La ilaha illa-Llah, Muhammadu Rasul-Allah,* ﷺ." Enter it; you should be in safety. Whoever is outside, *Hu-u!*—finished.

Allah-Allah, Allah-Allah, Allah-Allah, 'Aziz-Allah. Allah-Allah, Allah-Allah, Allah-Allah, Karim-Allah. Allah-Allah, Allah-Allah, Allah-

---

[4]"There is no deity except Allah."
[5]"Muhammad is the Messenger of Allah."

Allah, Subhan-Allah. *Allah-Allah, Allah-Allah, Allah-Allah, Sultan-Allah.* *Sultan mutlaq,* absolute sultanate, eternal sultanate for our Lord, Allah Almighty.

Accept our *mu'adharat,* excuse. We are weak servants. Send us one who may keep ourselves from being put under the guillotine, to save our necks from the guillotine that Shaytan and his followers are going to be under—not to be with them. Let us, *ya Rabb,* O our Lord, be with your most honored servant, most honored messenger, Sayyidina Muhammad, ﷺ. *Bi-hurmati-l-habib, bi-hurmati-l-Fatehah.* ▲

15

THE POWER OF HOPE

> People need hope to go on living. When hope finishes, life finishes. Those who are working for the sake of this world or for their egos' pleasure easily lose hope and go down, but those who work for the sake of Allah and *Akhirah* keep their hope, their strength and vitality up to the end. Most people, although they are still in this life, are dead. But Allah's *awliya* are living ones, keeping their powers, like Sayyidina Zakariyah who asked for and was granted a son at a very advanced age. We must try to look for a living *wali* to give to us from his power.

Allah-Allah, Allah-Allah, Allah-Allah, Allah-Allah, Allah-Allah. Meded, ya sultan al-awliya. Meded, ya rijal-Allah, meded, meded, meded, meded, meded, meded. Every moment we must ask for heavenly support, and heavenly support is reaching to the hearts of pure-hearted people and going through their hearts. Whoever is asking for divine support, it is running to their hearts and giving power and pleasure and satisfaction and contentment to people because we are in need of living hope.

Hope—when you lose your hope, you are finished. Therefore the Prophet was saying, "You must work." You must work because you have been ordered to work. But to work for whom, for what?

Everyone works but their intentions are different. We may say, as a summary, that the majority of people are working for their egos or egotistical desires, or they are working for their egos' pleasure. Another, a handful of people in comparison to the first group who are working for their egos, those who are working for Allah, are a handful of people, so small a group of people. If there are six billion people working for their egos, for their desires, for their physical being's pleasures, you may find perhaps, *perhaps*, one million—not billion, one million—people who are living for Allah or for working for Allah.

Don't say, "What about Muslims?" Muslims, also, they are following Western people and they are asking to be westernized Muslims, Westernized people whose only aim is to live an enjoyable life, to make themselves in pleasure and nothing else. And Muslims, they are imitating Western people and they are saying, "We must also enjoy ourselves more. As much as possible, we must enjoy our physical being." And when people are running after their egos or physical beings' desires, they are going to be slaves to their egos or egoistical desires, their lives passing only for fulfilling the desires of their physical being.

Now, their hopes are continuing up to a limit. When they are reaching to that limit, they are going to finish.

What is that limit? When a slave of Shaytan or slave of his ego reaches a limit and sees that he is going to be unable to fulfill his physical being's desires, he is going to be hopeless, his hopes finishing there.

When their feelings signaling that they are finishing, it is like the measure of petrol in a car. If it is full, you are such a hopeful person, saying, "Oh-h, I am full." Yes, and a man also is full when he is young. Young ones' tanks are full but they are beginning to waste, quickly wasting; then coming, looking, "Oof, this needle is coming down. Oh! What we shall do now? It was like this, now falling down like this. What shall we do? Finishing—our time is finished to put any more."

No more [claps hands together to indicate finished]. Finished; hopeless. He must die, she must die. Then they are not asking to work—no, because no hope; they can't work, no. Therefore, European people, they are building some places for old people. That means that whoever has lost their life-hope, they can't do anything now. They must sit and they must wait for their last moment. When the last moment comes, angels are coming.

At that time he is feeling his loneliness, understanding loneliness. There may be there thirty or forty old people but everyone is feeling that now they are lonely, alone. When they were with their children, they were not thinking of loneliness, but when they are taken among themselves—when their children, grandchildren, are throwing them away, saying, "We don't like you more than this. Go away," sending to *iftiara* house, old people's places—everyone is sitting like this and feeling loneliness, and the *adhab*, punishment for their souls, is beginning from that time. No hope from their lives, no hope to be with another one; they are alone. They may be millionaires but they must be in that place. Even if they have a big castle, she or he is going to feel loneliness, cut off, his life-hope just finished. He has died.

Those who were working for their egos, their aim only to enjoy themselves through fulfilling physical desires, they are finished. Now perhaps youngsters, without being old, are going to finish their life-energy. They may finish at the age of twenty-five years, and now in Western countries people are not saying, after twenty-five years, "young people". They may say "finished people," their engines just burned. From an outside view it is okay, but the engine . . . [claps hands to show finishing]. But those who are working for Allah, they are never losing their hopes, they are never feel loneliness; no. The one who is with Allah, how can he feel loneliness?

Sultan Selim, a great sultan who inherited the holy flag of Rasul-Allah, ﷺ, the conquerer of Egypt, Yavus Sultan Selim Khan—when he was passing away, the one closest to him was saying to him, when he saw that with every breath he was going to finish, "O sultan, now you must not think of anything else. Now it is the time to be with Allah."

Then the sultan was saying, "O my *nadīm*,[1] O Mehmet Jan, with whom do you think I was before? Why are you saying this? Do you think that I was with another one up to today and you are saying to me, reminding me, 'O sultan, now it is the time to be with Allah'— do you think that I was with *dunya* or with Him?

"I am not alone. As long as I am with my Lord, I am not alone." No loneliness for the one who is with Allah, and Allah is saying, "*Ana jalisu man dhakarani*."[2] And Allah Almighty is saying, "Whoever is making *dhikr*, whoever is calling Me through *dhikr*, I am going to be with him. I am not leaving him alone."

Therefore, a believer is never going to lose his hope, never going to be hopeless and to die hopeless, and to be hopeless, that means to fall into a deeply dark place. That hopelessness gives a darkness; hopeless people have just extinguished the lights in their hearts. And people are feeling fear in themselves 'till those lights are coming and opening.

Therefore, the Prophet was saying, "O people, work—work hopefully, as if you are never going to die." Make death far away from you because you are working for Allah. If you are plowing, you are plowing for Allah; if you are planting, you are planting for Allah; if you are building, building for Allah, if you are trading, trading for Allah, if you are fighting, fighting for Allah, anything that you are

---

[1] Sheikh Nazim explains the meaning of this word parenthetically, saying, "What is *nedim*? *Aqrabu shakhs lil-insan* [the closest one], *nedim* means that a *sultan* may have some people always in his presence and speak to them, and his heavy burden may be taken from him"—that is, an intimate, a confidant.

[2] "I am companion to the one who thinks of Me."

doing, doing it for Allah, not for yourself. Therefore, no hopelessness can come to you.

You must not think about death when you are working. You must be full of hope for working, so that people may think, "Oh, this person is never, *never* going to say 'Enough' for doing more, for doing more when he is working," that he is *harisun 'ala ad-dunya.*[3] They think that that person is eager, eager for *dunya, shatana ma baynahum.*[4] Whoever is working for *dunya*, he is finishing, but whoever is working for Allah, doing the same work, he is not going to lose his hope, and he puts death far away and works because he is working for Allah. Up to the last moment, last breath, they may work, and their work is acceptable because they are working for Allah.

Now people they are *amwat*, dead ones. The whole world's people are dead ones because no hope of another life for them. Therefore they are dead ones, going-coming, but they are dead ones, they are not living ones. Living ones are only those who are working for Allah, for the Eternal Life, and they should be paid in the Eternal Life. They are never losing their hope; yes.

I am eighty years. I am running, and I don't like *dunya* but I am working for Allah, everything to be for Allah. I am not going to be hopeless, no. I don't like to be in an old people's house, no. *Insha'Allah, Rabbi yataqabal,*[5] Allah Almighty is accepting and giving much more power. I would like also to fight against *kufr* and to destroy the Satanic kingdom on earth and to build the heavenly building, to put the holy flag of the Prophet, ﷺ, heavenly flags, from East to West, from North to South. [All: *Amin.*]

---

[3] Desirous of this world.
[4] Attached to what is with them.
[5] God willing, my Lord accepts [it].

At one of the entrance doors of Istanbul Castle, there was one person, ninety years old, who was fighting to destroy the satanic kingdom. And someone was saying to him, "O shaykh, you are now such an old one. For what are you going now to fight? You sit."

And he was on his horse and he was passing under Topkapı or Edirnekapı. There was a heavy iron, used for breaking down the doors of castles, and he was passing on his horse. And he was putting his legs under his horse, catching this and doing like this, and he was taking his horse up and saying, "I am such a person. This power, I must use it to destroy the satanic kingdom, for building the heavenly kingdom." Yes, Allah gives such power to the one who is working for Him Almighty.

Hope makes people live. When you lose your hope, *ahli dunya*,[6] those who they are working for *dunya*, for their ego, they are dead ones, not living ones—no.

The Holy Qur'an is giving, for everything, what we are in need. Zakariyah,[7] *shaykh ul-anbiya*,[8] the old one among prophets, he was asking for a descendant from Allah Almighty. And Allah Almighty was sending Jibril, saying to him that Allah is going to grant to you a descendant. And this event that is mentioned in the Holy Qur'an,[9] I am bringing as an evidence for what we are saying now.

He [Zakariyah] was saying some words, but when he was speaking, he was speaking on the level of common people. "How can it be?" he was saying, suddenly surprised. "I am an old one. How can there be a child for me?"

---

[6] Worldly people.
[7] The prophet Zechariah, father of John the Baptist.
[8] The elder of the prophets.
[9] 3:38-41, 19:2-11.

Then Allah Almighty was sending Jibril, saying, "You are not on the same level [as other people]. You are always on another level so that you are not getting to be an old one, you are not going to finish or vanish or to die.

"You are speaking about dead ones. At your age, there are very few people [alive]. Under your age, also, so many people just passed away, cemeteries full of them, because they were dead ones, going-coming, working, marrying and bringing children, but they were dead ones. I am addressing you, your Lord saying that I granted to you never-ending youth power. That power—don't look at your age. You are not from dead ones, you are a living one. By My divine grant, I am granting to you real life, and don't say to Me, 'I am an old one'—no." Therefore Zakariah, as, *tubtu wa raj'atu ilayhi*. "*Tawbah, ya Rabbi. Tawbah, ya Rabbi. Tawbah, ya Rabbi.*"[10]

"I am granting to you a power; never-ending power you have. Don't say this! They are dead ones. I am addressing *you*, speaking to *you*, and you are saying, 'How can it be?' bringing a comparison between dead people and yourself. You are not a dead one. *They* are dead ones but if they follow you, they should be alive ones, living ones."

And that power is going on now—*must be*. The majority they are dead ones, even though running, going-coming, eating-drinking, but dead ones. Alive ones *must be*. Six billion people are dead ones, running, working, but one million are alive ones. Try to reach to those alive ones who may give to you that power, also, to be alive here. In your grave, you will come and stand up with your real being on the Day of Resurrection.

---

[10]"I repent and turn to you. Pardon, O my Lord. Pardon, O my Lord. Pardon, O my Lord."

Never going to be dry, their powers—no. Therefore, hopeless people they are going to die. [He corrects himself.] Not *going* to die—ask them; originally they are dead ones. Therefore, *awliya* are looking at people, running, going-coming, going-coming—dead ones. Alive ones are very few. If you can reach to alive ones and you may drink what they give to you, you should be like Sayyidina Khidr, the Green Man, Saint George. Never-ending, never-dying, secret power should be granted to you.

Allah-Allah, Allah-Allah, Allah-Allah, 'Aziz-Allah . . . . For the honor of the Seal of the Prophets: *Fatehah.* ▲

16

SEEK THE HEAVENLY WAY

> Anything that moves requires a power to move it, either from
> outside or from inside. And everyone has a goal or aim,
> which it requires power to reach. The people who are with
> *dunya* require external power to move them toward it, while
> those who are with their Lord are moved from inside, by di-
> vine power. To reach our destination, we are in need of di-
> vine help and power. There are only two ways: to be on the
> side of material powers or on the side of heavenly powers.
> But now material powers are finished. At this time there is
> only one way—the heavenly way. The other road is closed
> and its adherents done for.

*Bismillahi-r-Rahmani-r-Rahim. La hawla wa la quwatta illa bil-Lahi-l-
'Aliyyi-l-'Adhim. Meded, ya sultan al awliya, meded, ya rijal-Allah.*

Nothing can move by itself. Everything that moves either must
be pushed or pulled, or it is sitting in silence, no movement. A
stone, a horse, a car, a man—for everything that you want to make it
to move, you must use a power. And among mankind, each one
individually needs some power to make him to move, and that power
is going to be either from their inside or from outside.

Those who have lost power through their inside, they are in
need to be pushed or pulled from outside, like a car: if no petrol,
petrol finishing, it can't move by itself; it must be pulled or pushed
from outside. But do you think that a coach [bus], when its petrol
finishes, people are coming down and making it to move by pushing,
some of them pushing it from behind, some of them pulling it from

in front? What is the benefit, what is the benefit? They are getting tired and very few may reach their goals, with countless difficulties. If they must reach to somewhere, they must be tired; they must carry it, pulling and pushing. But if they have petrol, petrol inside is giving movement; power inside is carrying the coach, and the people are resting and it is moving.

Now people are in such a way. Allah Almighty, He knows everything from the beginning up to the end, everyone's destination. He is informing us that mankind, they have been created weak ones, with no power, and they have, individually or generally, a goal that they must reach to that limit or target or aim or idea. And on this planet, it has been so difficult, from the beginning up to today, for the people who are living on it to reach to their goals without any power in themselves. For people to reach to their destinations only using external pushing and pulling power, it should be such a heavy and difficult way for them.

Grandshaykh was saying, so many times, "*Olay geçecek hayatı çok muşkilat den geçiyor bu insanlar devar.*" That means, "This short life, it was so easy to pass it without harming people, hurting them, disturbing them—so easily it was passing. But I am wondering," Grandshaykh was saying, "that people they are always taking the difficult way to reach to their destinations and leaving the easy, very, very easy way that also reaches to their destinations."

Two ways—two ways for all mankind to reach to their destinations, and everyone has a destination that is different. Everyone's destination is different; can't be same destination, no. Everyone is created as one, unique; each one is carrying a oneness among his kind. You can't find anyone who is one hundred per cent similar to another. No. Look at faces, look at souls, look at colors, look at their bodies—can't be one hundred per cent similar to another one, never.

And their destination, also, it is just different, one hundred per cent. You are thinking something, that one is thinking something else, that one is thinking another thing, and men must move toward their destinations. And the Lord of the Heavens is showing two ways for them for reaching to their destinations—easy way, difficult way.

Easy way, that is the heavenly way, those heavenly powers coming to the hearts of those people who are accepting the easy way, and the heart is the *sultan*, the king of our physical bodies. When heavenly power comes through the heart of a person, that power makes them to move easily. They are not in need to be pushed or to be pulled; no, easily running on it.

The difficult way is for those who are not interested in the heavenly powers that have been granted to the children of Adam, never interested, and they are saying, "No, we are not accepting such a thing. We must make ourselves to move as we like."

Because those who are surrendering to heavenly powers, they are surrendered and giving their free wills to their Lord, their Lord is taking them on an easy way to their destinations. Those people, the first group of people, they are humble people; they are accepting that our Lord can do everything for them; they have surrendered. But the second party of people, the second group, they are proud ones. They are saying, "No, we are not in need of heavenly orders or we are not accepting heavenly rules. No, we have minds and we have will. We can do as we like. It is an honor for us not to surrender."

They are thinking that whoever surrenders to Allah they are going to be slaves, but really they are surrendering themselves more to Shaytan. But they are drunk people; they are not understanding. When they are proud and refuse divine orders and rules, they are thinking that they are free ones. No! Like a magnetic iron, two poles—one positive, one negative; one useful, one useless, harmful;

if you are losing one, the second must catch you, and you can't be in both poles. You must run to one of them.

Those who are surrendering to Allah are servants, and they are more honored people, more honored servants. But if they are losing that, they must be caught by the second pole; they must surrender to Shaytan, and Shaytan is making them more enslaved. Either one of two: men must be caught either by the heavenly side or the satanic side. Can't be in the middle—difficult, so that those who are surrendering to Allah Almighty, He is giving that power through the hearts of people and then that power makes everything easy for them, so easy. Therefore Grandshaykh was saying, "It was so easy for people but they are not preferring the easy side. They are asking for the difficult side, not choosing easy ways but choosing difficult ways."

Now whole world is in it. They have fallen into crisis; no one knows the beginning or the ending. When it began is unknown, and no one can say that this crisis is going to be ended on that date. No limits now, finished [claps hands to show finished]—finished, because they chose difficult ways for themselves to their destinations. They must be tired, they must be finished and vanish because some of them are trying to push, some of them trying to pull, and they are finishing. Hundreds, thousands, millions and billions people are going to die, and they are not going to be able to save themselves or to move to their destinations. They should be finished and vanish.

Therefore, when I was beginning, I was saying *"Meded."* We are in need of moving, a power must be. If we remain with what we know and say, "I am not in need of someone to carry me, to push me. I may take from books, I may know," in a hundred years you can't take anything, only a heavy burden.

I am asking, I am saying, "I am nothing. O my closest one to the Divine Presence, O my Grandshaykh, give me power because every time I am finishing. I am finishing, I am in need of something new.

And he is saying, "Don't worry. We are not finishing; we are not finishing. Our taps are never going to be dry, our springs are never going to stop, our wells are never going to dry—no, always running." But those who are using water through *khazan*, water tanks, when the tank finishes . . . [claps hands to show finishing.]

And people, still they are insisting on finding a way—here, in Turkey, in Russia, in Europe, in America, in China, in India, in Japan, in the East, in the West, North, South, they are asking for a way. I am saying, "Finished; I am closing on you. I am that one that is closing on you. You can't reach a millimeter, you can't take a way for saving yourself—finished. You must come to this side."

It is a big sign, "Road closed." What does it mean? "Road closed" means you can't pass there. Now I am putting this writing, "Road closed," for all nations. I am here, and if they do like this, it may fall it down, but I am laughing at them. You may take that, but yet my order is "Road closed," finished. You must come this way now, *mecburi istikamet*[1]—diverted. They are saying "Diverted—you can't use this way. You must use *this* way by force."

Finished now; the whole world is diverted. You can't go this way. That is my mission from the Day of Promises; finished. I am nothing, but I am doing like this—finished. I am looking if anyone is going to save himself from crisis. I have code numbers and big keys like the keys of London Tower; I am carrying them. When the order comes, I will open this way.

May Allah forgive. Therefore, you must try to take that power from inside you, heavenly powers. Material powers are finished. No

---

[1]One way.

fear now of anything that they invented of weapons, of fires. They can't do anything except each one destroying the other.

Allah-Allah, Allah-Allah, Allah-Allah, Allah-Allah, 'Aziz-Allah. Allah-Allah, Allah-Allah, Allah-Allah, Allah-Allah, Karim-Allah. Allah-Allah, Allah-Allah, Allah-Allah, Allah-Allah, Sultan-Allah. Mutlaq sultan Allah—absolute sultanate, eternal sultanate for Allah Almighty. May Allah accept our humble servanthood, to be in His endless sultanate, honored for His divine servanthood. For the honor of the most honored one in His Divine Presence: *Fatehah.* ▲

17

MANKIND HAS LEFT GOODNESS

> We are asking for firmness on the right path, the *Shari'ah* of
> Islam, which contains holy orders coming from the Heavens.
> In our time, virtually all people are on the wrong way. It
> may happen that people go along with sinners and their do-
> ings out of weakness, and if they express their dislike of the
> matter to their Lord, they will be forgiven, helped and
> blessed. Sins are the main reason of crises, and dark dark-
> ness is in the hearts of the people who are following ego. The
> whole world now is out of control, and if nations do not ac-
> cept divine control, Allah will leave them to control them-
> selves, with terrible results.

Her gün yeni dir, her gün yeni bir başan mıştır—every day is a new
beginning. *Bayat şay satmas, canabu Allah*[1]—no *bayat*, old things, for
Allah, everything is new. Therefore, we are looking for a new page.
What They are sending, we must say.

*A'udhu bil-Lahi min ash-Shaytani-r-rajim, bismillahi-r-Rahmani-r-
Rahim.* O our Lord, *wa la tunsina dhikrak*, don't let us forget Your
Holy Name, to say *"Bismillahi-r-Rahmani-r-Rahim."* Every time that
we are saying *"Bismillahi-r-Rahmani-r-Rahim,"* it is going to be a new
beginning, new grants coming from Allah Almighty. *La hawla wa la
quwatta illa bil-Lahi-l-'Aliyyi-l-'Adhim.* And we are asking from Allah
Almighty to send us from His heavenly powers, to stand on it. *Alla-*

---

[1]"Allah does not sell stale things."

humma, thabit aqdamana[2]—O our Lord, make our feet to be on the right path.

What is the right path? The right path, it is *Shari'ah*. For wrong ways around the right path, you can find so many exits, all of them wrong ways. The right path, that is *Shari'ah*. *Shari'ah* means holy orders coming from the Heavens.

Why is it the right path, *Shari'ah*? Because the *Shari'ah* leads people to Allah. Therefore it is the right path, and other ways never lead to Allah. Therefore all of them are wrong ways. And in our days, in the twenty-first century, people, the majority or hundred per cent, they are on wrong ways.

You may find some people that they are not accepting wrong ways but by force they are sent towards wrong ways, and because they are feeling weakness in themselves, they are obeying and they are following wrong ways. At the least we may say, "O our Lord, I know it is the wrong way but in my weakness I am not able to face those people, to find an opposite way. They are carrying me, but I am never happy to be with them or to be on their ways." You can save yourselves by this.

Sodom and Gomorrah were two sinful cities that Allah Almighty destroyed. When Allah Almighty ordered Archangel Gabriel to turn those two cities upside-down, and he put his wing under the two cities and took them up, he was looking and finding thousands of people who were praying night prayers, and he was confused, thinking, "How can I turn this upside-down while so many thousands of people are praying.

And Allah Almighty ordered "Don't be late, don't be late! I am that One who never accepts anyone to be late in standing up and

---

[2]"O our Lord, make our feet firm."

keeping My orders. If in less than a unit of time you are going to delay, I will destroy you, also, taking you out of existence.

"Yes. I am looking, also, and I am seeing who is there. They were praying but they were living with those sinners and they were not leaving them, not leaving those cities and going away. Therefore, My divine anger has come on all of them, but finally I am going to delay them with another judgment—with another judgment. But now you must make them upside-down."

Because they were feeling weakness in themselves and giving too much tolerance to those people, therefore all of them together with those sinners were punished, their cities becoming upside-down. But finally angels were taking them away from that area that divine anger fell upon.

Now the whole world is worse than Sodom and Gomorrah, worse. Therefore, a punishment is coming to all mankind, and that punishment is only going to be taken away from those people who may say, "O our Lord, that is something Your servants are doing that is against Your divine rules, and we are unhappy with them and with their beliefs and actions. We are never happy with them, but we aren't able to leave and to go another place. Therefore, everywhere we may go we are finding same old, dirty scenes. O our Lord, forgive us and make for us a safe way or a safe place with a safe way, not to come under Your divine anger." Anyone who is going to say this should be saved, should be sheltered, should be protected, should be forgiven, should be blessed.

Sins, that is main reason of crisis, nothing else. The Lord of the Heavens, He is not happy; He is not happy with those people that are living on earth. And now He is beginning to cut down their provisions, to close every open door for them, and to imprison them in their egoistical prisons because they like to be in darkness.

They are not asking for lights, divine lights. Therefore, Allah Almighty wants to make their *dunya*, their lives on this planet, in darkness, and that darkness, if ten suns rise, their lights can't take it away because that darkness is coming through their hearts. And the darkness of their hearts is coming on their faces, and the faces of those people are just covered by a dark darkness, not any attraction in their faces, such wildness and violence in their faces because no more mercy is remaining in their hearts. They are like rocks, no more mercy, no more justice, in their hearts.

Therefore, everyone must ask forgiveness from Allah Almighty and also say, "O our Lord, let us to leave them for a place where they are not there. Let their illnesses not come on ourselves," because an ego is much worse with other egos. The servants—not servants, the *slaves* of their egos—are worse than shaytans. Shaytans, you may think of them but you can't see them, but people who are representing their egos, hundreds, thousands, millions and billions of people are following their egos and they are saying, "Our pleasure is with our egos, our good feelings are with our egoistical desires, and we are living only to fulfill the desires of our egos, nothing else. There is not any philosophy, not any ideas, not any belief that we are proclaiming or accepting. We are throwing them away. Everything that is against our physical desires, it is unacceptable, just removed and thrown away."

People who are living in our times, they are worse than people that lived in centuries that passed away because even though they were idol-worshippers, they were defending their idols and saying to prophets, "We are keeping the ways of our fathers, of our ancestors." But those shaytan people who are living on earth now— mostly they are Shaytan, representatives of Shaytan or just becoming Shaytan—they are not saying, "We are keeping the ways of our ancestors. Our nation is saying that our ancestors were on the wrong way and now we have found the right way," and cursing their ancestors, not keeping their ways and becoming the worst people on earth.

The people of the time of Ignorance, they were keeping, defending, the ways of their ancestors. Now our nation is saying that our ancestors they were on wrong way; now we have just found the good way, the perfect way, the enlightened way. Towards which direction? To Allah? Never! To Shaytan. We never found such days and such ways that are guiding us to fulfilling our egoistical desires.

Therefore, no hope, no hope. It is so difficult. If the Prophet came, it would be difficult for him to have an affect on them. Therefore, Allah Almighty is asking to cut it, from all nations. In Cyprus, they are cutting some olive trees when they get old, cutting everything on them and only a piece of wood is remaining. You can't see any branch, any leaf, any flower on them, nothing, only a piece of wood, just cut. And after a while, the second year, the third year, you may see that from that dry trunk there is going to be a new green, a new life coming. Therefore people must be taken away now.

Therefore, Grandshaykh was saying, "Don't be sad about what is happening on earth or what is going to happen to mankind, because not millions but billions of people should be taken away. It is a whole cleaning, and after a short while, you can find a new refreshment for that tree, new life coming, everything new—branches, new greenness on them, and quickly getting more power, and as many as went away through Armageddon or the Great War, very soon will come more of the *ummah*, filling this world. And they should be a pure generation, pure in their minds, in their eyes, in their tongues, in their hands, in their legs, in their organs, inner and outer, and in their hearts—clean ones, no illness; no illness, just perfect beings, and for the sake of the Seal of Prophets, a new generation is going to fill East and West, from North to South. The best times of this world, from the beginning up to the end, should be that time,

Darkness will just be defeated; no more darkness on earth for forty years. And this is a divine promise for Sayyidina Muhammad, pbuh, and after that the Last Day must come for judgment for everyone, for every nation. We are just approaching it. Today we are closer than yesterday, and tomorrow we are going to be closer to those huge events that should be and *must be* on earth.

Therefore, it is a warning. No matter how many days as we are speaking, They are making me to speak on different aspects, different subjects, but they are, all of them, only to warn people about the coming terrible and dangerous events, not to be taken away. It is only for sheltering people from that divine punishment, so that they should reach to Mahdi, as, and after a short while they may reach to Sayyidina 'Isa, Christ, pbuh. We are going towards it now.

O people, crises are never going to stop now. No; finished! The whole world now, it is out of control. No control; anywhere, you can't find control. Every country is out of control. Americans claim that they are the boss of world but they are in such a terrible position, and they are not able to control even among their people, and they are asking to take control of nations from East to West. And throughout East and West, every country is out of control, also, like a motorway with all cars running out of control.

What is going to happen? No one is in control. If there is a controlled one, uncontrolled cars are coming on it, also, to destroy it. Only if it may be taken far away from the runway, it may be saved, but whoever is on the runway, on the motorway, every means on it is out of control. America is out of control, Europe is out of control, the Middle East is out of control. The whole world isn't able to control a small place like Palestine and Israel—the whole world! Do you think they can take control of it? For years and years, the superpowers haven't been able to stop, to make a control on Arabs or on Jewish people, and they are such small states. What about the whole world?

Who can say now that the whole world is under control? I am asking, "Under whom?" Who is controlling them now, because the people living on this planet they are saying, "We are not asking for heavenly control. We can control ourselves," from the beginning of the twentieth century, and before, also. And Allah Almighty is saying, "Yes. Do your control, *masha' Allah!*"

Why are they not controlling themselves, and heavenly control is not on them now, just forsaking them now, leaving them? "Yes, look after yourself—look! Control yourself, all nations." True or not? Yes. No more control on earth, finished, because they said, "We can control ourselves," and the Lord of the Heavens is saying, "If you don't like My control, I am taking My control from you. Do your control on yourselves, *masha' Allah.*"

So happy, nations, all nations, all Number One people, generals, presidents, kings—all happy now because they may control. *Yahu!* This is Cyprus, northern Cyprus; no control, also. Perhaps it is undeclared—a very small state, very small, and no control. I am not thinking about the Turkish Republic, if they have control; I am hearing that they have enough control. Hah! I am laughing at them because they refused divine control on themselves. I am saying, "Oh-h, oh-h, hip hip hooray for you! You may do your best for people." Even Number One of whole nations, President Number One in the US, is trembling every night, taking one handful of tablets to make his nerves calm. We are not in need, we are sleeping. And they are not asking, "O our Lord, reach to our weakness. Please control us"—no one is saying that. Yet they are fighting, saying, "Crisis."

Allahumma, la hawla wa la quwatta illa bil-Lahi-l-'Aliyyi-l-'Adhim. Subhanallahi-l-'Aliyyi-l-'Adhim. Subhana Malik al-Mulk, Dhal Jalali wal-

Ikram. Anta Rabbuna, Anta Allah, la ilaha illa Anta. Subhanaka! Sub-hanaka! Subhanaka! All glory to you, O our Lord. *La hawla wa la quwatta illa bil-Lahi-l-'Aliyyi-l-'Adhim, la hawla wa la quwatta illa bil-Lahi-l-'Aliyyi-l-'Adhim.*

O our Lord, forgive us, forgive us. We are saying "Pardon" to your Divine Presence. For the honor of Your most honored one, that the whole of creation was created for His honor, forgive us and grant Your pardon to us. *Bi-hurmati-l-Fatehah.* ▲

18

THE MAIN MISSION OF GOD'S MESSENGERS

The main mission of the Prophet, ﷺ, was to change people's bad characteristics or attributes to good ones. There are true ones who are able to do this work, but also fake ones who make such claims but aren't authorized to do it. Paradise is only for clean people, and if you don't get cleaned during this life, you will be cleaned hereafter. The divine punishment in Hells is not Allah's revenge but is His cleaning so that His servants may come out of Hells and enter Paradise. It is so important to give complete respect and obedience to Allah's orders, lest there be punishment and cleaning in Hells.

A'udhu bil-Lahi min ash-Shaytani-r-rajim, bismillahi-r-Rahmani-r-Rahim. La hawla wa la quwatta illa bil-Lahi-l-'Aliyyi-l-'Adhim. The Seal of the Prophets, Sayyidina Muhammad, ﷺ, he was saying about his real mission, "I have just been sent to change people's bad characteristics into good characteristics, I have just been sent to change their bad attributes to good attributes."

Is it possible? If it was not possible, he would not have said this, and if there was no possibility of changing bad characteristics into good characteristics, all *sahabah*, his disciples, would never have left the bad characteristics they had before coming into Islam. One hundred per cent they were changed;

the power of Rasul-Allah, ﷺ, just changed them from the worst to the best, from the lowest level to the highest level.

"*Innama bu'ithtu li-utamimu makarim al-akhlaq.*"[1] That is a hadith, holy hadith from Rasul-Allah, ﷺ, that is saying that the only real purpose of my message or my messengerhood or prophethood is to complete mankind's good characteristics. They have a foundation but they are in need of completing it, to build on that foundation the best manners, best characteristics.

A foundation is okay for everyone, but if we are not building on it, Shaytan is coming and building the worst and most dangerous, most harmful building on that foundation. "I just came, I have been sent, if I am finding people who are not yet building on that foundation, to make them to build on it. Whoever was beginning to build on it and they do not know how it is to be built and how to reach the level, the high level that they are asking to reach, I just came for that purpose, to teach people."

Therefore, a bad one can be a good one—yes. An ill person, if going and doing a treatment for himself, should be treated, should be healthy, but if not taking care of his illness, he is never going to save himself from that illness. Therefore, those who are asking something for themselves of goodness, they must follow the treatments of heavenly people, and heavenly people are never going to finish; must be up to Last Day. But you must ask, you may ask, because at every time you can find, together with real ones, also imitation ones, *sahte*,[2].

If you reach an imitation one, you will lose everything, and it is cheating. Whoever hasn't been authorized by heavenly

---

[1] "I have just been sent to perfect excellent characteristics." (*Muwatta*, 47.1.8)
[2] False, counterfeit, sham.

people and they are saying, "We can treat people," they are cheats, and the Prophet ﷺ was saying, *"Man ghashana fa laysa minna*[3]—whoever is cheating us, he is not from my nation, just discarded."

Therefore, it is difficult for anyone to address people if he is not authorized. At least he must say, "I am only a person reminding you about bad characteristics and the ways for treatment. I am only reminding you but I am not claiming that I can treat you." At that time, their responsibility is going away. If not saying that and claiming, "I am advising you, I am able, I can treat you," and he can't, that is a liar and a cheat. He should be punished.

Therefore, everyone must see about that point. And in our time, during this period of the twenty-first century, there are unauthorized people, thousands. All doctors, those whose titles are doctors, they are cheating people because they can't treat people in a true way and they are cheating people, everywhere.[4] Those people going to be punished muchmore on the Day of Resurrection.

Everyone who is sitting on a seat in mosques, going up to *mimbars*[5] and addressing people, and people are thinking that they may be able to change their characteristics but they can't do it, they have that responsibility. At least they must say, from the beginning, "By your permission,[6] that one who authorized people to advise the whole nation [*ummah*], I am humbly asking

---

[3]"Then whoever cheats us is not of us."

[4]That is, our modern doctors of religion or Islamic studies. Since they do not possess the characteristics, training and methods to produce a deep, permanent change in people's outlook, characteristics and actions, it is false and deceptive.

[5]Pulpits.

[6]That is, by the permission of the Holy Prophet, ﷺ.

for a support, a light from you, because I am here such a weak and unauthorized person, and people here, they are asking something from me. Please send your heavenly support, even one ray, to address the servants of my Lord so that it may be useful, that they may take benefit from this gathering and meeting." But if not saying this, their speech, their addressing is poisoned, poisoning people.

Yes. When speaking, authorized people, they have been authorized for changing, taking people from level to level. You may understand it or not, but they are carrying people from level to level, and you must find such a person to treat you because if you are not taking care of yourself, not being treated, you should be treated at the last moment of your life, when you are leaving this life, and you should be treated in your grave or you should be treated on the Day of Resurrection. If not enough, you should be in Hells for treatment, to be clean so that you may enter Paradise because Paradise is only for clean people, pure people, good people, not for bad people, not dirty people, not poisoned people; no. They can't get in; it is impossible.

And most people now they are not taking care, and punishment it is not only a revenge from Allah Almighty. His revenge is not like your revenge, no. Man's revenge it is to take that one from existence, throw him away, to destroy him; our revenge is in such a way. But Allah's revenge gives life, gives treatment, gives purity, because they are not clean and no one can enter Paradise if he is not clean. It is not like a prison of governments, your governments; no. Prisons never take anything from people; prisons are only for destroying their personality, physically and spiritually. Therefore, in *Shari'ah* there is not prison; no. The only prison is seclusion, and you may put yourself into seclusion as a prison for cleaning, for pureness.

Those prisons are against humanity, *Shari'ah* never accepting because they are not treating people—killing and destroying, individually and generally, spiritually. From every direction prisons are destroying humanity, and no one is happy with prisons because they are such a terrible punishment for destroying the personalities of people.

That is revenge of people's governments. But Allah Almighty, His revenge can't be the same as the revenge of mankind, no, because He is asking to put those who are in Hells in Paradise. Allah Almighty is not happy for His servants to be in the Fire, putting them there for cleaning, cleaning everyone; then taking them out and sending them to Paradise, cleaning and giving to them real life, because in Hells people do not know if they are living or dying. Hells' people they never know if they are alive ones or dead ones, *bayn al-hayat wal-mawt.*[7]

There is a secret point; we are not speaking on it, *sirr.*[8] But Allah Almighty is asking to put His servants in Paradise because all the descendants of Adam, they were in Paradise. Not anyone was outside; all were with Adam. He was carrying the miniature personalities of his children, descendants, up to the end—miniature beings; perhaps they were like *dharrat*[9] (atomic particles). Billions of his descendants they were with Adam and Eve in Adam.[10] If Adam had not put them in Hawa, Hawa

---

[7]Between life and death.

[8]Secret.

[9]Atoms, tiny particles, specks.

[10]The Holy Prophet ﷺ said:

> God took the covenant from Adam's back at Na'man, which is 'Arafat, and He brought forth from his loins all his descendants, whom he multiplied and scattered before Him like tiny specks. He then spoke to them face to face, saying, *"Am I not your Lord?" They said, "Yes, we bear witness [to it]," [lest] you should say, "It was only that our fathers previously took others as partners with God, and we were [merely their] descendants after them. Would You*

124

wouldn't have been able to bring forth any descendants. Hawa wasn't carrying them; Adam was carrying his descendants up to the end.

That means, as Grandshaykh was saying to me, also, that for each one of mankind, Allah Almighty just parcelled Paradise with everyone's name written on it, "This, this, this." When they are prepared, when they are clean ones, when their cleanliness is suitable to be in Paradise, they may come here and everyone may come to their estates. Therefore women are washing clothes in hot water. For what? For cleaning. Putting detergents and other washing powders, and putting in that washing machine, turning, turning, turning, turning—for what? To make it clean. And seven Hells, they are only for cleaning, because He, Allah Almighty, likes to put His servants into Paradise, and dirty ones can't be in Paradise.

"*La yadkhulu-l-jannata man fi qalbihi mithqala dharratin min al-kibr.*"[11] The Prophet was commenting that whoever has in himself the smallest amount of pride, it is impossible for him to enter Paradise, and pride is only one bad characteristic of our egos. What about the others? Everyone must be clean. Then they should be in Paradise because Allah Almighty He is not happy for His servants to be in Hells, *Arhamu-l-Rahimin.*[12] But also His command is not to have dirty ones put into Paradise. Must be clean ones in it.

---

then destroy us for what the perpetrators of falsehood did?' [7:172] (*Mishkat al-Masabih*, 0121)

Other *ahadith* related to this subject are Abu Dawud, 4686; *Mishkat*, Book I-Faith, Chapter IV, II; *Muwatta*, 46.1.2.

[11]"The one who has in his heart a particle of pride will not enter Paradise." (Muslim, 164-166)

[12]The Most Merciful of all merciful ones.

O people, we are speaking about the main mission of the Seal of Prophets, Sayyidina Muhammad, 襻, and he was saying, "I have just been sent to clean you from your bad characteristics and to bring to you good characteristics—*Innama bu'ithu li-utamimu makarim al-akhlaq.*" You must try as much as possible to be clean ones. If not, at the end of your life, the last day that you are leaving this life, you should be in a difficult situation with treatment for cleaning. They are saying "coma". Coma is only is a way of purification that a person has lost during his life. If it is enough, enough. If not enough, in the graveyard will come another treatment, and if that person going to be clean, okay. If not, on the Day of Resurrection will come another treatment for all people on the Plain of Gathering of Judgment Day. Therefore, angels will quickly come for pure ones with special mounts, They will be taken away and sent to Paradise. But those who are not clean should be there, to be cleaned.

If that treatment is not enough, they must fall from the Bridge of Paradise[13] into Hells, and according to their treatment, they should be there *ahqaba, huqub*[14]—like a century but it is only eighty years, and each year is twelve months or each year is 365 days. Eighty years is one century in Hells, and people, till they are going to be treated and become pure ones, they should be inside one year out of eighty years, 355 days, and each day one thousand years.

Therefore, the Prophet was warning, "*Man taraka salatan hatta mada waqtuha uzzilat fil nari huquba. Al-huqub thamanuna sana, kullu sana thalatha miyatu khamsa wa sittun yaumin, kullu yaw-*

---

[13]The *Sirat*, a bridge in Paradise thin as a wire which is excruciatingly difficult to cross.

[14]A long time, a period, an age.

126

min alfa sanatin min ma ta'uduna." The Prophet was warning his nation, "Take more care about your prayers. If a person leaves one prayer out of five and does not pray it, his punishment in Hells should be eighty *huqub*, eighty centuries." One *huqub* it is eighty years, and each year is *thalatha miyatu sittuna yaumin*, 360 days, and each day it is going to be one thousand years of our calendars, only for *one* prayer. Because He is Allah; His order is so great. If you are putting it down, it is punishment for that person.

Keep prayers. You should be saved here and Hereafter. If not, you should be punished, you should be treated for cleaning here and there. When you are going to be clean, Paradise's doors will open and you may enter it.

O people, we are not coming to play in this life, to be slaves of our egos and to try to fulfill our physical desires—not for this, but we are coming for high respect of the high commands of Allah Almighty, for fulfilling His great orders, not to let them fall down. And when the time comes or His order comes, we must see to it. If not taking it and letting it fall down, that is a punishment.

May Allah forgive me and bless you. For the honor of the most honored one in His Divine Presence: *Fatehah.* ▲

19

SEEK TO MOVE UPWARDS

Despite having reached the age of adulthood, in our time virtually all people are at the lowest level, animals' level. This is evident from the prevalent understanding of the Qur'an. And people are insisting on remaining at this level, not wanting to change or improve, feeling that it is suitable for themselves and that other understandings are wrong. But while our lower selves remain at the lowest level, our souls are asking for higher levels. All prophets came to save people from the darkness of their material being, but people rejected them and even killed them. In our time, even children are abandoning their parents. That results in negative loneliness that destroys people spiritually and physically. And Allah is calling us to be with Him, in his Oceans, in which we are in all and all is in us, and because the drop has dissolved in the sea, there is no more loneliness. Therefore, people are in need of new understandings, but knowledge and science cannot give such understandings to anyone.

Ya Mufathi al-Abwab, ifta lana khaira-l-abwab.[1] Always, always good things are coming from Allah Almighty, but people are running after bad things. Without stopping, mercy is coming, but people are running under cursing lines.

A'udhu bil-Lahi min ash-Shaytani-r-rajim, bismillahi-r-Rahmani-r-Rahim. Dastur, ya Sayyidi, meded. La hawla wa la quwatta illa bil-Lahi-l-

---

[1]"O Opener of Doors, open to us the best of doors."

128

'Aliyyi-l-'Adhim. Meded, ya rijal-Allah, meded, ya sultan al-anbiya, meded, ya sultan al-awliya.

We are like small children. Always we are in need to catch the hands of our parents, as a small child runs to mom or dad, running after them to catch them. We are not at an age to be free, we are not on a level that we know what we are doing.

Even though we are reaching the age of maturity and more, now people they are like mongoloid-type children. No matter how old they may be, maybe forty years, forty-five or fifty, they are on the same level of understanding as when they were seven years old; if reaching seventy years, they are on same level, their understanding the same at seven years and at seventy years.

Now people on earth, millions of people, from the beginning of the age of maturity up to the last year of their lives, they are on same understanding-level, never changing. *Subhahallah!* What is their understanding?

Their feelings, when they are reaching to the age of maturity— what is that? Under maturity, they are pure. After maturity, they are opening, an opening coming to them, changing in their physical being. They are looking, they are listening, they are tasting, they are thinking, they are doing. Their thoughts, their ideas, are changing.

But if you look, all people are on the same level, no difference between two persons now on earth about their thoughts, about their ideas or about their understanding. They may educated people or graduates, but their understanding or their vision never changes. Everyone is on that lowest level of life, looking there. No one is asking to change or to reach another opening more than their own understanding.

And for understanding, there are countless levels, but we have been imprisoned only on the level of our animal being, because people, in their physical being, they are on the level of animals, and their understanding is the same understanding as animals, no more. They may dress in so many fashionable clothes, expensive or cheap, they may graduate from different universities, but their understanding of life is the same because these teachings never change their understanding. Their teachings revolve around this life, the platform of animals' life, nothing else. They may be president, may be prime minister, may be king, queen, may be professor, may be any kind of business man, but they are never changing their understanding, and they are not asking for any other level for understanding.

There is the Holy Qur'an. People are trying to translate the Holy Qur'an and it is impossible, but people are trying to take the meanings of that Last Testament, the Holy Qur'an. And people, according to their levels, are giving an understanding.

So many translations are coming to me. I am looking and quickly I am understanding the level of those people, that they have never changed their level from the physical, animals' level—quickly. When you look, the people of animals' level are never interested in other commentaries of the Holy Qur'an. They say, "We are not accepting this. From where are you bringing this meaning? We are not seeing this." Yes, how can you see? You are still on animals' level, the most primary level for mankind.

Not any understanding for that level; all nations now, all people, are on that level, insisting, also. They are saying, "It is okay for us. We are not asking for anything else," because they do not believe that there is another level, because their understanding-level is preventing them from looking for another level and they think that there is only *our* level, no further level for understanding, and they are leaving it there. And that level of understanding is so cursed. It is not suitable for the nature of man.

The nature of man is above that level, calling them. *Istiadad*,[2] their real creation that is granted from Allah Almighty, that belongs to their souls, is asking to move up, but they are imprisoning their souls to be with their material being at the lowest level and lowest understanding.

"*Wa man jahida, fa-innama yujahidu li-nafsihi.*"[3] Therefore, we have been offered and ordered to try to save ourselves from the prison of material being. And all prophets came as saviors for people, to save people from the prison of the darkness of material being. But people were fighting those enlightened, heavenly ones, fighting them and they were saying, "Oh! Why you are coming? We are so happy with our lives. Why you are coming? Go away or we shall kill you!"

Therefore, now the whole world's people are on the same level of understanding. They are not understanding who they are because they are occupied by their physical beings' desires, nothing else. Therefore, they are saying, "What is that? No. Don't involve in our lives. We are free ones. We like to live as we like." Even children are saying to their parents, "I must live my life. You don't care about me, no, and I don't care about you. Leave me—finished. No connection with you, no. You are an individual in your world and I am going to live in my world, also, as I like."

Subhanallah, that is negative loneliness—negative, asking to carry people to a dark loneliness, not any connection with anyone else. The closest ones to a child, they are parents. They are trying to cut it, to be alone—alone, asking for loneliness. Therefore, they are renting a flat to be alone. They may bring someone there, but still they are not asking to be with that one forever. Their connection with each other may be for a short time. Then everyone is just

---

[2] Aptitude, capacity, disposition, readiness.
[3] "*Whoever strives, strives only on behalf of himself.*" (29:7)

thrown into their loneliness, and that—that is a negative loneliness that is destroying people through their spiritual being, as well as destroying their physical beings.

Yes, we are alone. We are coming alone to this life; from our mother's womb, we are coming alone. Even though we are living now with so many people, we are alone. When we are passing away, we are in our coffin alone. When we are going to be buried in our grave, we are alone. But those who are asking to leave their loneliness, the Lord of the Heavens is saying to His servants, "Come to Me! I am inviting you. I am that One who is never leaving you alone. Go and be with My representative, the Seal of the Prophets, not to be alone. Jump into his Ocean, but don't be like a stone that never melts. Be like a cube of sugar. When it falls in water, it is going and melting, and no more loneliness."

Therefore, our souls are running to reach the Unity Oceans of Allah Almighty because we are now like drops, and drops are running to an ocean to *be* the ocean; no more loneliness for them. And that is endless enjoyment for everyone in a positive way, but that understanding is just finished now. All people are never understanding.

Everyone is asking to be alone, to be Number One, alone. A president is Number One, but he is alone. A king is Number One, but he is alone. And loneliness—we have been thrown on earth alone, but we are suffering from loneliness. Therefore, people, when they are coming together, their feelings are changing. When they are lonely, sadness and darkness are covering them; therefore, people are running to people. That is our souls.

But now, people are no longer understanding that very important point for their beings or for their existence in this creation. Therefore, Sayyidina 'Ali was saying, "The whole universe is just in you." Therefore, if a person reaches that level of understanding, he is never going to be lonely, no. He is with them and everything is in him, also. He is in all, as well as all are in him.

This understanding gives honor to mankind and opens endless horizons of understanding. *He*, that *Who*, Allah, is in all and all are in Him. No more sadness, no more hopelessness, no more fear, no more darkness for those people who have reached to the Oceans of Unity. A drop is coming from the clouds and falling into the sea; that is becoming the sea. You can't find where it is—finished. No more loneliness.

But now people are just imprisoned, each one in himself, in herself, and sadness and darkness and fear have just been dressed one after another over them. That is a terrible crisis for people but they are not understanding.

No understanding for people; they are not understanding about themselves. Their understanding is like common people's understanding 7,000 years ago, about which they are saying that their and animals' worlds are near each other, only they can't speak but we can speak, nothing else.

What we are speaking about, animals do without speaking. [Laughter.] That is the difference, nothing else. Look at an ox. [Laughter.] The ox should be surprised. "Who are you? Who are you? What you are doing? You are doing what I am doing, but you are too much [blah-blah]. For what, for what, writing, reading—for what? Anything else you are doing more than me? Nothing. What is your honor over me?" it is saying. *Subhanallah, subhana Malik al-Mulk, Dhul Jalali wal-Ikram, ya Fattah, ya Mufatih al-Abwab, subhanallah!* And prophets were coming to open that understanding-level, calling people to them, "Come! Leave the level of animals. Come and look, O people. You are living in the basement. Come and look what is on the roof. Come!"

And people are saying, "No, go away. Go away! We are so happy here. What is the basement? It is an excellent place."

May Allah give us understanding. People, they are in need of understanding. And knowledge and science will never give anything, any new understanding for man. However much technology gets more and more developed, it can't give any different understanding to mankind—the same. Therefore, we are in need to change our level, but technology is never giving that. Therefore Allah Almighty is sending heavenly people; must come.

Therefore, people, *mumins*, the Muslim world, they are asking for Mahdi, as, and 'Isa, as. The Christian world, everyone in it is hopeless now; they are asking for Jesus Christ to come to them to prepare, to arrange everything. Jewish people, also, they are saying, "We are fed up, fed up with paper money, with gold, with jewels. We must have someone else," and they are asking the Messiah to be sent to them. The Messiah just passed but they are still asking; they were sleeping when he came. May Allah give us a new understanding for an opening. We are waiting. For the honor of the most honored servant of Allah Almighty, Sayyidina Muhammad, ﷺ: *bi hurmati-l-Fatehah.*

And now our understanding level, in Western countries, they are understanding about technology, they are understanding about new weapons, new machines, new *jihaz*, instruments. All their minds are on it, to find a new one. Their understanding level is that level. Oriental people, they are thinking how we can cook a better *tandoori* or *chapatti* or curry. They are saying, "Turkish kitchen." Say, "French kitchen." Oh-h! Pakistani chicken or *tandoori* chicken or Uzebekistan pilau or Ajemistani rice or Turkish *muhalebi* or Arabs' *baklava.*

Oriental people, they are working for their stomachs, using their understanding for that purpose. Europeans working on iron, working to make new instruments. From morning up to evening, from evening up to morning, they are only thinking how we can do this, how we can do that, how new a model Mercedes or new a model princess or new a model, new fashion Rolls Royce, new fashion plays, new fashion washing powders. [Laughter]. Their minds are just occupied with that understanding; oriental people, for their eating. True or not? [Sings.] "Wel-come to you, hap-py birth-day to me!" *Fatehah.* ▲

20

THE SOUL IS OUR SULTAN

People are complaining of bad thoughts or impulses, and are asking to save themselves from them. The soul is the *sultan* of our real being being, and there must always be a *sultan* in every human system. Indeed, the lack of *sultans*—a single sovereign authority in charge of nations—since the time of the French Revolution has wrought havoc among human societies, bringing only troubles and crises. The Prophet, ﷺ, went to *Me'raj* with his real being, of which his soul was the *sultan*. On the Day of Promises, God took from all the descendants of Adam up to the end the commitment to acknowledge Him as Lord. The Prophet, ﷺ, was sent at the end of the prophetic line, in charge of all human beings up to the Day of Judgment, and the Qur'an that was revealed to him contains everything that mankind may be in need of.

A'udhu bil-Lahi min ash-Shaytani-r-rajim. So many people are coming and complaining, complaining of some thoughts, of some ideas, of some actions that no doubt all of them are from Shaytan. And they are asking a cure and to be saved from such bad thoughts, bad ideas, bad actions because they don't like them but they can't prevent themselves from that. And we saying, "*Bismillahi-r-Rahmani-r-Rahim.*"

Everything that mankind is asking to reach or to save themselves with must be in heavenly teachings, because people are between good things and evil and devils, and at every time, people are asking to reach good aspects and they are asking to save themselves, at the same time, from bad thoughts, bad feelings, bad actions. You can't imagine the number of good things to reach, or you can't imagine counting the bad feelings and ideas that are knocking [knocks] at your head, [knocks] your heart, and saying this and that.

When Allah Almighty was bringing the souls of people or their real beings into existence, our real being it is not only the soul. Soul, that is the *sultan* on our territories; everyone's soul is *sultan* over their beings. If you are taking away the *sultan*, no meaning for his territory, or territory without the *sultan* it has no meaning. It will collapse.

Therefore, people, when they are asking to be in a good condition through their lives, they *must* have a *sultan*. If a person fails to reach or to find or to have a *sultan*, he is nothing; going to the sewage—finished. Therefore, the whole collapse now on earth is because people have lost their *sultans*, individually and generally. The period of kings and *sultans* has finished, and those who are not *sultans* are coming. People are saying, "You are like me, as I am. Not any reason for me or for you that I must obey you because your level it is not above my level." Therefore, common people, when they are going to be without a *sultan*, they are like a flock that has just lost its shepherd—finished.

The systems of nations that they are calling "democratic," that is false, collapsed, and crises are coming after this, because even though their titles are different, their realities, real beings, are the same, no difference. Therefore, in the democratic system obedience has just finished. Therefore they are in need to put, each day, more rules to make people to obey them, and it is impossible, also. As often as they are putting a law preventing them from something, they are looking for a weak side, to get out; if not, they are digging under the prison and getting out. No success, during two centuries and the beginning of the twenty-first century, no success for mankind through the democratic system. Democracy has brought only cursing on nations and prepared nations to fall in a depthless collapse, depthless crisis.

Yes. The *Sultan* must be obeyed. All nations must change their ways now. I am warning the whole world. I am nothing here but something in the Heavens. If I am warning something and they are disobedient, curses and punishment are ready for them.

The *Sultan* is to be obeyed, and souls they are *sultans* in our real being. Our real being it is not only our souls. The Prophet, pbuh, during the Night Journey, *Me'raj*—*'ulama*, scholars, are saying that he was with his physical being or only with his spiritual being, and *awliya* are saying, "Either one of the two. You are on wrong way."

His real being was never going to be only his soul. He traveled not only by his soul but he was, that Night, with his *real being* in the Divine Presence; with that he traveled. No doubt; if they are saying, "By his soul," they are denying that the Prophet, 鷺, traveled by his physical being, denying that it was impossible. If they are saying, "By his soul," everyone may say, "That is like a dream; we can understand. No objection to it, no." But they are objecting that the Prophet was, with his real being, traveling first from Makkah Mukarramah[1] to Jerusalem and from Jerusalem up to the Heavens and above the Heavens to the Divine Throne. And who was on the Divine Throne? He was going to look at the empty Throne? That is reason their heads are trembling, trembling, trembling; empty, empty, empty, empty, empty a like football, never understanding anything.

Yes. The *sultan* in our physical being; without that *sultan*, this is nothing. The life of our physical being is through the *sultan*, the *sultan* giving. Also through territories, the *sultan* is giving life to his people. When the *sultan* is finished [claps hands], nations just died, like this—to dustbin. Then will come a big brush, *superge*, broom—

---

[1]Mecca the Blessed.

brush (not Bush. Doesn't matter; Bush coming to clean all dustbin people away).

What we are saying now from that is that people must have *sultans*. They tried since 1789; from the big French Revolution, that collapse just began, every bad thing coming out. They took their kings and *sultans*, killing them. Then they are now in deep darkness, never knowing how they can save themselves.

And Allah Almighty, He called all the descendants of Adam up to end of this life, so many millions of descendants, calling them into His Divine Presence. And they were like the smallest particle of matter. You may say "atoms"; we are saying "*dharra*," something that you can't imagine a particle of matter smaller than that particle. They were in the Divine Presence, and each one was carrying the personality, perfect personality, of *you*—each one, representing your perfect personality. Now they are trying to say "DNA," but it only gives *so-o-o* distant a meaning about those representatives, such a *noksan*, imperfect understanding, DNA, to give your personality.

The perfect personality that Allah Almighty was calling in His Divine Presence was taken from the back of Sayyidina Adam. Every *dharrah*, every atom, represented one person from Adam's descendants, and *never* were two of them the same. Impossible; each one was just granted a perfect, individual personality.

Now we are in '*ama*', we are in darkness. If our hearts' eyes were just granted heavenly lights, we could look and could see that *mashad*,[2] that vision [of the Day of Promises]. You must see, when Allah Almighty called and said, "Am I your Lord, your Creator?" and said, "*Bala*, yes. You are our Founder, Creator, Manifestor; You are our Lord," Still this has not finished in the Divine Presence, continuously going on.

---

[2] View, scene, spectacle, meeting.

And Allah Almighty was taking the first oath from all the descendants of Adam, and all of them they said, "You are our Lord, you are our *Mahmoud*,[3] our God, to be praised, to be glorified. Only You are our Creator, and we are swearing our oath that we will glorify You forever." And, as they said, it is going on, glorifying from our souls without *tawaqquf*[4]—non-stop glorifying. But our egos are forcing this not to be heard, not to be seen, not to be known.

Therefore, Allah Almighty sent thousands of prophets who are still on that vision. They are seeing and hearing Allah Almighty's *khitab*, addressing, *never* stopping from that up to eternity, asking *"A-lastu bi-Rabbikum?"*[5]— going, saying, giving their oath, going away; another group coming, just to be someone in His Divine Presence to be addressed with that, going on. Another coming, going on; another coming, going on; another coming, going on, and each one is still in their remembrance. It is something that our minds can't reach; with your minds and intellect you can't reach to that point. Only when you are using your spiritual power, when you are going to be free from your physical being, giving all authority to your *sultan*, you may see, you may hear, you may know.

And Allah Almighty, through that vision, He was addressing to the Seal of Prophets and saying, "All of mankind, I just granted all of them to you. Look after them, keep them and bring them to Me, My Divine Presence, on *Yawm al-Din*, on Judgment Day. And I just granted to you what you may be in need of for all mankind's inner problems and troubles, or what will happen around themselves of troubles and actions that are harming people, hurting them, making them unhappy. I just granted you keys of everything, that you may

---

[3]Praised, praiseworthy, laudable.

[4]Halt, break, ceasing, stopping, discontinuing.

[5]*"Am I not your Lord?"* (7:172)

use those keys for any purpose that you may be in need of for nations. From prophets up to the end, it is your period."

Therefore, we began to say that everything that you may be in need of, you can find in the Holy Qur'an that was granted to the Seal of the Prophets. He may open and he may give to you what you may be in need of for reaching the highest levels here and Hereafter. And to save yourselves or to protect your beings here and Hereafter, you may find that in it.

May Allah forgive me and bless you. For the honor of the Seal of the Prophets, for the honor of the most honored servant of Allah Almighty: *bi hurmati-l-Fatehah.* ▲

21

INDIA AND PAKISTAN: ONGOING TROUBLES

> Concerning the debacle partition of India and its aftermath.

Everywhere you can find them, and particularly in Pakistan and Hindistan, India—wrong people, so many. . . .Such wrong groups of people, they are coming to destroy the beliefs of *Ahl as-Sunnah wa-l-Jama'ah*,[1] and mostly in India.

It was India but non-Muslim countries, they did a trick for the Indian people. They played in the minds of Muslims' imitation leaders, who were not real guides, and they said we must partition India into two parts, which never happened in any historical period. India it is a continent. It has a specialty among other continents, and India is still a virgin area not completely well-known.

And all kings and *sultans* and emperors, they were running to conquer Indian territory, and it was the highest *rutbah*, rank and honor, for them, and therefore finally the British, they conquered India, and the title of Great Britain's kings was the King of England and Emperor of India. That was their title, "Emperor India," to make their titles high. They used this up until after the second world

---

[1] The People of the Prophet's *Sunnah* and Congregation; that is, the followers of the Prophet's example as taught through the four schools of Sunni jurisprudence (*madhahib*, i.e., Hanafi, Shafi'i, Maliki and Hanbali).

war, through '50, when they were granted their freedom, but really it was not freedom but slavery. They were more happy, more free, in the colonial time, but now, no.

We do not know anything; we are not taught about your history. Everything wrong was just taught to them. I am sorry to say so, but we must say it: people, to come from India, to run away from India for living, for asking their provisions outside of India— what is that foolishness? And India is so rich, perhaps the richest, richest territory in Asia, on earth, also. How are they running away and coming, asking for work, these people?

Like these people, millions of people were running away from Pakistan. Yes. Before Pakistan, people they were living in a continent and it was so easy to reach to their provisions. After partition, Muslims were cheated and they were given the useless part, all deserts. Pakistan is all deserts, no rain, not anything growing. In Karachi, perhaps twenty million people are living, like *naml*, ants. What are they doing?

In seven years, no rain. I was there last year; I went to Islamabad by car. If you go up to the north, you are passing all through deserts, and Islamabad is just built on a desert plain, useless. People, what should they do? Therefore they are running away, running away to look for something other than that huge continent.

But our guides during this last century, they were the worst. They were servants of Western people, servants of non-Muslims; they were prepared for that purpose. People are saying, "Oh-h, Qaidi-Azam, Qaidi-Falan, Qaid. . . !" What did they, did he do for you? Now he is imprisoned under a *kubbe*, a dome, and the government is putting two soldiers, not to allow him, if he comes up, to escape—two guards with arms, waiting there. If Qaid comes out, saying, "Lie down!"

Therefore, I am sorry about what happened after *khilafati-l-Osmania, devleti-l-Osmania*.[2] They were its defenders. More than Turks, Indian Muslims they were supporting the defense of the Ottomans from aggression of other powers in Anatolia; they were supporting with *everything*. They were supporting Turkey—not Turkey at that time but the Ottoman Empire, because their belief it was to support *makam ul-khilafah*,[3] to keep the *khalifah*.[4] Therefore they supported it as much as possible. May Allah reward them.

But then their beliefs they were just broken. When Turks took away the *khalifah*,[5] throwing him out, they were so sad. There were so many writings against the new Turkish government, but finished. If they had known that they would do that, they would never have supported them, and if not supporting them, that movement could not have been successful.

And then when their ancestors did this, non-Muslims punished them, saying, "You must have a separate part to be only for yourselves and you may call it 'Pakistan, Clean Land.'". Yes? Clean land, Pakistan? What do you think—is it clean now, very clean, very clean?

Pakistan. Hindu people they never changed its name, saying "India". And they are saying, "We are coming on you, to take away from you the second part, also." Therefore they are preparing, and they are a billion people now. You understand what I am saying?

Look at your people: they are from London, Pakistani people. Millions of people ran away, and people are also coming from India,

---

[2] The Ottoman caliphate, the Ottoman government.
[3] The seat of the caliphate.
[4] Caliph.
[5] Referring to the abolition of the caliphate in 1924 after the formation of the Turkish Republic.

and they are much more powerful than Muslims, everywhere, supporting each other and growing. They have power. Even the government must obey to their beliefs.

The British government is ordering everyone to put on their heads that helmet, but they [Sikhs] are putting on turbans, never taking them off. They are fighting the government and they are saying, "We are not wearing it, we are not putting on helmets. We must keep our turbans." Now look how many people in England are wearing the crown of Islam! This [turban] is the crown of Islam. They are only putting such a thing, like this, looking like that, and 'ulama are putting another, big one, saying "Maulana." I am saying, "Maulana is putting such a *charpoosh*, hat, on his head. Where is the Islamic 'crown'? Why not putting it?"

Therefore, we are living in the worst time because people are all drunk people, never defending real Islam. Young people, you must try to learn about your past and present times, and you must think about your future. We are not created to be laborers, workers, servants to Western people. *Why?* Turks, also; Turkish people are the same, going to UK, Germany, Euro countries to be servants. *For what?* Eat dry bread but don't be servants. Arabs, also.

Therefore a punishment is coming, two for Muslims, one for Europeans. May Allah forgive me and bless you. *Bi hurmati-l-habib*, who is the most honored one in the Divine Presence: *Fatehah*. ▲

22

THE UNIQUENESS OF EACH CREATION

Each individual creation has its own private independent existence with its Lord.

Eternal... that is *ebedi*. Eternity.

For the Lord of Heavens, and He created us. That declaration from servants to say "O our Creator! You are our Lord and we are Your servants." That declaration making our Lord Almighty Allah to be pleased with us.

Meded ya Sultan al-Anbiya, O Most Glorified and most Honored, most Glorious Servant of Allah Almighty.

We are proud to be your nation. To be one from your countless nation. It is such a big prize, such a big honor, it is impossible to say anything for description [of] that honor.

O people! Be believers.

O people! Try to believe!

O people! Try to take away your ego and give your most high respect and glorifying only to Your Creator, al-Haqq, *subhanahu wa ta'ala*, Allah Almighty.

That is as a introduction, or you may say preface. If we are going to follow Preface, may take that speech on it, up to end of this world. And may finish if whole trees going to be pens or pencils it is so small for glorifying or trying our Lord's glorifying or our Lord's Glory.

Everything just granted from Allah, the Creator to creatures according to their understanding or according their *maqdirah*, possibilities for understanding. Because everything has a possibility according to their positions for understanding. Don't think that an ant's understanding is going to be the same as a bee's. Don't think that the understanding of a bird is similar to the understanding of a bee. Don't think that a falcon's understanding is the same understanding as a pigeon's.

Everything in existence has a private position for understanding of its Lord. Because everything in existence if we are looking in it, we are looking and seeing an appearance from its Creator. And everything has special appearances in Divinely Mirrors. If there are no mirrors, no one can see himself or anything else. Therefore every creature created must have a special mirror. If it is looking at that mirror, it can understand about itself, herself or himself.

That is a deep ocean, a very deep ocean. It is not enough for giving an explanation on that pre-appearances that are coming as a reflection through minutes, and seconds and moments, and even less and less (fractions of time), to never-ending endless time. If you are looking up, that appearance is going to appear endlessly up to infinity; up to the last point of glorifying at the last point of being in existence through eternity.

May Allah forgives us. We are very weak ones as well as we are the weakest ones for understanding becuase every time our souls are asking to know about the Lord of heavens, the Lord of spirits, the Lord of souls, the Lord of *suret*, images of everyone. So different, so different. Countless differences among two ones. And this is an endless ocean. *Allahu Akbar, Allahu akbar al-akbar, subhanallah.*

And He is eternal, the Lord of Heavens. Eternity only for Him Almighty Allah, but from His Endless *Sakhawa, Karam* [generosity] from His endless Generosity, giving to everyone from His Endless Mercy Oceans, that Mercy Oceans including countless kinds of creation. Countless.

That is Divinely Glory for our Lord's Glorious, Most glorious Being. And you must happy. We must be happy on our levels, because there are endless endless creation and endless creatures, countless, countless, only belonging to our Lord and we are speaking only on our levels that it is different from every levels of creation. Because you can't find two levels similar, at the same time. And it such *'Azhamat, Heybet*, appearance of glorifying our Lord that He is creating, creating countless worlds, countless universes, countless *'awalim,* [worlds], countless creation and each one it is only in its position, only one. Not a second one from creation going to be the same or similar to anyone else. [*Masha' Allah*] Even *ya* Shaykh Hisham Efendi, even they say there is atoms, they are similar. They are saying, for example, Hydrogen atoms, they are similar. And I am saying that I am nothing, I am saying "If they are all similars, why they are not getting altogether to be one?"

If I am identical to Sahib, why is there going to be one Sahib and another one, myself, tht I am here? As whole mankind, they are similar, but not hundred percent similar, no. If they were 100% similar there must be only one, not many. Like Hydrogen atoms, if every one they were the same why going to be millions, billions or quadrillions of atoms. Why not coming altogether? Which thing making them to make each one appear by itself as a private , private being in existence? Must be all of them one. That means each atoms has a special being and everyone, each one just *harisan*, they are so greedy to keep its personaltiy. Each atom, another personality it has. Therefore not saying, "O all are alike—you should be one block."

There should be just one block of Hydrogen atoms. That is coming to me so often: if Hydrogen atoms or other atoms if they are (exactly) the same why they are going to be different so that millions or billions or trillions of atoms are in existence? Why are they not coming to be one mass of one atom only? Who is making them to be different? That means every atom has its own and independent *mustaqill*, and *iwanlik* being, in existence. So no one of them is going to be happy to be with another one, together.

Everyone asking to be independent in the Divinely Presence to grant their glorifying of their Lord independently and freely. This point was coming to my heart. I would like to ask this point from scientists, which is coming to me such idea, that why atoms—if they are all (absolutely) the same—why are they not coming altogether to be one atom, one mass? If I am saying this, I may say if the whole mankind are the same, why are they going to be this one, that one, this one? They must all be in one *qalib*, one form, one form, one man. Why making so [many] different billions and trillions people to be each one separated and independent? What is their independency that is making them to be alone in their positions, not accepting to be with that one? What is that?

That is a secret of the Lord of Heavens, a secret of the Creator that He is putting that He is not accepting to be sharing in its independency. No. That one is independent and that other is independent and that other is independent and He is filling the world with mankind. If they are similar then there is only needed to be Adam and Eve. Why coming from Adam and Eve, billions and billions, for what that huge number of people? What is the reason? Why the Lord of Heavens not keeping them all in one man and one woman, [Rather] making them to be countless independent beings?

Always I am thinking on that regarding those atoms. Why all those atoms are not going to be happy to be similar to the silver atom? We must ask also which thing is making silver atoms to be independent and never asking to be golden atoms? Why? Who is making them to insist to keep their personality and all are happy with their being and with their existence? No silver atom is asking to be a golden atom nor a golden atom is ever asking to be a silver atom. Each one they are happy being silver, being golden, being copper, being *hadid*, iron, being *teneke*, tin, why?

That (reality is) showing that the Lord of Heavens, Allah Almighty He is doing and granting them a special Name in the Divine Presence. *Subhanallah*, Hisham Effendi.

I don't think that a fish, a shark, is asking to be like *usral*, dolphin or a dolphin asking to be like a *balena*, whale. No, everyone saying, even small ones, they are never asking to be like gigantic fish and gigantic fish are not asking to be like small fish.

Everything in its position is happy with its Creator and. May Allah forgives us, Hisham Effendi.

And, O people, don't waste your valuable times to be empty, because everyone is running to their destination. That destination it is another endless ocean to be granted everything in different destinations. Maybe one hundred whales but everyone's destination is so different.

It may be one thousand small blue fish. No one is asking to be *yumaththal*, to be represented by, another one. No, everyone is saying "I am independent. I don't like anyone standing on behalf of me and he is saying 'my representative.' I am giving to you because you are like me and I am like you."

No, all are different and we are speaking on atoms and no any atom is happy to say to a second atom [saying] "you may represent myself in yourself." No, [rather each is] saying "I am something else, and you are something else. You are in the Divinely Presence an independent being as well as I am myself an independent being in the Divinely Presence."

Why I am going to lose my independency through yourself? No. I am standing up and I am glorifying My Lord myself, not through yourself, no. To be, to grant my glorifying to My Lord it is an honor for me, independently."

You also are granting your endless glorifying to Your Lord and it is all for you. No one is asking to me to *mumaththal*, be represented by another, no."

That is the Lord's endless, endless Power Oceans, endless Knowledge Oceans, endless Greatest Creation Oceans. Such things, when you are hearing or listening or trying to understand something, giving to your from *ma'rifatullah*, from Holy Knowledge of Creator, Allah Almighty.

O people look. Leave useless things and come and listen and accept real diamonds and pearls that granted to you through heavenly beings, through prophets, peace be upon them. One day you may be *peshman olma* [enemy] *dushman deyil*. One day you may be *yarayt ma fa'alta hadha*, [wishing that I didn't do it] another one [regretting] regretting why I am not using what granted to me alone and I left this to that one, when the greatest opening coming to everyone on the Day of Resurrection, Resurrection making everything to wake up and understanding and that understanding beginning from the Day of tem... Trumpet. From [time of] Trumpet and on, you can't imagine that people ask "Why, why, why, we wasted a chance to know such a things through our short life and may Allah forgive us!" O Shaykh Hisham.

It is a deep ocean coming today that I never thinking on it but suddenly coming to my heart and going to my mind and opening through my speech.

May Allah gives us *maqdirah* ability to understand something that has no scale, its amount.

Bismillahi-r-Rahmani-r-Rahim. May Allah forgives us. Such a knowledge preparing people for big events, big visions that they are running on it and they are coming on them. But people now they are only *khaddam* [servants] servants of their stomachs and they were mostly they're servants of their rides, nothing else.

Now we are living in the 21st Century, but people they are occupied themselves with such a things that have no value, and leaving most precious things that canot be reached a person after death, after this life. They should be on their levels no more getting up. Therefore prophets asking, "O people, leave that *muwaqqat*, temporary life and come and ask permanent delights of your life that you are running on it.

May Allah forgives us. ▲

23

UNSEEN FOUNDATIONS

> Everything in Creation Has its Foundation in the Unseen
> World. Each existing thing has One Who originated it. And
> each smallest particle is utterly unique, reflecting that Divine
> Attribute.

Bismillahi-r-Rahmani-r-Rahim. Because everything beginning with
it and ending with it, is as He likes. He Almighty has no beginning or
no ending.

Dastour ya Sultan al-awliya, we are asking heavenly support for
our meeting and for every good acting, we must ask a heavenly support. Or our *juhud,* effort going to be *suda,* meaningless, as long as
people are forgetting their Lord, no chance for them to be happy
here or hereafter. That is some *qa'idah,* principle, it is unchangeable
principles, must be known and must be learned. That we are not by
ourselves. No. If no any relationship for mankind on this planet it is
impossible to be in existence, to move, to act, to think, to learn, no.
They should be like statues.

First of all man must learn about themselves, about their positions. Glory for Allah and His Glorious from pre-eternal up to eternal. Absolute Glory for the Lord of heavens, for the Creator that He
created. No one can claim that I am creating something. We may ask
'show us what you created." If he is saying, "I created myself" they
are liars, unacceptable, cann't be. because you are coming from your
mother's womb. Think on it, Holy Quran.

That whole knowledge appeared from the Holy Quran. and everything that belonging for knowledge it is coming, not growing in ourselves. Man taking everything from his outside. Because everything begining with Him everything belonging on knowledge it is coming not growing in ourselves man taking everything from outside it is impossible for a person to feed himself by himself to feed herself by herself, to feed their descendents through their wombs; it is impossible. Must be granted to them something from unseen worlds.

It is a principle something if it is seen must be unseen on same level. Now we are seeing something, here. If we are looking and seeing something, must be behind that our side, another side, that it is unseen. Yes, we may say this atmosphere. Atmosphere it is unseen, unseeen waqi`a, incident. we are saying that there is atmosphere. If you are asking them, "can you see it?" no one can say, "yes I am seeing." If you are saying "I can't see" and you are saying "there is an atmosphere but I can't see it," that means for everything you can find an unseen, unseen happening about that one. "Happening" means to be in existence and something to be in existance as a happening must have a Happener Who (is making that) Happening. There must be a Happener for something to be able to be in existence and to be in the universe that we are looking and we are seeing something and then beyond that distance we are seeing nothing.

That is something that if you are speaking a little bit deeply about it, we must say for everything in existence, there must be a "room" that it may be through that room, and through that room it must have something about its happening.... or can't be a happening for that thing, that atom, because that atom it is in existence. And it has a space, yes, it (occupies) a space. If it has no space, an atom, can't be in existence.

And we may ask, what is an atom's space? Is its space bigger than the atom? Or is the atom bigger than its space? We may ask if the atom is much more powerful, or its *qa'idah*, its base? The base is more powerful, not space.

More important we may ask: "Who is that One that is making for an atom its base?" I am asking from learned ones and scientists and academic people for an answer.

For an atom, it is a "happening" that just "happened." It never happened by itself! But it is in a space and that space contains possibilities for everything. If no possibility for that space, nothing can be in space. Then that atom, without a base, cannot be in existence and it can't be seen. If it is seen, and it has a base, there must be another power that is covering and catching that atom and making it to be on its base.

That is a very important question that no existing one can be without a base. If you are saying this world is without a base, it is foolishness and it is a ignorance. This world must have a base. If no base, no moment. If no base, no existence. Because base is carrying existence for everything. Beginning from atoms or less than atoms. Look! There is nucleus, the center of atoms and we are saying its position is positive and scientists are saying that it has electrons around itself and their positions are negative. How can a positive happening be friendly with a negative one? And they are turning around itself. What is the base of the nucleus? And what is the basis of electrons? You can say their base is the nucleus, but really that cannot be, because that is positive the electrons are negative. So what kind base exists for the nucleus, and which kind of base is there for electrons?

How are they denying an Unseen One and saying "because we can't see it, it is out of existence or no existence for it"? That is 21st century's ignorance. A base is so important that everything has just been put on its base.

What do you think? Who is that One putting an atom on its base? And what is the base of its nucleus? What is the base of electrons? Which thing is making them to be fixed. The nucleus is on its base. So which one is making and forcing electrons to keep their bases and to move?

How they are saying that nothing is unseen? That is the utmost level of ignorance. But they are such heedless people. No one is asking what I am asking them up to today.

We have power from our Holy book to speak on such positions. No doubt, no doubt! But atheist people they cannot answer me. I never heard a physicist to speak on such a subject. No one is saying there is a base for an atom and no one is saying about the base of electrons and what about that nucleus which is carrying different pieces from creation.

Everyone, if they are in existence, must have a base because without a base, nothing can be appear, finished! Therefore, I am warning whole scientists, that if they are going to continue on their ignorance something may happen through their heads leaving them as a *majnun* crazy one. They should lose. Yes, man they have bases. Each one if we have a base in existence, and our bases each one is independent from all others. My base is never going to touch to your existence, to your base.

The sun must have a base. Without a base it cannot be in existence. What is that base? It is something that may be known or not? No one knows what carrying sun from east to west or Who turning our globe from east to west? And without a base, how it can be moved, or how it can be in existence? A base is the real reason for happenings for everything. The Creator just created and His creation is most perfect. It is in absolute perfection. Absolute perfection is for Allah.

Why they are not saying this? They are afraid? Why are they afraid?

I am asking and waiting, looking for an answer for that happening. I am knowing nothing but sometimes my heart going into relation, connection with some centers. We are reaching to bases, through our unexpected or impossible-to-be-known powers carryng some people to some realities.

Some people are saying they are realists. What is a realist? If you are a realist say about your real being what your base is. Now our base is here, and after one hour our base is there, moving. Like your shadow, a base must be there.

But its base is not the shadow. The real reality of being belongs to that base, (not to the shadow).

What is that base? That is the secret of secrets that it is impossible to reach. If you are reaching one secret, appearing another secret ocean. And beyond it you should find another secret ocean. Never-ending oceans.

Therefore the Lord saying, all glory for Him, "I am that One who creating. I am that one that giving a base for creatures. I am making creation and creation going on with its bases. All bases tasbeehaat, are praising and glorifying Me. I am your Lord, so glorify Me." All bases glorifying the Lord.

Those ignorant ones that they only know 1, 2 3, no more, their heads can never carry such things and we are speaking only very very very very simple description to carry that description for the understanding of mankind.

Yes. The sun what is its base? When it is in the east and what is its base when it is reaching to the west? Where is its base? Holy Quran saying that sun coming and setting down in a black sea,

in a black ocean which is mentioned in Surat ul-Kahf about Dhul -
Qarnayn.

*hatta idha balagha maghrib ash-shamsi wajadahaa taghrubu fee `ayni
hamiyatin. Till, when he came to the setting of the sun, it appeared to him that it
was setting in a dark, turbid sea;* (18:86)

That is base that when the sun is moving from one point to another point its base is getting different. It is not same base that the
sun is reaching at the end of the day. Holy Books and particular the
Holy Quran are signing, giving some signs about that and saying the
sun is just setting and it has another base for it. Beginning with a
different base, like a train beginning from one station and reaching to
another station.

The sun is also moving. Don't say it is not moving. No it is
moving. And without a base it can't be moved must be has a base, if
no base, no sun. *Allahu Akbar.*

Who its base appearing running appearing according to Holy
Commands of heavens and coming and reaching to its last minute
for a day and disappearing it has another base there. But people now
so *suthi*, superficial, shallow. Reality is something, shadow is something else. And through the shadow appearing and setting, rising and
setting. Where is Real Being that it never needs a base? It is in Unseen climates of Unity of the Lord of creation. Beyond that no one
can reach to that point. Only that is belongs to the Creator. Therefore, He is Wahidun Ahad, (One and Unique). *Wahidun Ahad. Qul
Huwa Allahu Ahad. Say! He is Allah the One, the Unique.* Such a things
in our days it is going to be unexpected positions people they are
asking to learn something that it is so cheap. But like plastic toys. But
no one asking to enter in it.

Therefore we are saying for every seen happening must be another happening in unseen worlds.

That means *'alamul-mithaal.* that there there is no need for a base. That when the Lord, the real positions of everything it is under Holy Commands of Lord of heavens. When He asking in that plane it is unseen. When he is asking it to be seen, the way of creation, He knows, *hal min khaliqun ghayrullah, Is there a creator, other than Allah?* (35:3) . Only One may create and bring in existence with its base for without base nothing is going to be in existence. It is going to be only for the Lord's endless creations.

Naas, people now, are running to know very cheap knowledge about creation.

And we are saying that if something just appeared in creation it must have a real Being through Unseen worlds. Look and think on it to know something. Don't run directly to know the Creator. No, no! First give what I am asking you, say to me a reply, an answer. Say to me what is your reply about what we are saying. Say! Then we may speak another page and endless pages through creation that belongs to the Lord of creation.

May Allah forgives us. I think it is a heavy ocean and I don't think that it is a too difficult for understanding. It is giving something to people for understanding that they can catch it and that catching may lead them to real reality. Because reality you can't find here by your mind. Mindly-production it is not enough. Another Being or another happening that is going to happen through a man, it is something else. And you may get up one degree after another degree. Different levels. And you can find in front of you endless levels.

Therefore, the Lord He is the Absolute Power, with Absolute Knowledge with Absolute Wisdoms according to His Absolute Will-power. And you, O man, you are so small. But according to your position the Lord of heavens giving something to you for understanding, from a small bubble endless expansion.

May Allah forgive us.

It is something that most, or perhaps all people living in this world, are heedless about and they are denying. The reason for denying, is they are not using their thinking power for such a thing. It is so small, yet so important. *Allahu Akbar, Allahu Akbar!* My Allah forgive us.

Today it is something that is unexpected.

Allah keeps us not to fall through the valley of objection. Therefore if asking more, Allah gives more. If they are happy to be on their real level, the first level, they should be there forever. But whoever is moving they may move eternally and through eternity they should find something that belongs to eternal worlds, to eternity. And that is real pleasure for a person from mankind: not this world or the simple enjoyable levels after death (physical pleasure Allah grants to common believers in the afterlife).

No, the enjoyment for wise men, prophets and their followers it is something else. It is something else: asking and approaching as a fish always has its mouth is open and never closing it. They have an endless *ihtiras*, greed. Someone was asking why a fish is always opening its mouth. Just he asked from a holy one (a saint, *waliullah*) and he was answering, "Because that fish is running to drink the whole ocean. Therefore always opening its mouth and its last desire and demand is to reach to the whole ocean."

Men on earth now their mouth has been open and they are asking to drink or to reach everything through this life. And it is impossible.

May Allah forgive us.

That is the teaching of the Lord Almighty to His prophets, and prophets are teaching to their real followers who are believing in unseen worlds, unseen happenings, unseen power oceans, unseen wisdom oceans. Who is asking endless beauty oceans and endless endless oceans, that is only for the Lord of heavens (to grant). May Allah forgive us. *Fateha.* ▲

24

SPARKLING LIGHTS IN ENDLESS DIVINE OCEANS

> Highest respect is for the Lord's most honored servant Prophet Muhammad. Eternity was created for his sake, and gifted to mankind. Stop running after this worldly life and turn towards the heavenly life. If you were to taste even a drop of the Divinely-granted oceans that the Lord has provided for His sincere servants you would never enjoy a single moment in this life.

A'udhu bil-Lahi min ash-Shaytani-r-rajim, bismillahi-r-Rahmani-r-Rahim.

Dastur ya rijal Allah meded. Meded!

Holy Ones, *meded.* Our holy masters.

(Mawlana stands up)

Welcome. *Allahu Akbaru, Allahu Akbar, la ilaha ill-Llah, Allahu Akbar, Allahu akbar, wa lillahi 'l-hamd*

That is our honor that granted by our Creator. And we are giving our high respect to His most respectful and honored, glorified servant and His Deputy and who is representing the Lord of heavens, theLord of creation, from pre-eternal up to eternal. We are giving high respect to him and asking his intercession here and hereafter.

Alfu 's-salat alfu 's-salam, endlessly our greetings on him as long as Allah Almighty honoring him and greeting him (stands) Sayyidina Muhammad ﷺ.

It is an honor for a weak servant like me - weakest servant - to address My Lord's servants. I am knowing nothing but if my holy master sending me something for addressing people it is ok, even an ant can address to you and gives to you honor.

As-salamu 'alaykum, peace on you, whole servants of Allah, whom they are giving their high respect, highest respect and endless glorifying and endless greetings, endless majesty to our Creator, Allah Almighty.

Allah Almighty: (stands) we are standing up for His Honor that He created us and granting us endless Mercy Oceans to be His servants; to know Him and to give our most high glorifying, most and majestic addressings to Him, Almighty Allah. He may grant us a tireless life that we can stand up from beginning up to end for His Majestic Presence.

O people! Listen and obey and take your Lord's endless blessing oceans. Listen and obey and reach our Lord's endless Glory Oceans.

Everything in His Divinely Presence, endlessly from pre-eternal up to eternal. Eternity. O people! Come and ask eternity. So sweet word to say "eternity".

Allah, Allah, no one can give a person such a pleasure as to say "eternity". That is biggest, biggest grant from our Lord to His servants. He is so Majestic that granting to His creatures eternal life and promising them eternity. *Allah, Allah*.

So sweet word: "eternity".

O people! Run after eternity.

Huuuuuw. Here we are like sparkling, a small light, sparkling and He Almighty from His Majestic Lightening Oceans, endless oceans, He is granting to His weak servants and saying, "O My servants, come to Me and take from My endless Lightening Oceans."

Each one of that oceans is majestic and most glorified. Through that oceans one spot of lightening may give life such a universe thousands and thousands ones.

He is Allah Almighty is Great and His Greatness is Mighty Greatness. His Greatness is Majestic Greatness. His Great most and endless Glorified Oceans' Greatness. Absolute Greatness for Our Lord Almighty Allah.

O people! Come and run to Him and fall into *sajda*, bow yourself in front of His endless Greatness (Mawlana bows), Majestic Oceans.

And say, "O our Lord! We surrender to You. You created us. You granted us everything and we are giving everything to You and we are trying to give everything as a grant from You to You."

O people! O mankind. Don't fear for surrendering to Your Lord.

People are running away now from surrendering. Shaytan is urging them that "you must run away from the Lord of heavens and you must not be ever surrendered to that One."

Surrendering, that is the meaning of Islam. Therefore it is most high honor for mankind, that their Lord, their Creator asking from them, "O people! Surrender."

As He was asking for, from every prophet and particularly from Abraham 🕊 the father of prophets, saying to him, "Surrender O My servant! Surrender to Me and be a Muslim." Therefore first surrendering one that named as a surrenderer is Abraham, peace be upon him, Our Lord's Friend. Friend. He became, accepting Allah to be His Friend, and His Friendship. And giving to him from His heavenly love and when Abraham tasting that Heavenly Taste, he was runninng and moving to his Lord Almighty Allah Who granted to him to be Friend from the Lord of heavens, friendship.

Masha-Allah.

And Abraham, peace be upon him, the Friend of Allah, that friendship so high, so high honor that no one can understand that friendship except the Seal of Prophets Sayyidina Muhammad ﷺ.

Whole respect is to him, the Seal of Prophets Sayyidina Muhammad ﷺ. Please O glorified Prophet we are asking your intercession, here and hereafter. That is our honor.

Try to give your respect, your High respect to Allah Almighty. The Lord of Creation is One. There is no second creator and He has no wife. He is only One.

Through that ascension, through Divinely Presence, he only can know and understand, that word only, to be (in the) Divinely Presence. That is only for one. No second one to reach to that position, to reach heavenly position, no one except the Seal of Prophets Sayyidina Muhammad, peace be upon him. Whole glory, whole magnificent lightenings, whole majesty that was just granted from the Lord of heavens and the Lord of the Divinely Beings—that is only for Sayyidina Muhammad, peace be upon him. Not a second one.

Others on the line of heavenly position, but Divinely (position) only for one.

Allah Allah, Allah Allah, Allah Allah, 'Aziz Allah.

Allah Allah, Allah Allah, Allah Allah, Sultan Allah.

Allah Allah, Allah Allah, Allah Allah, Subhanallah.

Allah Allah, Allah Allah, Allah Allah, Karim Allah.

Whole angels they are singing and if one of them making his singing and glorifying through his singing, if it was, if it can be possible for hearing, the Children of Adam, they should fall down as dead bodies, leaving their bodies and riding on their spirits, their souls, rides to reach to the stage of heavens.

And they are not going to ask anything, any treasures, any materials. They are leaving, they are running away, they are running to hear that holy singings from heavens.

O people! Let us go to reach that stations that you should forget everything from materials; you should run away from... from treasures. If whole world full with diamonds and pearls and emeralds and full with rubies you are going to kick them away but asking to hear that holy singing through angels, through heavens.

O people! Don't waste your precious lives; your lives are precious. Don't live to pass away and you are losing endless glorifying from heavens.

O people! Now reduce your running. Now reduce your speed a little bit less for understanding the pleasure, endless pleasure from heavens that whom they are tasting, even one second, they should kick away the whole world. If may be from golden or from ruby, but no value. When they are reaching to a level and appearing to you from real reality, you are running to reach it and to enjoy yourself and to give your high respect (to) the Lord of Creation.

O people! Please reduce now your speed. Enough of your running after *dunya*, because *dunya* is like a carcass. Don't run after it, but run to reach heavenly stations to be granted endless pleasure, endless beauty, endless peace, endless lights, endless pleasures, endless enjoyment, endless lightenings, everything endless through that level.

Run on it. Leave this imitated life and leave this short time of life to make full enjoyment for your egos. Leave your egoistic enjoyments and run after spiritual enjoyments; heavenly enjoyments. Run after it, you should be happy and in safety and in endless pleasure that time.

May Allah grants us His *Huwww...*, endless Mercy Oceans; grants us a small spot for understanding it is enough to leave everything and run after that station of enjoyment; station of pleasures; station of lightenings; station of majestic beings.

May Allah forgive us and send us someone to make our faces to turn to reality and to leave this imitated life and to run after a real life through angels, through Lightening Oceans, through Mercy Oceans, through endless Beauty Oceans.

May Allah forgive us. *Allah Allah, Allah Allah, Allah Allah, Allah Allah. Allah Allah, Subhan Allah. Fatehah.* ▲

GLOSSARY

Abu Bakr as-Siddiq—the closest of the Prophet's Companions and his father-in-law, who shared the Hijrah with him. After the Prophet's death, he was chosen by consensus of the Muslims as the first caliph or successor to the Prophet. He is known as one of the most saintly of the Prophet's Companions.

'Abdul-Khaliq al-Ghujdawani—the eleventh grandshaykh of the Naqshbandi *tariqah*, one of the Khwajagan of Central Asia.

Abu Hanifa—the founder of one of the four schools of Islamic jurisprudence, the Hanafi *madhhab*.

Abu Yazid Bistami—Bayazid Bistami, a great ninth century *wali* and Naqshbandi master.

Adab—good manners, proper etiquette.

Adhan—the call to prayer.

Ahl al-Bait—People of the House, that is, the family of the Holy Prophet 🕌.

Ahl ad-dunya—people of the world, i.e., those who are attached to its life and pleasures.

Akhirah—the Hereafter, the Eternal Life.

Alhamdulillah—praise be to Allah, praise God.

Allahu akbar—God is the Most Great.

Amir (pl., 'umara)—chief, leader, head of a nation or people.

Anbiya (plural of **nabi**)—prophets.

'Aql—mind, intellect, intelligence, reason, discernment.

'Arafat—a vast plain outside Mecca where pilgrims gather for the principal rite of Hajj.

'Arif—knower; in the present context, one who has reached spiritual knowledge of his Lord.

Ar-Rahim—the Mercy-Giving, Merciful, Munificent, one of Allah's ninety-nine Holy Names

Ar-Rahman—the Most Merciful, Compassionate, Beneficent, the most often repeated of Allah's Holy Names.

Ashhadu an la ilaha illa-Llah wa ashhadu anna Muhammadu Rasul-Allah—"I bear witness that there is no deity except Allah and I bear witness that Muhammad is Allah's messenger," the Islamic *Shahadah* or Declaration of Faith.

Astaghfirullah—I seek Allah's forgiveness.

A'udhu **bil-Lahi min ash-Shaytani-r-Rajim**—I seek refuge in Allah from Satan the accursed.

Awliya (sing., **wali**)—the "friends" of Allah, Muslim saints or holy people.

Bait al-Maqdi— the Sacred House in Jerusalem, built at the site where Solomon's Temple was later erected.

Barakah—blessings.

Batil—vain or false; falsehood, deception.

Bayah—pledge; in the context of this book, the pledge of a disciple (murid) to a shaykh.

Bi-hurmati-l-Fatehah—for the honor or respect of Surat al-Fatehah (the opening chapter of the Qur'an).

Bismillahi-r-Rahmani-r-Rahim— "In the name of Allah, the Beneficent, the Merciful," the invocation with which all a Muslim's actions are supposed to begin.

Dajjal—the False Messiah whom the Prophet ﷺ foretold as coming at the end-time of this world, who will deceive mankind with pretensions of being divine.

Day of Promises—the occasion in the spiritual world when Allah Almighty called together the souls of all human beings to come and asked them to acknowledge His Lordship and sovereignty (7:172).

Dhikr (zikr, zikir)—message, remembrance or reminder, used in the Qur'an to refer to the Qur'an and other revealed scriptures. Dhikr (or dhikr-Allah) also refers to remembering Allah through repetition of His Holy Names or various phrases of glorification (for the meanings of the phrases of dhikr mentioned in this book, see the footnote entries under individual phrases).

Dhulm (zulm)—injustice, oppression, tyranny, misuse, transgressing proper limits, wrong-doing.

Du'a—supplication, personal prayer.

Dunya—this world and its attractions, worldly involvements.

Efendi—mister, sir.

'Eid—festival; the two major festivals of Islam are 'Eid al-Fitr, marking the completion of Ramadan, and 'Eid al-Adha, the Festival of Sacrifice during the time of Hajj.

Fard—obligatory, prescribed.

Fard al-kifayah – an obligation which suffices to be met by one or a few persons in a community.

Fatehah—al-Fatehah, the opening surah or chapter of the Qur'an.

Fitnah (pl., **fitan**)—trial, test, temptation; also, discord, dissension.

Grandshaykh—a wali of great stature. In this text, where spelled with a capital "G," "Grandshaykh" refers to Maulana 'Abdullah ad-Daghestani, Shaykh Nazim's shaykh, to whom he was closely attached for forty years up to the time of Grandshaykh's death in 1973.

Hadith (pl., **ahadith**)—a report of the Holy Prophet's sayings, contained in the collections of early hadith scholars. In this text, "Hadith" has been used to refer to the entire body of his oral traditions, while "hadith" denotes an individual tradition.

Halal—lawful, permissible.

Hajji—one who has performed Hajj, the sacred pilgrimage of Islam.

Halal—permitted, lawful according to the Islamic Shari'ah.

Haqq—truth, reality.

Haram—forbidden, unlawful.

Hasha—God forbid! Never!

Haqq—truth, reality.

Haram—prohibited, unlawful.

Hasan al-Basri – a great scholar of the seventh century C.E.

Hawa—desires, lusts, passions of the lower self or nafs.

Hidayah/hidayat—guidance.

Hijab—barrier, screen, veil or curtain; the covering of Muslim women.

Himmah—desire, zeal, eagerness, ambition, determination.

Hu—the divine pronoun, He.

Ibrahim—the prophet Abraham.

Imam—leader; specifically, the leader of a congregational prayer.

Iman—faith, belief.

Iman—faith, belief.

Insha'Allah – God willing, if God wills.

'Isa—the prophet Jesus 簃.

'Isha – night; specifically, the night prayer.

Jababirah—tyrants, oppressors.

Jinn—an invisible order of beings created by Allah from fire.

Kafir—a denier or rejector; in an Islamic context, one who denies Allah (an unbeliever or atheist) or does not acknowledge or is ungrateful for divine favors.

Khalifah—deputy, successor, vicegerent.

Khidr—a holy man, mentioned in the Qur'an, 18:60-82, to whom God has granted life up to the end of the world..

Kufr—unbelief, denial of Allah.

La hawla wa la quwwata illa bil-Lah al-'Aliyi-l-'Adhim—"There is no might nor power except in Allah, the Most High, the All-Mighty," words that Muslims utter frequently during their daily lives , signifying total reliance upon Allah.

La ilaha illa-Llah, Muhammadu rasul-Allah—there is no deity except Allah, Muhammad is the Messenger of Allah.

Mahdi--the divinely-appointed guide whose coming at the end-time of this world is mentioned in several authoritative hadiths. He will lead the believers and establish a rule of justice and righteousness for a period of time prior to the events preceding the end of the world and the Last Judgment.

Masha'Allah—what or as Allah willed.

Masjid—literally, a place where sujud, prostration, is made, i.e., a mosque.

Maula—master, lord, protector, patron, referring to Allah Most High.

Me'raj—the Holy Prophet's ascension to the Heavens and the Divine Presenc.

Muezzin—one who makes the call to prayer (adhan).

Muluk (sing., **malik**)—kings, monarchs.

Mumin/muminah—male/female believers in Islam.

Munkar--that which is disapproved, rejected or considered abominable in Islam.

Murid—a disciple or follower of a shaykh.

Murshid—spiritual guide, pir.

Musa—the prophet Moses ﷺ.

Muwahhid – one who proclaims the Unity of Allah Almighty.

Nafs—(1) soul, self, person; (2) the lower self, the ego.

Nasihah—good advice or counsel, admonition, reminder.

Nur—light.

Qada wa qadar—the sixth pillar of Islamic faith, referring to the divine decree.

Qiblah—direction; specifically, the direction of Mecca.

Qisas—retaliation.

Qiyamat/Qiyamah—the Day of Resurrection.

Rabi'ah al-Adawiyah—Rabi'ah Basri, a great womansaint of the eighth century C.E.

Rabitah—bond, connection, tie, link, in the context of this book, with a shaykh.

Rak'at—a cycle or unit of the Islamic prayer (salat), which is repeated a specified number of times in each prayer.

Ramadan—the ninth month of the Islamic lunar calendar, the month of fasting.

Rasul-Allah—the Messenger of God, Muhammad ﷺ.

Sahabah (sing., sahabi)—the Companions of the Prophet, the first Muslims.

Sajdah (also sujud)—prostration.

Salat—the prescribed Islamic prayer or worship.

Sallallahu 'alayhi was-salam—the Islamic invocation on the Prophet ﷺ, meaning, "May Allah's peace and blessings be upon him."

Salawat—invoking blessings and peace upon the Holy Prophet ﷺ.

Sayyid—leader; also, a descendant of the Holy Prophet.

Sayyidina—our chief, master.

Sayyidina 'Ali—the cousin and son-in-law of the Prophet ﷺ and the fourth caliph of Islam.

Sayyidina 'Umar—'Umar ibn al-Khattab, the Prophet's eminent Companion and the second caliph of Islam.

Shahadah—the Islamic creed or Declaration of Faith, "Ash-shadu an la ilaha illa-Llah wa ashhadu anna Muhammu rasul Allah, I bear witness that there is no deity except Allah and I bear witness that Muhammad is His messenger."

Shah Naqshband—Grandshaykh Muhammad Bahauddin Shah-Naqshband, a great eighth century wali, the founder of the Naqshbandi Tariqah.

Shari'ah/Shari'ah—the divine Law of Islam, based on the Qur'an and the Sunnah of the Prophet ﷺ.

Shirk—polythism, ascribing divinity or divine attributes to anything other than God.

Shaykh Sharafuddin—the shaykh of Grandshaykh 'Abdullah ad-Daghistani.

Shaytan—Satan.

Sohbet (Arabic, **suhbah**)—a shaykh's talk or discourse ("Association").

Subhanallah—glory be to Allah.

Sultan al-Awliya—lit., "the king of the awliya,' the highest ranking saint.

Sunnah—the practice of the Holy Prophet; that is, what he did, said, recommended or approved of in his Companions. In this text, "Sunnah" is used to refer to the collective body of his actions, sayings or recommendations, while "sunnah" refers to an individual action or recommendation.

Surah—chapter of the Qur'an.

Takbir—the pronouncement of God's greatness, "Allahu akbar, God is Most Great."

Tarawih—the special nighly prayers of Ramadan.

Tariqah/tariqat—literally, way, road or path. An Islamic order or path of discipline and devotion under the guidance of a shaykh (*pir, muli*); Islamic Sufism.

Tawaf—the rite of circumambulatin the K'abah while glorifying Allah, one of the rites of Hajj and 'Umrah.

'Ulama (sing, **'alim**)—scholars, specifically of Islam.

'Umar—see Sayyidina **'Umar**.

Ummah—faith community, nation.

'Umrah—the minor pilgrimage to Mecca, which can be performed at any time of the year.

Uns – familiarity.

Wali (pl., **awliya**)—a Muslim holy man or saint.

Wa min Allah at-taufiq—And success is only from Allah.

Wudu—the prescribed minor ablution preceding prayers and other acts of worship.

Ya Rabb—O Lord.

Zakat/zakah—the obligatgory charity of Islam, one of its five "pillars" or acts of worship.

Zakat al-Fitr—the obligatory charity of 'Eid al-Fitr, the festival marking the completion of Ramadan.

Other titles from

INSTITUTE FOR SPIRITUAL & CULTURAL
ADVANCEMENT

Online ordering available from www.isn1.net

The Path to Spiritual Excellence

By Shaykh Muhammad Nazim Adil al-Haqqani
ISBN 1-930409-18-4, Paperback. 180 pp.

This compact volume provides practical steps to purify the heart
and overcome the destructive characteristics that deprive us of
peace and inner satisfaction. On this amazing journey doubt, fear,
and other negative influences that plague our lives - and which
we often pass on to our children - can be forever put aside. Simply by introducing in our daily lives those positive thought patterns and actions that attract divine support, we can reach spiritual levels that were previously inaccessible.

In the Mystic Footsteps of Saints

By Shaykh Muhammad Nazim Adil al-Haqqani
Volume 1 - ISBN 1-930409-05-2
Volume 2 - ISBN 1-930409-09-5
Volume 3 - ISBN 1-930409-13-3, Paperback. Ave. length 200 pp.

Narrated in a charming, old-world storytelling style, this highly
spiritual series offers several volumes of practical guidance on
how to establish serenity and peace in daily life, heal emotional
and spiritual scars, and discover the role we are each destined to
play in the universal scheme.

Classical Islam and the Naqshbandi Sufi Tradition

By Shaykh Muhammad Hisham Kabbani
ISBN 1-930409-23-0, Hardback. 950 pp.
ISBN 1-930409-10-9, Paperback. 744 pp.

This esteemed work includes an unprecedented historical narrative of the forty saints of the renowned Naqshbandi Golden Chain, dating back to Prophet Muhammad in the early seventh century. With close personal ties to the most recent saints, the author has painstakingly compiled rare accounts of their miracles, disciplines, and how they have lent spiritual support throughout the world for fifteen centuries. Traditional Islam and the Naqshbandi Sufi Tradition is a shining tribute to developing human relations at the highest level, and the power of spirituality to uplift humanity from its lower nature to that of spiritual triumph.

The Naqshbandi Sufi Tradition

Guidebook of Daily Practices and Devotions
By Shaykh Muhammad Hisham Kabbani
ISBN 1-930409-22-2, Paperback. 352 pp.

This book details the spiritual practices which have enabled devout seekers to awaken certainty of belief and to attain stations of nearness to the Divine Presence. The Naqshbandi Devotions are a source of light and energy, an oasis in a worldly desert. Through the manifestations of Divine Blessings bestowed on the practitioners of these magnificent rites, they will be granted the power of magnanimous healing, by which they seek to cure the hearts of mankind darkened by the gloom of spiritual poverty and materialism.

This detailed compilation, in English, Arabic and transliteration, includes the daily personal dhikr as well as the rites performed with every obligatory prayer, rites for holy days and details of the pilgrimage to Makkah and the visit of Prophet Muhammad in Madinah.

Naqshbandi Awrad
of Mawlana Shaykh Muhammad Nazim Adil al-Haqqani
Compiled by Shaykh Muhammad Hisham Kabbani
ISBN 1-930409-06-0, Paperback. 104 pp.

This book presents in detail, in both English, Arabic and transliteration, the daily, weekly and date-specific devotional rites of Naqshbandi practitioners, as prescribed by the world guide of the Naqshbandi-Haqqani Sufi Order, Mawlana Shaykh Muhammad Nazim Adil al-Haqqani.

Pearls and Coral, I & II
By Shaykh Muhammad Hisham Kabbani
ISBN 1-930409-07-9, Paperback. 220 pp.
ISBN 1-930409-08-7, Paperback. 220 pp.

A series of lectures on the unique teachings of the Naqshbandi Order, originating in the Near East and Central Asia, which has been highly influential in determining the course of human history in these regions. Always pushing aspirants on the path of Gnosis to seek higher stations of nearness to the God, the Naqshbandi Masters of Wisdom melded practical methods with deep spiritual wisdom to build an unequalled methodology of ascension to the Divine Presence.

The Sufi Science of Self-Realization
A Guide to the Seventeen Ruinous Traits, the Ten Steps to Discipleship and the Six Realities of the Heart
By Shaykh Muhammad Hisham Kabbani
ISBN 1-930409-29-X, Paperback. 244 pp.

The path from submersion in the negative traits to the unveiling of these six powers is known as migration to Perfected Character. Through a ten-step program, the author--a master of the Naqshbandi Sufi Path--describes the science of eliminating the seventeen ruinous characteristics of the tyrannical ego, to achieve purification of the soul. The sincere seeker who follows these steps, with devotion and discipline, will acheive an unveiling of the six powers which lie dormant within every human heart.

Encyclopedia of Islamic Doctrine
Shaykh Muhammad Hisham Kabbani
ISBN: 1-871031-86-9, Paperback, Vol. 1-7.

The most comprehensive treatise on Islamic belief in the English language. The only work of its kind in English, Shaykh Hisham Kabbani's seven volume Encyclopedia of Islamic Doctrine is a monumental work covering in great detail the subtle points of Islamic belief and practice. Based on the four canonical schools of thought, this is an excellent and vital resource to anyone seriously interested in spirituality. There is no doubt that in retrospect, this will be the most significant work of this age.

The Approach of Armageddon?
An Islamic Perspective
by Shaykh Muhammad Hisham Kabbani
ISBN 1-930409-20-6, Paperback 292 pp.

This unprecedented work is a "must read" for religious scholars and laypersons interested in broadening their understanding of centuries-old religious traditions pertaining to the Last Days. This book chronicles scientific breakthroughs and world events of the Last Days as foretold by Prophet Muhammad. Also included are often concealed ancient predictions of Islam regarding the appearance of the anti-Christ, Armageddon, the leadership of believers by Mahdi ("the Savior"), the second coming of Jesus Christ, and the tribulations preceding the Day of Judgment. We are given final hope of a time on earth filled with peace, reconciliation, and prosperity; an age in which enmity and wars will end, while wealth is overflowing. No person shall be in need and the entire focus of life will be spirituality."

Keys to the Divine Kingdom
By Shaykh Muhammad Hisham Kabbani
ISBN 1-930409-28-1, Paperback. 140 pp.

God said, "We have created everything in pairs." This has to do with reality versus imitation. Our physical form here in this earthly life is only a reflection of our heavenly form. Like plastic fruit and real fruit, one is real, while the other is an imitation. This book looks at the nature of the physical world, the laws governing the universe and from this starting point, jumps into the realm of spiritual knowledge - Sufi teachings which must be "tasted" as opposed to read or spoken. It will serve to open up to the reader the mystical path of saints which takes human beings from the world of forms and senses to the world within the heart, the world of gnosis and spirituality - a world filled with wonders and blessings.

My Little Lore of Light

By Hajjah Amina Adil

ISBN 1-930409-35-4, Paperback, 204 pp.

A children's version of Hajjah Amina Adil's four volume work, *Lore Of Light*, this books relates the stories of God's prophets, from Adam to Muhammad, upon whom be peace, drawn from traditional Ottoman sources. This book is intended to be read aloud to young children and to be read by older children for themselves. The stories are shortened and simplified but not changed. The intention is to introduce young children to their prophets and to encourage thought and discussion in the family about the eternal wisdom these stories embody.

Muhammad: The Messenger of Islam

His Life and Prophecy

By Hajjah Amina Adil

ISBN 1-930409-11-7, Paperback. 608 pp.

Since the 7th century, the sacred biography of Islam's Prophet Muhammad has shaped the perception of the religion and its place in world history. This book skilfully etches the personal portrait of a man of incomparable moral and spiritual stature, as seen through the eyes of Muslims around the world. Compiled from classical Ottoman Turkish sources and translated into English, this comprehensive biography is deeply rooted in the life example of its prophet.

Lightning Source UK Ltd.
Milton Keynes UK
29 March 2011

170047UK00001B/164/P

Partially Sighted Chil

Partially Sighted Children

Gianetta Corley, Donald Robinson and Steve Lockett

NFER-NELSON

Published by The NFER-NELSON Publishing Company Ltd.,
Darville House, 2 Oxford Road East, Windsor,
Berkshire SL4 1DF, England.

First published 1989
© 1989, Gianetta Corley

British Library Cataloguing in Publication Data
  Corley, Gianetta
    Partially sighted children.
    1. Schools. Partially sighted students.
    Teaching
    I. Title   II. Robinson, Donald   III.
    Lockett, Steve
    371.91'1043

    ISBN 0-7005-1198-9

Printed by Billing and Sons, Worcester

ISBN 0 7005 1198 9
Code 8311 02 1

**Please note that the pronoun 'he' is used throughout the book. The
authors do not want to be considered sexist in their choice of the
masculine pronoun, which was selected for consistency of style and
convenience.**

Contents

Horizontal Section of the Eye   vi

Glossary   vii

Guidelines for Teachers of Partially Sighted Children   xi

1. Introduction   1

2. The History of Education for Partially Sighted Children   2

3. Partially Sighted Children in Mainstream Settings –
    Some Integration Issues   13

4. Equipment for Partially Sighted Children   23

5. Mobility Education   30

6. Talking and Listening   46

7. Pictures and Illustrations   51

8. Reading   54

9. Writing and Spelling   60

10. Mathematics   69

11. Sport and Leisure Pursuits   76

12. Future Prospects – Employment, Training and Careers   81

Appendix I   *'Walk and Talk' Assessment*   85
Appendix II   *Identification Checklist*   87
Appendix III *List of Addresses*   88
Appendix IV   *Reading List*   90

References   91

Horizontal Section of the Eye

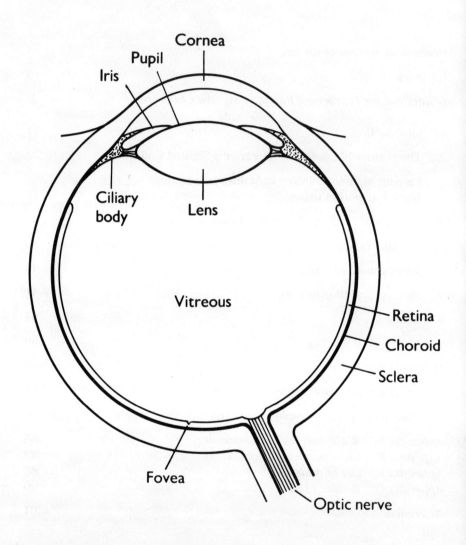

Glossary

Accommodation
> Adjustment of the shape of the lens to change the focus of the eye. This is brought about by the relaxation or contraction of the ciliary muscles.

Albinism
> The absence of pigmentation in the skin, hair and eyes, often associated with lowered visual acuity, nystagmus and photophobia.

Aniridia
> The absence of an iris.

Aphakia
> The absence of the lens.

Astigmatism
> A refractive error caused by abnormal curvature of the cornea and/or lens. Light rays are, therefore, prevented from coming to a single focus on the retina.

Binocular vision
> The ability to focus both eyes on an object at the same time and so see one image of the object. This enables judgement of distance and perception of depth.

Blind
> Blindness is total if there is no perception of light. A person may be registered as blind if visual acuity is less than 3/60. If the field of remaining vision is contracted, then a person with visual acuity of up to 6/60 might also be registered as blind.

Cataract
> Opacity in the lens of the eye producing blurred vision.

CCTV aid
> A closed circuit television aid consists of a television camera and a screen (either a standard TV or a video monitor) mounted on a frame with a light source. The material to be viewed is placed under the camera and the resulting image appears on the screen.

Clue

> A term used in mobility training to signify an object, sound, smell or other sensory aid to confirm a person's position.

Cornea

> The transparent circular part of the front of the eyeball which can be affected by disease or damage.

Cortex

> The central processing area of the brain. Visual impairment can be at this level and is referred to as cortical loss.

Field of vision

> The area in front of the eye in which an object can be seen without moving the eye.

Glaucoma

> High pressure inside the eye causing pain and loss of vision.

Hemianopia

> Defective vision in half of the visual field.

Hypermetropia

> Longsightedness. In its relaxed state the eye cannot focus. Focusing power comes either from strong use of the ciliary muscles of the eye or prescribed lenses.

Landmark

> A term used in mobility training to denote a fixed reference point which is easily identified, such as a pillar box or telephone kiosk.

Low vision personal aids

> Individually prescribed lenses to use in addition to regular glasses or separately for viewing near or distant objects.

Microphthalmos

> An eye which is smaller than normal.

Monocular vision

> Vision with one eye only.

Myopia

> Shortsightedness. This refractive error can usually be corrected with appropriate lenses.

Nystagmus

> Rapid involuntary movements of one or both eyes.

Ophthalmologist
  A medical eye specialist.

Optic atrophy
  Degeneration of the optic nerve leading to the cortex.

Partially sighted
  A general term used to cover a wide spectrum of defective eyesight.
  There are three main categories: 1. acuity between 3/60 and 6/60 with
  full visual field; 2. acuity up to 6/24 with moderate field contraction
  or certain other pathological eye conditions; 3. acuity of 6/18 or above
  but with very contracted visual field.

Photophobia
  High sensitivity to light.

Ptosis
  A dropping of the upper eyelid.

Refractive error
  A defect in the eye which prevents light waves from being brought to
  a single focus exactly on the retina. Such errors can often be corrected
  by lenses.

Registration as partially sighted
  Registration is not compulsory and is completed, if wished and
  appropriate, by an ophthalmologist on completion of Form BD8,
  under revision.

Retinal aplasia
  Maldevelopment of the retina.

Retinitis pigmentosa
  Degeneration and atrophy of the retina.

Retinoblastoma
  A tumour arising from retinal germ cells.

Retinopathy of prematurity
  Damage to the retina associated with oxygen inhalation.

Sighted guide
  A method of safe travel whereby a fully sighted person guides a visually
  impaired person through his environment.

Strabismus
  Squint. Any abnormal alignment of the two eyes.

Subluxated lens
> Partial dislocation of the lens from its position.

Trailing
> A term used in mobility training which means using the back of
> the fingers to trail lightly over a surface for location or for travelling
> parallel to that surface.

Tunnel vision
> Contraction of the visual field to such an extent that only a small area
> of central visual acuity remains.

Vision testing
> Distance vision is tested using a Snellen chart set at six metres from
> the person, or at three metres if the chart is viewed through a mirror.
> Vision is measured from 6/60 top letter, through 6/6, normal vision,
> to 6/3 on the bottom line. If the top line cannot be read, the person
> is asked to count fingers (CF), or detect hand movements (HM). The
> minimum vision recorded is perception of light (PL).
>
> Near vision is recorded from N5 the smallest print to N48, the
> largest print size. These print sizes are to be found in a book of
> reading test types.
>
> Colour vision is usually tested using Isihara plates. The person with
> normal vision can read all the letters or figures but the one with
> defective colour vision cannot. The accurate charting of peripheral
> and central fields requires equipment which is usually found only
> in eye clinics.

Visual acuity
> The ability of each eye separately or together to perceive the shapes of
> objects in the direct line of vision. Testing is as above. For educational
> purposes both near and distant vision needs to be known, as well as
> colour vision. For the partially sighted child it is also important to
> know about the child's visual field.

Guidelines for Teachers of Partially Sighted Children

General points

The following eight points are designed as guidelines for teachers of the partially sighted.

1. Always announce your identity when you enter the classroom so that the partially sighted child is aware of your presence. Also tell him when you are leaving.
2. Always address the visually impaired person directly, head gestures are not sufficient, nor is looking at him direct as these visual clues in conversation cannot always be identified by the visually impaired.
3. Never speak to the child through a third person, e.g. 'does he take sugar'.
4. Never be afraid to use phrases like 'did you see'; words such as 'look for these' are common words used in everyday language. The avoidance of these phrases and words can often lead to a false and stilted conversation.
5. Try to remember that a visually impaired person can appreciate the environment through the eyes of a fully sighted one.
6. When approaching a visually impaired individual to offer help, e.g. to cross the road or to guide him, always ask first if he wants any help. If help is accepted allow the visually impaired person to take your arm so that you are half a pace ahead. If you are unsure of what to do there is a free booklet produced by the RNIB called 'How to Guide a Blind Person'.
7. Always tell the partially sighted child when anything is being moved, this is a common oversight of the fully sighted.
8. Remember to keep doors fully open or firmly closed and also when using steps or stairs indicate whether they go up or down.

These eight guidelines may help communication with a visually impaired child run smoothly and all eight can be adapted for use outside the classroom and/or with the older partially sighted individual. Perhaps the most important consideration is never to assume that the visually impaired person cannot do certain activities, sometimes it pays just to ask them if they can do, or feel confident about doing something.

1 Introduction

This practical volume is intended mainly for class teachers in mainstream schools and nurseries to cover some of the needs of partially sighted children, as distinct from blind children, whose needs have been catered for in other volumes. Some sections of the book will also be of value to staff in day nurseries and play-groups where young partially sighted children are present. It is certainly aimed at the non-specialist in visual impairment, although there are certain reference points, hints and pointers to more detailed information elsewhere.

It should be emphasized that some teachers take a specific training course to become qualified teachers of the visually impaired and their advice is required concerning visually impaired children's needs as set out in DES Circular 1/83 (revised 1989) where a Statement of Special Educational Needs is made, and, of course, in all cases of severe visual impairment, long before this official step is taken. These specialist teachers are a major source of early support to visually impaired children and their families, from the child's earliest years. This book is not intended to replace their advice but rather to supplement it. A class teacher of a partially sighted child having read this book might consider taking the specialist training which can be undertaken either in Birmingham or from the teacher's own locality by means of a Distance Course. The address for further information about this training is shown in Appendix III.

This book begins with general chapters on the history of the education of partially sighted children, integration issues, equipment, mobility, communication and the processing of visual material, followed by chapters on key curriculum areas such as reading, writing, mathematics, sport and careers. There is much cross-referencing between the topics presented in the separate but interrelated chapters and thus the whole volume gives a complete overview.

Partially Sighted Children was written by three authors with considerable experience of the needs of partially sighted children, and brings together a wide range of knowledge and experience about their educational needs for the benefit of mainstream teachers and educators. Donald Robinson is a qualified teacher of the visually impaired and Headmaster of a school for visually impaired children in London. Steve Lockett is a qualified teacher of physical education and has also taken the additional training to become a qualified mobility teacher for visually impaired children. Gianetta Corley is a qualified teacher and Educational Psychologist for the school and for visually impaired children in day nurseries, school nurseries, primary and secondary schools in one quadrant of London.

2   The History of Education for Partially Sighted Children

The following chapter describes how a teaching method and a curriculum specifically tailored to the needs of partially sighted children came to be designed and how this differed from that developed for blind children. It also encompasses the kinds of damaged eyesight which fall under the umbrella term 'partial sight', and an introduction to how the class teacher in a mainstream school might identify and begin to overcome some of the common problems associated with partial sight.

Background information

The incidence of partial sight is low. If you have a partially sighted child in your class, you have quite a rare student, for the ratio is just over two partially sighted children to every 10,000 fully sighted children. This child will need particular teaching, and the skills, knowledge and craft of teaching partially sighted children, gained over the last 80 years by their teachers and educators have been documented here for this purpose, making the task accessible to the mainstream teacher.

Perhaps the main factor which distinguishes the education of the partially sighted from that of the blind is that their education is based on sighted methods. Partially sighted children learn to read print and to write script either by hand or by the use of a typewriter. Given the correct teaching and where necessary the correct equipment, they can do as well as their fully sighted peers. If a partially sighted child is failing in school, you, as the teacher, must check your teaching method and the child's equipment and then seek advice – if this has not already been done – from the peripatetic advisory teacher of the visually impaired and from the psychologist.

An early question many teachers ask is 'How will I know if one of my pupils is partially sighted?' A list of signs or symptoms is given in Appendix II and a class teacher may notice one or more of these which may suggest that the child's eyesight requires medical investigation, but most often information on a partially sighted child's eyesight comes from the child's parents and from medical sources. For the teacher it is the educational implications of impaired vision which are important. The Glossary gives a brief introduction to some of the main medical conditions and terms associated with impaired eyesight, and the References and Reading List suggest further reading.

In many instances impaired eyesight is diagnosed in the first few months of the child's life, however, in some children it is not recognized until later in life, by which time eyesight has deteriorated still further. In a few cases eyesight is not actually damaged until later in life. Partial sight tends to affect both boys and girls equally. In an area in which there was no special school any of the problems in Table 1 might be found in a mainstream classroom.

Effects of visual impairment

As an educator and lay person attempting to understand the implications of impaired vision it is important to consider the following effects of visual problems, for example:

- near vision which affects how the child will react to print;
- distant vision which affects how the child will be able to see or not see the blackboard or bus numbers; and,
- colour vision which affects how the child is able to appreciate pictures and also how the child copes in different intensities of light.

The following points may help to differentiate between the different visual problems.

1. If near vision is good, there is no reason why the child should not manage print perfectly well but he may have to go very near to things to do so. Thus myopic children should be able to learn to read and write without much fuss but they will have trouble with blackboard work and with wall displays. If distant vision is good the child will be able to see the blackboard but will have difficulty in bringing close work into focus and so print may constantly seem fuzzy.

2. It is important to know the difference between field of vision, which can be damaged as in tunnel vision, leaving only the central area for clear focus, and central vision. If central vision is impaired then looking at things will be like looking at a fragment. The child will have difficulty in focusing on what he wants to see and may have to learn to look out of a small corner of the eye, using a small patch of well functioning retina, as in retinal aplasia.

3. The eye can be the wrong shape or size so that light entering through the lens does not fall cleanly or regularly on the fovea — this is the case in myopia, hypermetropia and astigmatism. These refractory errors of the eye can usually be rectified by spectacles and lenses.

4. The musculature of the eye can be faulty and give rise to squint, amblyopia, ptosis or nystagmus. Muscles can be strengthened by patching of the good eye and ptosis can be operated on to raise the lid.

5. The liquid inside the eye can be too great and the pressure raised, as in glaucoma. Intraocular pressure can be painful

and, of course, the clear passage of light through to the fovea is affected.

6.   The lens of the eye may be damaged as in cataract and so may present a fuzzy image or one with blotches where the opacities of the lens occur. Sometimes part of the lens becomes detached or slips and this is referred to as subluxated lens.

7.   There may be damage to the retina, the blood supply to the eye, and in conditions such as retinitis pigmentosa or retinal aplasia there are some non-functional areas of the retina – areas of the visual field through which nothing is seen.

8.   Lack of pigmentary substance throughout the whole body affects the whole skin area and leaves the person concerned highly sensitive to light as in albinism.

9.   Alternatively the messages may simply not be relayed to the central processing areas of the cortex as in optic atrophy or damage by anoxia or tumour or other adventitious means.

This book does not intend to go into medical detail – but some practical details to ask are:

Table 1: Problems and their frequency in a special school for partially sighted children

Problem	No. of cases
Myopia	16
Cataract	14
Albinism	8
Glaucoma (buphthalmos)	5
Aniridia	5
Retinal aplasia	4
Subluxated lens	4
Retinitis pigmentosa	3
Corneal dystrophy	3
Cortical vision loss	3
Microphthalmos	2
Nystagmus alone	2
Aphakia	2
Hemianopia	1
Retrolental fibroplasia (Retinopathy of prematurity (ROP))	1
Optic atrophy	1
Retinoblastoma	1
Obscure undiagnosed deterioration of eyesight	1

Unusually neither tunnel vision nor hypermetropia (longsight which can be associated with marked educational difficulties) were present in this group of children.

- what can the child see best?
- what is blurred and fuzzy?
- what can be seen near to?
- what can be seen far off?
- is there too much light or too little light for this child?
- what is the best size print and the best colour of paper for this child?
- are the pictures too fussy and detailed?

It is worth recalling as an educator that if the input can be clarified as far as possible at the peripheral level then the central areas of the brain can do their work and the differences between fully and partially sighted children lie at the peripheral processing level rather than at the central level.

Provision

Partially sighted people are often referred to as 'in betweens' for they are neither blind nor are they fully sighted, the repercussions of this are explained in Chapters 3 and 4 on Integration and Mobility. At the beginning of this century when services specifically for the partially sighted were first developing, they were called 'part blind'. It is valuable for the educator to remind himself of this because partial sight is often so hidden an impairment that its existence and the educational implications of it are ignored or denied. The opposite view is that what is required by partially sighted pupils is so special that their education can only be carried out in special schools or classes. Whilst this remains true for some, it is not true nor possible for all, and so this book addresses the midway position, acknowledging that special thought, advice and approaches will be needed, but seeing that these can now be within the grasp of the interested and committed mainstream teacher.

In some local education authority (LEA) areas, there is a well developed visual impairment team which works on a peripatetic basis, in other areas the special school acts as the resource base and bank of expertise and specialist equipment. It is valuable to be able to try out equipment with an individual child before it is purchased and the reasons for this will be covered in Chapter 4. Any specialist team would include not only teachers qualified in teaching visually impaired children but also a mobility teacher, for travelling and transport are key concerns for the partially sighted as for the blind.

History

The history of the education of partially sighted pupils has its own identity, separate from that of the blind. It consists of three main phases. The first phase begins in 1908 with the opening of the first known separate special class for myopes and finishes with the Education Act of 1944. The second phase runs from the enactment and implementation of the 1944 Education Act to the 1981 Act and the third phase concentrates on the present day situation, post Warnock Report, and looks at the enactment and implementation of the 1981 Act.

The first phase

Following the Education (Blind and Deaf Children) Act of 1893 there was an onus upon school boards to provide an education for blind children from five to 16 years of age, but there was no direct provision for the partially sighted until the beginning of the 20th century when funding was provided for this purpose.

The first class in the London County Council area opened in 1907 within a school for the blind. This coincided with the case of an eight-year-old girl with impaired vision who did not attend school for a year because her parents would not allow her to attend a school for the blind and the medical officer refused to sanction her attendance at an ordinary elementary school. This dilemma was solved by the opening of a special class for part-blind children in the grounds of a regular elementary school in Camberwell. The main concerns when setting up this class and later ones were not only curriculum content, but also where the finance would come from, because the Education (Blind and Deaf Children) Act of 1893 did not include provision for partially sighted children. These same difficulties prevail today: it is harder to convince the public of the needs of partially sighted children than it is to convince them of the needs of the blind. This issue was resolved in the London County Council area in 1912.

> The Board of Education have now approved generally the Council's proposal to establish special classes for those children (i.e. those suffering from high myopia) and are prepared to pay grant under the Elementary Education (Blind and Deaf Children) Act 1893 in respect of such children.

This was the beginning of the first phase in the history of specialist provision for partially sighted pupils and the funding of it, which made it possible to develop and increase the number and the quality of the classes.

There are two descriptions written by Dr Harman, Ophthalmic Surgeon to the West London Hospital, of those first classes, one written in 1910 and the other in 1919. The first class for myopes was regarded as experimental and one at least, as mentioned earlier, was in a school for the blind. This was not regarded by Dr Harman as at all satisfactory. He found the presence of high myopes in schools for the blind absurd and potentially damaging to their employment prospects. Learning braille was a waste of their time and, as they tended to peer at the braille characters, it was actually damaging also to their vision and posture. He made a strong bid to have the classes for myopes removed from the sphere of blind education altogether and in that he was successful.

Writing briefly in 1910 he described the class for myopes at Boundary Lane School in Camberwell. First, the class was for those children whose sight was too poor for them to be educated in ordinary elementary schools and whose sight was too good for them to be educated in blind schools. These were mostly myopes but also included some with other eye conditions. Obviously those whose eyesight could be corrected by glasses wore them. Selection for the class was on the basis of future prospects, 'If there is a prospect that they will retain useful vision in later life they are entered for the myope class'. Dr Harman described the curriculum of the myope class in this way:

> The curriculum of the myope class is arranged under three heads – oral teaching, handicraft, literary work. So much as is possible of mental training is given orally in the ordinary school with their normally sighted mates . . . but the use of class books is forbidden: they are trained to listen and think of what is taught.

> The rest of the training is undertaken in their own special classrooms. Every sort of educational handwork, anything upon which a lesson of thoughtfulness and order can be hung, any device of an instructional nature the teachers can bring into usefulness, is taught. Modelling, matmaking, beadwork, simple carpentry, every kind of work which requires a minimum of inspection and a maximum of feeling, is used. The literary work comes last. These days, some knowledge of the ordinary means of communication is essential to everyone: to this end we teach reading and writing and such ciphering as script needs, but as little as possible is taught, for we do not wish to cultivate the desire for literature, and this is taught in such a manner as will, we believe, inculcate habits of care which may become second nature to the child.

There were two items of classroom furniture which were needed – first, a specially designed desk by Dr Harman. This had several special features to it – it was larger than the ordinary desk and had a sloping top, so that it could be used flat for handcrafts and sloping for writing. The undersurface was a blackboard so that the children would do their own free arm writing on it. The second piece of furniture mentioned then was the blackboard and this is described in greater detail in the later article but here Dr Harman writes:

> All the reading and writing is done with the use of blackboards . . . The child writes free arm fashion in large characters, each upon his own blackboard . . . We want a library of large printed books or rather scrolls, such as can be hung up in sight of all the children and printed in letters of such a size that a child with say 6/24 vision can read with ease at the distance of two or three metres.

In his later article, in which Dr Harman expands on these same ideas, the number of classes had increased and they were no longer regarded as experimental. 'There, in brief, is the scheme of the myope class, it is essentially personal and lacking in that modern substitute for personal teaching, the book.'

By 1919 he saw provision for the visually impaired as being of four kinds: 1. elementary school for easy treatment as regards eye work; 2. elementary school for oral teaching only; 3. myope class; 4. school for the blind and partially blind. He regarded the second option as a temporary option only, pending the provision of more special classes.

The ethos of these early classes was far sighted in terms of integration. Dr Harman writes:

> The first necessity for the successful establishment and working of such a class or school is that it shall be associated with an ordinary school for normal children. The myope class must be considered and worked as an integral part of this school.

The need for natural lighting in the classroom is stressed. Artificial lighting was unnecessary, because as soon as lighting was needed, all work other than oral, drill or games was stopped. The classroom had a band of blackboard running around the walls at a height which both children and adults could see and use, or there might be oiled baize on rollers. The special desks and the boards were marked with bold white lines and thick chalk was used for writing on them. Twelve pupils to a class was considered a viable number. For the older children, printing blocks were provided so that they could make a permanent copy of their work. With regard to the rest of the curriculum, pictures show the girls knitting by touch and the boys making baskets, again by touch – other important subjects were drill and games. Dr Harman made it clear that for the myopes, learning manual skills was not intended to be vocational – but a general education and training that would,

> fit them for positions of usefulness and responsibility of the indoor and outdoor type, such as small traders, collectors, agents, visitors, etc. This kind of occupation presents no risk to the eyesight.

One-third of the roll of the myope classes then suffered from eye conditions other than myopia but they were pupils for whom this regime was considered suitable. One of the advantages of these special classes was that the pupils in them had regular ophthalmic reviews and oversight which was a great benefit in the time when there was no National Health Service.

Moving on in time to a colleague and fellow practitioner of Dr Harman to Dr James Kerr, Medical Officer to the London County Council, writing in 1916 in the 14th Edition of Newsholme's *School Hygiene* he refers to myopia schools which count with the blind for grant purposes and he goes on to state,

> The pupils are not allowed to look at any book or write on paper. Literary work is entirely done in large broad lined letters on the blackboard, or handprinted in letters about 2″ square with india rubber face types.

Writing a little later in 1926 about school health, Dr Kerr redefined the myope classes or schools but in much more severe terms (Kerr, 1926). He also produced a checklist of class conditions which, he contended, should be instituted to save children with short sight from eye strain.

1. For all lessons that can be learned by listening to the teacher, the children in the myopic class go into the ordinary class.
2. Lessons that need reading and writing are given in the myope class. Instead of using books, pens and paper, each child has a large blackboard on which he writes with chalk, just as the teacher does.
3. In the myope class a speciality is made of handicraft – various forms of carpentry, bent ironwork, model making, printing from blocks, and drawing. The children enjoy the work immensely and the instruction is most profitable.
4. The children learn to dance and drill, and for those lessons most of them are able to join in with the ordinary children.

Dr Kerr then urges parents and teachers to put more emphasis on games and outdoor play than on reading and writing.

Other particular points of interest are that Dr Kerr considered that the attainments of children in a myope class should not be compared with those of children in an ordinary class. There should be no close work. The arm's length was the nearest a child should be to his work. Dr Kerr suggested that children should use a pen and ink, provided the pen had a shield which overlapped the writing point an inch in all directions. Then the art of writing would be learned first with chalk on the blackboard, then kinaesthetically with the pen, and there would be every chance that such writing would be more legible and better formed than if written visually. There should never be guiding lines on blackboard or paper.

In 1934 the Report of the Committee of Enquiry into the Problems Relating to Partially Sighted Children was published (Board of Education, 1934). This was the first report specifically concerning the education and needs of partially sighted children, for the 1921 Education Act amalgamated partially sighted children with blind children. There was, therefore, still no automatic claim on finance, and whereas legislation and funding were being interpreted broadly and generously, the definition of blind was still supposed to encompass partially sighted too. The 1934 Report stated that in that year there were about 3,200 partially sighted children for whom no special teaching or special education was being provided. The Report claimed that in the myope classes the regime provided did prevent sight deterioration. Success was claimed for the classes and advice was set out concerning print size for books.

A personal reminiscence from a former pupil of a special class in the late 1930s is very informative. There were five classrooms but only two seemed to be used for the 20 partially sighted children on roll. The classes were entirely separate from the ordinary school in whose premises it was sited. One of the classrooms seemed to have particularly good gas lighting which did not cast shadows. There was a blackboard which ran round the long main hall but in the classrooms there were roller boards which extended from floor to ceiling made of heavily waxed canvas. These roller boards were written on in chalk. The pupils had sloping desks and to ensure they sat upright and did not peer forward but wrote at arm's length they had to wear a harness around their shoulders and attached to the back of the chair. The younger children then wrote in large writing at arm's length – using printing not cursive writing. Metal clips were provided to attach things to the desks and items such as plimsolls were kept in bags on the backs of the chairs. Children over the age of 11 were allowed more freedom. Some of the children were brought to the school by green ambulances, others had a guide provided to take them to school and home again. By the age of 12, some, however, were independent travellers to school. The pupils from the special classes did not mix with those from the main school – not even at playtime, because they had separate playgrounds. Pupils from the main school *did* come to the classes to read to the pupils there but that seemed to be the only exchange.

The pupil mentioned above had actually learned to read before coming to the special class, so the manner of teaching was not recalled but what was remembered was that reading was not encouraged. The teacher read aloud to the pupils and they were trained and encouraged to memorize. They were also taught to be neat and orderly. Pupils learned to write first of all with chalk on the boards but then when they had practised they moved on to cursive writing and to hand printing. Greyish cartridge paper was used for everyday purposes but there was heavier glazed unlined paper for best use. The older pupils hand printed their own books, letter by letter on the good paper. This was bound between stout cardboard covers and laced. The curriculum included music, singing, country dancing, knitting, basket-work and, of course, writing and printing. No sports, including jumping and swimming, were allowed, but the pupils could do drill to music, running on the spot and they learned and performed country dancing to a high standard. There was a lot of learning by heart. There were some pupils who were not allowed to lift heavy objects – they were called 'care' children and had to wear a red arm band to indicate that they could not lift more than an ordinary chair's weight.

School leaving for the partially sighted seemed to be the same as for the fully sighted for this former pupil left school at 14 and then pursued a long and successful career involving much more study at a later date.

The second phase

Attitudes changed during the war years but not entirely. Many of the classes were evacuated or closed and there was general disruption of the service which had begun to develop so extensively.

A further reminiscence from a partially sighted pupil who attended a grammar school takes the account into the 1940s. This person refers to the 1940s when the sight saving era was ending. However, there were still anomalies – there was the option for a partially sighted pupil to attend a school for both blind and partially sighted pupils, so the two groups had not entirely separated. The school actually attended was an ordinary grammar school.

> There was one 'special' girl a year. I was allocated a magnifying glass on a stand which had to be used for all reading. I was also lent one for use at home when I was revising for public examinations. [During her teenage years she had been forbidden to read at home.] For the first year or so I was required to carry around a great wooden board about two feet by four to which I had to clip large sheets of paper and write with a black waxy crayon in letters half an inch high. As we moved around for each lesson you can imagine what it was like carrying this board and a loaded briefcase. After I'd been there a year or two the policy changed so that we were given oversized exercise books in which we wrote larger than average but not as large as as before, with a special thick pencil. There were two advantages to our status – only one if you were athletic. We were excused exercising and jumping from heights in PE and we were excused homework. We were not allowed extra time for examinations and I even did my O'levels using large handwriting.

Following the 1944 Education Act came in due course the special school regulations, and partial sight was then officially one of the ten forms of handicap for which local authorities had to make provision. But other events were also unfolding which will be mentioned in later chapters. There was the building up of the National Health Service with better provision of treatment and spectacles and other available aids, for those who needed them, and there was also the growth of the school health service with better and earlier testing of vision and screening for impaired sight. There were improvements in equipment with the growth of the computer sciences and improvements and refinements in eye surgery. This meant that treatment and surgery became available for conditions which would previously have led to blindness or part blindness. There was genetic counselling for those who wished it, to reduce the hereditary component of impaired vision. Educationally the provision moved away in many areas from the special class to a smaller number of special schools which were specialist and separate. The early ideal of Dr Harman at the beginning of the century faded away, maybe for practical reasons, such as deciding who was to be in charge of a special class on the site of an ordinary school. However, with the Warnock Report in 1978 the pendulum swung again and for the partially sighted this report embodied ideas which had been in the forefront of Dr Harman's thinking at the beginning of the century – namely the idea of integration. This principle is embodied in the 1981 Education Act which came into force in April 1983.

The third phase

Chapter 3, which covers the integration of partially sighted pupils will give details of how this is being effected in practice. The difference today as compared with 80 years ago is that there is now a considerable resource bank of specialist educational material within the teaching world which was not there before.

Moreover, research carried out in 1973 by Richard Lansdown showed that it was perfectly safe to compare the attainments of partially sighted children with their fully signed peers, despite Dr Kerr's fears, for their attainments are just as good and can stand comparison and scrutiny.

It is worth considering the children who have been in the classes or schools mentioned, i.e. the composition of special classes and schools. In 1908 one-third of the myope classes were suffering from keratitis or various eye conditions other than myopia. All other blind and partially sighted children were in schools for the blind. Now the myopic children are for the most part in mainstream schools whilst the schools for the partially sighted educated many children who would previously have needed to have learned to use braille. With improved print, enlarging, illuminating and clarifying facilities these children can now continue to learn by sighted means. Classes in mainstream schools and in special schools are much smaller than they used to be, quality of ordinarily available books and lighting have improved – though not yet sufficiently in some cases.

3 Partially Sighted Children in Mainstream Settings – Some Integration Issues

The purpose of this chapter is to draw together some of the experiences of partially sighted children in mainstream nurseries and schools and some of the questions, problems and solutions which have arisen. As each child interacts uniquely in each context there can be no ready-made prescription for any one partially sighted child, but general lessons can be drawn from the accumulated experience. The chapter will touch on some of the problems which partially sighted children may encounter, together with some ways around the difficulty. There are some points made, which concern in particular nursery aged children and primary or secondary pupils, but it is worth reading each section, even if you teach only at one particular phase, for the smooth and successful transitions from one educational phase to another is not only a task in its own right but success at the later stages depends crucially on the mastery of certain skills such as reading, writing and mobility at an early age.

In any area, it could be said that a visual impairment team for any partially sighted child in a mainstream setting will comprise a mobility teacher, a qualified teacher of the visually impaired, a resource base with specialist equipment and teaching expertise, a mainstream school with a philosophy of integration, and a psychologist working across mainstream and special schools. This is quite apart from the medical and ophthalmological aspects of impaired eyesight. The team needs to work in harmony and be in regular contact with each other.

As a teacher in a mainstream school, the information you are likely to receive from medical sources will concern any restrictions imposed on the child by virtue of impaired vision, such as the avoidance of lifting, diving or jumping, and then three further pieces of information. One might be N8 or N48. This refers to print size the child can read close to, and you should refer to the Peter Rabbit Print Type Tests (Keeler Instruments) for these different print sizes. The second fraction may read R 6/36 L 6/60. This is a measure of visual acuity, or distance vision, L and R refer to the left and right eye, tested separately. The top 6 refers to the standard distance from the vision chart – 6 metres – whilst the lower figure refers to the line the child can read correctly. The Glossary gives three definitions of partial sight for further clarification.

It is necessary for the teacher to know both the child's near and distance vision. It is also valuable to know whether the child is colour blind or has any restriction of the visual field. It may be the case that an eye condition is named and readers should consult an ophthalmological text for correct medical detail – a brief description is contained in the glossary. If impaired vision is accompanied, as it often is, by reduced hearing, there is a considerable teaching issue which is not covered in this book. All that can be said, is that the combination of slightly reduced vision and hearing and perhaps slight motor incoordination, together presents a very substantial teaching task.

What follows about integration is to be practical rather than philosophical or theoretical and is based on experience of carrying out the task. This chapter must be read in conjunction with those on curriculum matters, and the one on aids and equipment as well as on mobility, for they all belong together.

One important general point is that for each child and each setting, there has first of all to be an appraisal of both the child and the setting. Where has the child reached in acquiring the skills and milestones appropriate and necessary for that particular age group? What are the particular matters to consider, if the child has impaired vision?

The pre-school years

This represents an important time for the partially sighted child and is often not well utilized. There may be in your area a specialist adviser for visually impaired children in which case, his advice should be sought. But in the likely event of such a person being heavily overworked or of there being no such professional at all, this section could be valuable to teachers and day nursery staff who wish to build up their own skills.

It is essential for the young child to gain real experience of everyday objects. Therefore miniature or toy items should not be used until the child knows the size and shape of the real objects. Neither is it necessary to buy many special toys. As with any child, shopping is a useful means of feeling different shapes and smelling different smells. The young child must be encouraged to feel things, to explore and above all to look. Partially sighted children tend to be into everything with their fingers – this can be very irritating and messy, as well as tiring for the adults, but it is vital exploration, and later when the children want to do things for themselves it will be this early interest and exploration which will have laid the foundation for their growing curiosity and confidence.

As with all young children, the child must feel secure in his room or class to explore safely. It would be unrealistic and unhelpful to make a room so free of obstacles that it was more or less empty, and the partially sighted child will learn in the same way as all other children to negotiate things which stand in the way and to get up when he falls over. However, do not continually move objects. The partially sighted child may be able to see close objects quite clearly but distance vision proves more of a problem. The child may need, therefore, a very careful guided tour of a new room showing where everything is – the peg for his coat, the cupboard with the inset puzzles in, the milks, the sink and so on. If the child is at a loose end, he may explore all the puzzles without being able to see well enough to fit them back together again and so there has to be a careful structuring of activities to make them meaningful. Above all, as you will see from Chapter 6, there must be ample opportunity for talking things through with an adult, not necessarily the teacher but not just other children either.

The development of many partially sighted children does lag behind that of fully sighted children in many spheres – for example, if the child cannot see things clearly at a distance, exploration is likely to be more tentative. Motor skills will be slower to develop too, in part because it is harder to be confident and have a go at jumping or riding a trike if you cannot see clearly where you are going. But most importantly the range of words and the meanings of words are harder for the partially sighted child to acquire than for the fully sighted one. This is often unsuspected and ignored, but whilst the child is feeling and exploring, he or she needs considerable verbal interchange with an adult who will listen carefully for all the orientating questions the child will ask to gain an understanding of the situation or to be able to discriminate between similar items. Fine detail, in the course of time, has to be filled in and articulated, otherwise the child's categories remain too undifferentiated and everything which has four legs will just be an animal. Within that category the distinctions still have to be made.

In a nursery class the partially sighted child may go off into a world of his own unless the adult ensures that he is in the centre of activity. Other children of the same age are likely to be more advanced in what they can say and in the level of their play and so a partially sighted child may remain quiet and unnoticed: this is a particular danger if the group is large. Therefore, the setting must be structured and mediated or made meaningful by the adult's commentary. The partially sighted child must be included and encouraged to talk, not just to listen, for only by talking can some of the child's perceptions of what is only partially seen be understood and clarified. The silent unquestioning child is a cause for concern. Nothing the child says in seriousness should be regarded as a joke – particularly by the other children – because it represents the child's inner world, made up of blurred images and incomplete views.

Many nursery classes are a riot of colour and visual stimulation. If you shut your eyes and exclude that, the auditory environment may be very different. There may be a low hum of children's voices, or silence, or the voice of the teacher reading a story. Try shutting your eyes in a room of young children and gain an impression of the enjoyment or displeasure you experience. What can be done about this may vary, but the classroom which looks beautiful may sound boring.

Time is precious for the partially sighted child and there have to be aims and targets to pinpoint what he should learn from pre-school experiences. Much will not be picked up incidentally, it will have to be taught or the learning environment be so structured that the child learns within it. A very comprehensive manual of ideas and equipment, The Oregon Project (1977–78) has been produced by teachers and workers with blind and partially sighted children in the USA. It is easily available and details are at the back of the book. This provides a manual for the parent, teacher or key worker and sets out tasks, skills and activities for children aged from birth to six years. The manual gives a detailed guide of how some of these tasks should be tackled, using touch and language more than normal.

The manual and the ideas expressed in it are very like the Portage Project in style and approach (White and Cameron, 1987). Portage was designed for children with severe learning difficulties, but in this case the tasks and activities are specifically for the visually impaired whose abilities may be entirely normal but whose restricted vision prevents their appearance at a particular time. These ideas are preferable and the need for different modalities to be used is stressed, i.e. listening, looking and feeling.

The infant and junior school years

In the infant years the main educational tasks for the child are learning to read and write and understanding the basic concepts of number. These matters will be mentioned again and covered in part in Chapters 8, 9 and 10. It is possible that the partially sighted child will have spent time in hospital in the pre-school years and have gaps in his education, not just because of the original eye condition but because of the disruption caused by hospital visits and possibly surgery, so all the matters mentioned for the pre-school years still apply.

There has to be a reappraisal of where the child has reached in the various areas of skill acquired by others of the same age, and an appraisal of the classroom and the teaching style. There may need to be some modification made but all the same principles apply. The partially sighted child has to be a talker and a listener and he has to be active in exploring, in handling real objects and in learning to look efficiently.

As the child grows older he must learn to remember where things are kept which are regularly needed. For this reason, tidiness and order are important for the child and the class. If the child is to be able to move about the room freely it is important that things are not left on the floor. For many partially sighted children blackboard work is not viable. This is not important at infant level because blackboards are rarely used, but it does mean that the child will neither see wall displays, nor his own work up on the wall.

Teachers will probably be the first to notice that a child's eyesight is worsening, this may be the result of a known eye condition such as retinitis pigmentosa, which is known to be likely to degenerate, or it may be because of illness, tumour or accident. Alternatively, an eye condition may emerge which was not present before, or a youngster may become markedly more shortsighted in adolescence.

The RNIB have produced a very helpful leaflet called 'Information for People Losing their Sight', which is aimed mainly at adults, but if the teacher does notice that the eyesight of a child seems to be deteriorating, expert ophthalmological advice should be sought, and the situation in school held calmly until the child is ready to contemplate whatever changes, if any, in setting or circumstance are needed. This stage should not be hurried, however, as it may take years for the child and his parents to adapt to the new situation. For a checklist to enable the identification of impairment or deterioration of sight, see Appendix II.

A great deal of use can be made of computers and computer material from an early age and more is said about this in the Chapter 4. The illuminated screen and colour contrasts, if carefully chosen, can be well used but the partially sighted child must be seated in a position where he can see the screen adequately. A great deal of work is done at this level in groups and there is a danger of this child's view being obscured by the others, of the other children being over helpful and doing the work for the partially sighted child, or allowing the child to copy.

At this age the majority of children are likely to be brought to school and fetched at the end of the day by an adult. However, if the class goes swimming or goes to the zoo special consideration and thought should be given first of all to what the partially sighted child might feel when first in a swimming pool, without being able to see anyone more than a few feet away. Constantly calling the child's name will help, and making sure the child knows that he is being watched all the time is important, so that although the child cannot see far he knows he has been seen and so is safe. Going to the zoo or on any outing is perfectly viable, but needs particular preparation, for animals and birds or views at a distance will not be seen and will need verbal explanation. If there is an end-of-term outing to the sea or a Summer picnic in the park, the albino child may have to shade from the painful rays of the sun and may not be able to stay outside for much of the time. The pros and cons of each outing have to be weighed up. What will the child gain from a visit to the theatre? Would a visit to a farm be better for all the children rather than one to the zoo?

As the child moves through junior school, some games and sports such as football, netball or rounders may be inappropriate, for although the partially sighted boy is as well able to kick a football as any other boy, he may well not see the ball being passed to him from someone else (see Chapter 11).

The partially sighted child may well become so confident in a familiar setting that everyone forgets what is not seen, and it can be surprising to find that the child will not know that someone is sitting in the corner of the room unless it is pointed out or the person speaks. By the final year of the junior school, other children will be going out more on their own, perhaps coming to school alone or with friends, or travelling on the bus. The partially sighted child is unlikely to be able to do this and the information given on mobility teaching in Chapters 5 and 11 should be considered. Partially sighted adults have been heard to say that having overcome most hurdles on the way to adulthood, transport and lighting problems still remain.

Towards the end of junior school, there is preparation for secondary school. For many people there is no choice – all children in the area go on to one secondary school. For other parents and children in the area there is a choice and in the normal course of events the choice is made in the top junior year. For the partially sighted child, however, the preparation time which is needed is much longer, for the way has to be well prepared if the choice is to be a good one. There are two sets of circumstances to consider here. One is the child who has been in a special school or class at junior level and having acquired good skills in literacy and numeracy and having gained self-confidence, enters regular school; and then there is the child who has made his way through regular school from the start. The two cases are very different, although there are many similarities in their preparation for secondary schooling.

Preparation for secondary transfer

Whenever there is a change of context, the new context has to be appraised, as does the child who is to enter it. This appraisal consists of an assessment of the building and also of the teachers' willingness and ability to make some changes and modifications, if necessary, to what they already do.

The preparation may begin in the third year of junior school for the child who is in a mainstream school, with a visit to the Head of the secondary school which seems to be the one likely to be selected. This may be the nearest or it may be the one with a particular reputation. The Headteacher's willingness is essential, and unwillingness may be for a variety of reasons quite unconnected with the child but more connected with such matters as staffing or the layout of the building itself. So a frank and hard-bargaining session is realistic — patronage or halfheartedness is not.

Important preparation and sampling of the context for its suitability lies beyond the Headteacher, for it is the teachers with whom the child will have most contact on a day-to-day basis, and it is important to know the views of subject teachers above all. One way to start is to ask the Head of the Special Needs or Learning Support Department to send a questionnaire to each Head of Department. This could be quite short and concise but asking important questions to which answers are vital — for example:

> An application for admission to the school has been made by a child with partial sight. Please state from the point of view of your teaching subject and your department whether you foresee any difficulties in presenting your subject to such a pupil in the way you currently teach? What information would be helpful to you in making a considered reply and are there any aspects of your subject which you feel would present insurmountable problems?

Replies to this questionnaire would need to come back from all Departments if the school is to be committed as a whole to providing the child in question with a sound education. If too many of the replies are negative, another school should be approached if possible. If there is no choice, the next step is to go through all the objections one by one and see how to overcome them. If the replies are all positive, it suggests that people have not given the matter sufficient thought, unless the school has previous experience of the task — so it is necessary at this stage to elicit the doubts and anxiety and hidden objections which will be there if teachers are to make changes with inadequate or limited support or advice. Some typical replies might read like this:

Geography – there may well be problems with the following:
1. atlas work/maps/small symbols;
2. tracing tables and glare from the lights – the fine detail of maps;
3. fieldwork;
4. annotated sketches from slides and filmstrips;
5. blackboard work.

Religious Education
1. We would need expert advice and in-service training;
2. it would be a drain on office time if worksheets have to be typed;
3. the teachers will need time to enable them to prepare worksheets in advance;
4. we all use the blackboard a great deal.

Home Economics/Textiles
Can the child perceive potential hazards? We work mostly in groups so he would have the support of his peers.

French
The audio-visual course we have uses filmstrips and flashcards, and a large part of the course is teacher centred. The blackboard and visual materials are used extensively. It is difficult to see how he would function on a par with his peers in this situation or how we could modify the course.

Physical Education
'I have worked with a partially sighted child before and I feel all will be well. The most difficult part will be class acceptance, particularly when playing team games. There is no reason why swimming should not be his main sport.'

Science
'If he has come through a mainstream primary school, I imagine he will be able to function on a par with his peers.'

Business Studies
'Typewriting will be impossible but all our commerce and office practice worksheets are typed so I think he will manage those.'

(Comments from the teachers of a London Comprehensive School and the Head of the Learning Support Department).

These replies were considered sufficiently positive and realistic to move forward and there followed several visits to the school by the parent and child to look at lighting needs and to become acquainted with the layout of the building as well as to see if there were any potential dangers such as staircases or unexpected steps in badly lit areas. There were constant additions to the list of matters which needed consideration. One of these was what routine should be followed in the case of a fire – either a fire drill or a real emergency. The issues of transport also arose, for although it is quite usual for some parents to accompany their primary aged children to the nearby primary school, the same is not true of secondary aged children who are usually independent travellers by this stage. Providing a taxi service is a short-term solution, for ultimately the partially sighted child or youngster is going to need to learn the skills of independent travel. These problems are discussed in Chapters 5 and 11.

The transition will take a year to prepare, not only for teachers to assimilate their thoughts and to ensure that they have the correct equipment, but also for the child to get used to the idea of a new school and changing lifestyle.

Secondary school

Once at secondary school the partially sighted youngster may find that the amount of work and effort needed is very tiring. Even with all the right aids and with good lighting, the effort required to read the amount of printed material at secondary level is considerable and should not be underestimated.

The issue of transport has been mentioned. Another factor may arise which concerns friendships, for there may be children from the child's previous school who are over solicitous and who cease to benefit the partially sighted child. He, like all other children, will want to make new friends in the new school. One of the aspects of moving to secondary school is that it is another move into a wider environment and the partially sighed child's move into this wider circle could be inadvertently hampered by being restricted to a small set of friends who need him, more than the other way round.

For some partially sighted children transferring to secondary school from a special school, it may be preferable for the pupil to transfer into a year below his own age group. This is not a reflection on the child's ability or competence but it does acknowledge the fatigue element, the early lags in development which almost inevitably accompany vision loss. It also acknowledges the extra effort the youngster has to make to master almost everything.

It is useful to seek feedback from pupils who have transferred in this way. A structured interview with the parents and the pupil can provide a valuable insight. Youngsters interviewed at this stage, when they have made it, so to speak, often comment on the bullying or teasing which they have experienced, and this is one aspect of life in mainstream school which has to be expected and either prepared for or prevented, if possible. The preparation can be in the form of arranging in advance that if the child is bullied he is to go at once to a particular person. Another suggestion is to see that the child goes about with two other children. Lunchtimes and school canteens are quoted as sources of difficulty – they are times when supervision is lower than usual and the partially sighted child is in the position of not being able to read the menu, which can be overcome, but where once familiar people are in unfamiliar and unpredictable places.

Partially sighted pupils often find handwriting as opposed to print very difficult to read and particularly when teachers write comments on their work in varying scripts. They also often find their own writing hard to read back and it is no reflection on the writing but it does impose an additional burden on their time. The expectation must be that everything will be typed for them. Board work at secondary level is almost impossible. Whereas at primary level it is quite acceptable and customary to get out of their chair and go close to the board to read something, this is not so at secondary school and so prepared worksheets and notes are more necessary.

If there is a choice to be made between mainstream and special schools the child must be involved fully in the choice. The child, and not just the parents, must want to go to a mainstream rather than a special school, for it is the child and not the parent who has to attend the school and fight the battles. Some children prefer the larger size of a mainstream school with the wider range of curriculum choice it brings. One boy who transferred into a secondary school at a late stage did so because he was able to study subjects such as auto-engineering and metalwork there, following a long and thorough educational grounding in a special school. He did admit that the secondary school was unexpectedly tough in many respects and so other children may prefer the more personalized atmosphere of a special school or unit in which most of the main obstacles to learning have been removed.

One matter arises constantly in talking with young people and their parents about integration. They have often revealed their great concern that they will be prevented from doing or trying to do what they wish to achieve. There is still an attitude which must, therefore, be very prevalent that they will be making unreasonable requests, or that if they reveal their partial sight they will automatically be debarred from certain places, subjects or activities. This reflects the attitude of society: partially sighted children may still not consider it their right to use facilities if they have to be adapted or modified for their use. So their needs are kept secret and the danger then exists that some needs will not be met or those within the partially sighted person's own immediate circle will feel burdened with the sole responsibility for meeting them. Once again the need for realistic appraisal and assessment has to be stressed, both of the child, the context and the significant others within that context.

Transfer to tertiary education

By the age of 16, young people should be more fully involved in planning their next move than before and try to foresee for themselves where some of the hurdles may lie. With a group of such pupils moving from a special school, where they had mostly been for many years, into various sixth forms, Sixth Form Colleges and Further Education Colleges a short questionnaire was used. This helped to ensure that the equipment they needed was to hand in time and that they prepared for their own visits and interviews to the new establishments. Some did not see the need for this, for their own needs had been so well met until that point in a specially planned and equipped school that they did not realize that the special lighting, equipment and layout were not standard in all schools and colleges. This simply serves to underline the point that if a person's needs are met, they do not appear as needs and the person does not feel unnecessarily disabled.

4 Equipment for Partially Sighted Children

Several points should be clarified at this point to establish the basis on which later comments rest. First, the term partial sight covers a wide range of impairment and thus, each child is unique and individual and must be assessed as such for the equipment needed. This is a specialist task as some of the equipment is very expensive and needs to be tried out before being purchased. Lists of addresses of suppliers and low vision assessment bases can be found in Appendices I and III. Some items of equipment are individually prescribed as personal aids, and so whilst mentioned here in general terms, advice should always be sought from the medical specialists through the child's parents.

Equipment here is grouped into the following categories: low vision aids; lighting; classroom furniture; closed circuit television (CCTV); and typewriting and keyboard equipment. Further details are available from the RNIB and from the Partially Sighted Society. Exact prices and models are quickly out of date so emphasis is placed on the types of equipment now in use and where these items can be obtained.

Personal optical aids

Spectacles are the most obvious personal optical aids. Spectacles with thick lenses for myopia are usually made of plastic for lightness and safety. They are easily scratched and two pairs are needed for younger children. If the eye condition is one which can be corrected by spectacles or lenses, those with a more severe loss may have a supplementary lens mounted on the outside or normal spectacles for reading and writing. This can be mounted on one eye or both. These are cumbersome and many adolescents find them embarrassing to wear but adults use them more readily. Some partially sighted pupils have a monocular mini-telescope for seeing distant objects such as bus numbers or blackboards. For blackboard work these have only limited use, for scanning a large distant area with a narrow range lens is time-consuming and tiring, but a wider angle monocular can be obtained on request.

Many pupils now wear contact lenses, sometimes in combination with glasses and this gives a more natural appearance. Some forms of vision impairment cannot be corrected with lenses and this is often a surprise to visitors to a school for visually impaired children.

Hand-held magnifiers (manufactured by Keeler Low Vision Aids, Windsor) are an important low vision aid and are often individually prescribed. Some are battery-run and illuminated and can contain a measuring device. Other magnification aids are less complex and may be mounted on a small stand of black plastic. These are often nicknamed 'lobster pots' because of their appearance. They have the advantage of being easy to carry about, easy to use and they slide readily along a line of print as the child holds it at the best angle for him. The legs allow light through the base. Some pupils have cut the base out as shown in Figure 1 so that they can write under the lens.

Lighting

Depending on the eye condition, not all partially sighted children benefit from or need print enlarged. Lighting is of central importance – natural lighting and artificial lighting, task lighting and ambient lighting. In a specially designed school for partially sighted children one aspect immediately strikes the visitor. The windows in the classroom all have curtains and blinds. Overhead lighting is recessed into sloping wood panelled ceilings and additionally there are spotlights which can be turned on individually to illuminate work in a particular area. There is a blackboard with a light above it but this is seldom used. Each room is designed so that there are areas of maximum natural light for those who need it, and areas of shade for those who need shade. The overhead lighting is gentle to the eyes. Some desks have large angle-poise lamps attached and there are ample sockets in the room for the electrical equipment. It is, in fact, now possible to buy a security lantern with twin fluorescent lights, which has rechargeable batteries so that the partially sighted pupil is no longer so dependent on finding rooms with sockets to plug

Figure 1: A 'lobster pot' magnification aid

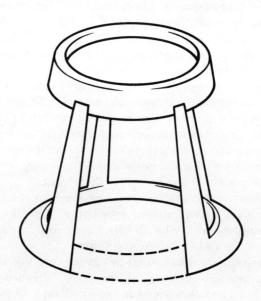

a light into. This should be of particular help to some pupils in mainstream schools and colleges who require additional task lighting.

The issue of individual lighting and the effects of different bulbs is the subject of an article by the PSS National Low Vision Training Officer (Collins, 1987). In this article, he mentions the difficulty of the heat generated by low lights and the heat given off by the bulbs giving rise to 'the burnt ear' effect. He also compares partially sighted adults' reactions to different types of light bulb. One well known disadvantage of fluorescent lighting is the flicker effect – this can be reduced by using two strip lights in parallel.

Lighting needs are very individual and the partially sighted child in any classroom needs to find the position in the room which is best suited to him. This position will vary from room to room depending on the source of the light and the time of day. One major aim is to reduce glare. Not only the paper the child uses but the surface the book rests on should be matt, if possible. Task lamps and overhead lighting can be fitted with anti-glare louvres. There is a reading aid called a typeoscope available from the Partially Sighted Society which consists of thick black matt card with a window cut out, through which the text can be read. The main purpose of this inexpensive and ingenious aid is not only to help with tracking but to reduce reflection from parts of the page not being read. This is helpful when using task lighting close to the reading matter. An antiglare screen can now be purchased for greater ease of viewing a computer or CCTV.

Classroom furniture

For the child, being in the right position for good lighting is the first essential, next comes the desk. In Chapter 2, there was a description of the 'Harman' desk with its sloping top which doubled as a large surface for handicrafts, and as a blackboard for free arm writing. One disadvantage of this desk apparently was that as the child got to writing near the bottom of the board it would tilt over and hit the child's head! It was actually very difficult to maintain a good working position at these desks and there was nowhere to store books, etc. This had been quite deliberate at the outset but became a disadvantage as attitudes changed.

The next desk was box type which provided good accommodation for belongings but did not slope. Finally a new desk was designed which had a hinged flap with two positions – one for reading and one for writing – and a place to stand the lens when required. There was a shelf for books under the desk and when closed the desk top formed a steady table for handwork. In some LEAs and schools now, the children are provided with a well made desk with a top which can be raised to a slope of varying angles – the surface is metal so that magnets can be used to hold books and papers in place, and there is a ledge to prevent things falling off when they are on the slope. Drawers at the side provide storage space and when closed, the desk top provides a wide working surface. The surface of the desk is a matt green to reduce glare and reflection. The slope can be varied according to the need and the task. It is intended to encourage a good viewing posture and many partially sighted children do use this facility. However, older students may need a work-station to accommodate their equipment if it is extensive.

An alternative to the sloping desk is to buy a book stand or typist's copy stand so that books and papers can be raised to a better reading angle and prevent the typical hunched and rounded shoulders of the child peering at printed material flat on the desk. This must certainly be more convenient at secondary level when pupils move from class to class. Even at primary school, partially sighted pupils either outgrow the sloping desk or complain that it makes them different from the other children. The RNIB and the Disabled Living Foundation both sell portable workboards which can be used on any surface and which therefore have advantages over the fixed desk with sloping top. For blackboard work, it is worth considering whether a portable white board would be useful. The advantages are that it can be positioned easily for the child in question, it can be well cleaned and the contrast of black pen on white may be helpful. But these boards do have a shiny surface, and the reflection may outweigh any advantages. It goes without saying that a chipped or dirty blackboard will be impossible for the partially sighted child to read. But also, it is evident when seeing a child using an enlarging device that any extraneous marks or dots on the page are a distraction – and whatever is presented to be read has to be quite free from marks, spots and chips which the child may think are words or punctuation marks.

A good quality photocopier in the school with enlarging facilities is often necessary for pupils who need print enlarged, and even public examination papers can be enlarged, but attention should be paid to any change in scale this may engender.

Print magnification and CCTV

Print magnification and CCTV can be considered individually or for the whole group. For the individual there are a variety of monitors available which have certain features in common. The screen is illuminated and the brightness and contrast can be varied. The print can be black on white, or white on black, and the print size can be enlarged and focused to the individual's need. If the set is a black and white one then coloured pictures and maps in books lose some of their interest and meaning, whereas a more expensive colour set would retain these advantages.

The printed material rests on a moveable trolley (an x-y table) below the monitor and can be moved from left to right or up and down at the required pace so that the print moves across the screen. Figure 2 shows the outline of such a reading aid and further details of systems and types of monitors are in the catalogues listed in Appendix III.

As previously mentioned, when items are enlarged less can be seen at one time, and viewing maps or pictures in small sections can be very different from viewing the whole at once.

Figure 2:A CCTV monitor above an x-y table

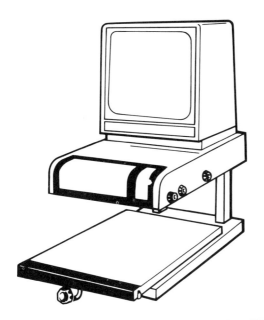

Some partially sighted children do not need print enlarged to this extent, or else they soon outgrow the device. For others the illuminated screen is unwelcome and tiring to the eyes. However, for some severely partially sighted children the Horizon illuminated print enlarger is what enables the child to read print at all and so is the mediator to the child of access to a regular school curriculum. If CCTV is used for a class, the teacher has the central monitor and the pupils can be grouped around individual receiving monitors in the room. Class teaching becomes more relevant for the older pupils studying for examinations and at any age it is important to be aware of the danger of the partially sighted child always being individually taught and so isolated with a monitor and separate from the group.

Typewriting and keyboard equipment

Keyboard skills and touch-typing need to be learned at an early age by a partially sighted child – usually at about nine or ten years of age once reading and writing fluency have developed. By this time, the pupil will have had considerable experience with computers. Materials can be commercial or specially produced by a media resources officer. Some commercial discs such as 'Paintbrush' give excellent colour contrasts and enlarged print if necessary, and provided the child can sit really close to the screen and can be well instructed this is a very popular and attractive learning vehicle.

27

However, the mastery of touch-typing and keyboard skills is more complex, and something needs to be said about different typewriters. The latest electronic typewriters such as the Canon Typestar can produce a variety of print according to the 'daisy wheel' fitted. These have proved to be very adequate for many partially sighted children. A back-up to the print is provided by a window displaying the lettering as it is typed and this can be corrected before each line is printed. For greater clarity nylon typewriter ribbon cartridges should be used. The availability of machines which run from rechargeable batteries means that students who have to move from room to room no longer necessarily have to depend on finding the electric sockets in each one.

For the more severely partially sighted student a more specialist machine may be needed and there are several available to enlarge the printout to a greater extent than the machines mentioned above, for example, Viewscan. This keyboard has a raised printout screen at right angles to the keyboard. The print is orange on black and can be altered in size up to a maximum of letters three inches high. The print scrolls by in front of the keyboard operator at a speed which can be varied. The machine has a memory store. It is compact and portable and can be run off rechargeable batteries. This allows up to two hours for use of the viewing screen. It has its own small printer which can be useful for the teacher, but only of limited use to the partially sighted student, so it would normally need to be attached to a printer. For that reason, in a school or college it might need to be sited at a work station rather than carried about.

Other systems such as Alphavision or Vista monitors are not portable, but are similar in concept, offering additional features such as a larger screen, and so a greater viewing area. When mastering keyboard skills, if material is to be copied, it needs to be raised to a good level by means of a copyholder. Many different ones are available commercially or through the RNIB and also available is a foot operated line finder.

Note taking is best done at school by use of a hand-held portable tape recorder, or by use of the microwriter available from the RNIB or the stockist listed at the end of the book. The microwriter is light (24 oz), portable and runs from rechargeable batteries. It is designed to be used with a printer. The student can learn to operate it after a short course of instruction. It is different from a typewriter in that it is worked with one hand only and the different letters are produced by combined use of the five keys and the sixth control key, so a letter code has to be mastered. It has a small in-built viewing window in which the text, 12 letters at a time, scroll by. This can be brought as close to the eye as need be and errors can be erased and the text amended. Some of the advantages of the microwriter are that it can be used on public transport, at home and at school and a good length of time is available for use between battery recharging.

There are many other pieces of equipment which the interested reader will find in the catalogues listed, ranging from large scale playing cards and dice to needle threaders and a large print telephone dialling disc. Some items are mentioned in the section on Mathematics and in particular in the chapters concerning mobility.

One point to bear in mind is that the partially sighted child does not want to stand out as odd, or as being so dependent on special equipment that he can hardly move from place to place. Some of the equipment mentioned is, of course, highly sophisticated technologically and so will be the envy of other pupils, and may have to be specially stored and insured. Some of the equipment mentioned is expensive and is provided by the National Health Service or the LEA. Some discretionary finance is available also for tertiary level students through the LEA or the RNIB. If a partially sighted student is continuing in full-time tertiary education which is not specifically for the visually impaired there is sometimes a grant available from the RNIB for equipment. The Manpower Services Commission also gives grants for equipment to enable visually impaired persons in work to carry out their work effectively.

Summary

This is an overview of some of the areas to consider under this heading, it is the layman's simplistic notion that all partially sighted people need everything enlarged and this is of course not the case. This is a specialist sphere and this chapter should serve as an introduction to further inquiry and search on behalf of your partially sighted pupil to ensure the best possible equipment is tried and made available.

5 Mobility Education

Introduction

This chapter is concerned with mobility training for the partially sighted child and is written to give the reader greater understanding of how the mainstream teacher can work, together with the specialists and parents, in managing an effective mobility programme. Much of the chapter is based on personal experience, specialist knowledge and training, and a practical approach to teaching mobility.

To clarify what is meant by mobility and who teaches it, bear in mind the following definition, 'mobility means the ability to travel safely and independently in the environment using the necessary skills to do so efficiently'. It is contended that any concerned adult with common sense can teach mobility to the visually impaired child. However, common sense is not always easy to find, especially when dealing with the many eye conditions that come under the umbrella of partial sight. Generally those concerned with mobility range from the specialist to the school teacher, to the parent or guardian.

The specialist

Specialist training is held at three main centres in Birmingham, Leeds and London, and training consists of both theory and practical sessions. The theory training incorporates study of the structure of the eye and eye diseases, audiology and the teaching and learning of mobility. Students will also learn braille, which, as with all the other theory subjects, is tested by written examinations.

Practical training comprises blindfold work, where the student assumes the role of a blind client undergoing a full mobility programme, in order to gain insight into the problems facing the blind client. The student will also undertake the same skills wearing simulation spectacles, which are designed to simulate many eye conditions.

Once qualified, the specialist may go into one of two fields: the social services or education. The specialist assumes the title 'Mobility Officer' or, where the specialist is also a qualified teacher, 'Mobility Teacher' is used.

The teacher

Most teachers of the visually impaired have gained a diploma in education for the visually impaired which includes some mobility work but to obtain work either in a special school for partially sighted children or in a mainstream a school as a support teacher they need not necessarily be specialists in mobility.

The parent or guardian

Although generally not specialists, the parents of the partially sighted child are perhaps the most influential people in the child's attitude to mobility, and the parents may work alongside the specialist or gain information and insight from the many booklets produced by the RNIB. Of course there are parents who are unaware of the information and the specialists available and who may over protect their visually impaired child.

The benefits of independent travel have been well chronicled in relation to the blind, however, such independence is just as crucial to the partially sighted. To be able to go to different places, to visit friends, go to concerts, travel into work or school, means a great deal to any individual, not just the visually impaired. However, the importance, for the visually impaired, of being an independent traveller cannot be too strongly emphasized. Consider the consequences of the non-traveller, that is a visually impaired person who has never ventured out alone, who has always had someone there to help. Such individuals are severely disadvantaged as Astrid Klemz suggests in her book 'Blindness and Partial Sight' (Klemz, 1977). They 'are dependent on others for nearly everything they need . . . This often reclusive existence may then lead to depression and total isolation'.

With such an existence the individual may then live the role of an invalid, becoming unwilling and unmotivated to go out and travel alone. Klemz illustrates this point when she says in her book

> the person who cannot go out alone cannot take part in the social
> activities normal to a person of his/her age, sex and interest. Being
> visited is not the same as going visiting, for the person who is
> always the receiver and never the giver of attention soon assumes the
> role of invalid.

But what does being mobile do for the individual? The answer is that they gain a feeling of self-worth and of independence. The social advantages of being able to travel all have beneficial results for the visually impaired. The confidence that being mobile brings to the visually impaired person seeps into other spheres of life, such as dealing with the general public and managing daily living skills like shopping and using public transport.

There are many factors involved in successful mobility for the partially sighted child. There are those who travel independently who have never needed or who have had little mobility training. This may be due to the degree of visual impairment and the personal attributes of the individual concerned, such as personality, intelligence, motivation and confidence. These factors are an individual mixture, therefore any mobility training is based on the needs of the individual. There are, however, common factors that contribute to independent travel whether at infant level or at secondary school level. These include sensory training, parental support, early experiences and previous learning and orientation skills.

31

Sensory training/orientation

Vision above all other senses is used to take in the environment, therefore, even when the visual senses are impaired the individual will still use his vision more readily than the other senses. The mobility teacher may then encourage as much functional use of vision as is possible, as well as training the other senses. There are those who may need to be shown how to use their vision. The earlier a child can be encouraged to use his own vision the better, so that the skill can be established from an early age.

Orientation can be described as the use of the senses to establish one's relative position in the environment. The skills of orientation and sensory training may well be taught at the same time. In the school situation this may be done on a one-to-one basis. One approach is to start at a fixed reference point in a vacant room in school. Here the child can play 'detectives' finding clues which are in the room. The child is encouraged to move independently in a controlled environment by exploration using his visual, tactile and auditory senses.

Another approach for the younger child is to start a simple route in the form of an errand, e.g. taking the class register to the school secretary. This route may contain a few simple clues for the child to remember. Also the encouragement of using vision and direction-taking can be done in a group situation. This can be done in a fun way as part of a PE lesson. Colour contrasting mats may be used as reference points and should be placed at either end of a clear space such as a gymnasium. On instruction from the teacher the children travel to each reference point. In such a game the child is being encouraged to locate a position visually.

Many partially sighted children are affected adversely by varying lighting conditions: too much or too little lighting in some cases rendering the child effectively blind. The vision of the child is no longer the dominant sense to be used and therefore audible, tactile skills become more important. Encouraging the child to use a combination of all the senses when undertaking different tasks with success and fun, may well be the approach to take.

Parental support

Partially sighted children have varying degrees of family support, previous learning and past experience. These range from those who have little support from the family or who are over-protected by the family to those who have a great deal of family support, who always travel with the family. Certainly the over-protected child who has little or no experience of moving or going out often builds up fears of the outside world which are based on the anxieties of the family. This can then lead to lack of confidence in dealing with the outside world. The family environment can deprive the partially sighted child of good learning experiences by over-protecting the child and never allowing him to escape from a prison of misplaced concern.

With positive family support, factors such as confidence and motivation can be built up from an early age so that anxieties and fears can be eliminated. A successful mobility programme is a team effort of both teachers and parents. This means active support from the parents to carry over and reinforce the learning of concepts after school and during school holidays.

Of course, it is not always possible for parents to spend so much time with their visually impaired infant especially the working single parent who is often stretched for time trying to provide for the family. One example of economical use of time is to use audible toys so that the child may walk towards the sound and be rewarded with the feel of an interesting and/or colourful shape. Unlike the fully sighted infant who can see an interesting object to go towards and play with, the visually impaired child does not have this immediate information and so physical encouragement from the parents or any member of the family is very important so that walking and moving becomes a pleasurable experience. A free environment at home is very important, and keeping furniture in the same place and allowing plenty of space for the child to move without too many obstacles all help to make walking and moving a pleasurable experience. The parents may also allow the child to experience bumping into objects as long as there is no danger of the child being injured or hurt. Supportive parents when the child is at school can take on all the aspects of mobility training.

Body awareness

The parents can encourage the child to identify different body parts, first on the child and then on a doll. The 'Simon Says' game is equally as effective at home as it is at school and is a game that parents and child can play together. Also, every opportunity can be given to encourage the child to move in different ways – one approach is to make an obstacle course of furniture to climb over and under. Outside the home the parent can give the child the opportunity to experience rolling down grassy slopes, or to splash in puddles, or to swing on the swings, or to slide down the slides in the play area of the local park. If the child has access to a garden the parents may attach a rubber tyre to a tree branch. Encouraging the child to climb on to a small wall can also be beneficial to balance if the child walks along the wall and then jumps off with the parent's assistance. The parents can also, by covering an old mattress with polythene, simulate 'soft play'. The 'follow my leader' games of moving in different ways can be used with the child copying the movement of the parents, e.g. stretching long or high, or rolling up small.

Sensory training, orientation and understanding of the environment

From an early age the child may need help to grasp the meaning of his surroundings and orientate himself by the use of his senses. Parental support is also extremely important in such skills. It is argued that whatever functional vision there is present, should be encouraged to be used by the child at an early stage, so that this skill is established in the child's behaviour. But how can the parents encourage the child to use his vision? Using colour contrast may help the child in this field. This can be present in the toys the child plays with, such as brightly coloured shapes in jigsaws or footballs. Also a colour contrast environment within the home may help the child in orientation and many daily living skills. This is relevant especially in the kitchen where there are so many potential dangers. This colour contrast may take the form of red plates on a white table, for example, to assist the child in locating the food when feeding, or using coloured beakers and jugs for pouring liquids. Of course, the use of good lighting conditions in the home environment, as the case illustration on page 45 shows is also essential to encourage the child to use the visual sense in orientation and understanding of the environment. The parents can reinforce all the approaches used at school by using them at home.

The remaining senses such as hearing, touch, smell and taste can be encouraged by the parents before and during the school years of the child as the home provides a very wide range of sensory experiences. The child may be asked to identify objects not only by their visual appearance but also by the sound the object makes or the feel of the object, its smell and so on. This full investigation by the child can enable the child to build up a picture of everyday objects and their environment and begin to understand it.

This early experience and learning can only be beneficial to the child's future mobility. In fact, for children to have a wide variety of experiences outside the home is a great boost to their confidence in their own ability to understand and master the environment. In the outside environment many of the mobility skills can be reinforced by the parents. For example, when walking to the local shops the child may hold the parent's arm just above the wrist and follow the parent at half a pace behind. This way the child holds on to the parent. However, some children may need to be held by the hand to stop them running off into potential danger. In this way the parent and child walk together on a meaningful route. This situation can also assist in helping the child to understand the environment. Explanations of which landmarks are used for telephone boxes or post boxes, for example, is relevant as is encouraging the child to post letters or to use the telephone. In this way physical features begin to have meaning and assist in the building up of a picture of the environment. Once at the parade of shops the child may be encouraged to identify each shop by its visual clues, its smell – as in the local chemist, greengrocers, or bread shop – and also the understanding of what each shop sells.

The child can also be encouraged to understand the design of his environment. Basic concepts of having a pavement for people to walk on and roads for cars to travel on and that there is pavement on either side of the road can be built up and reinforced by the parents on such a route.

A valuable approach is for parent and child to experience public transport together. With regular travel on all forms of public transport, confidence and early experience in this skill will be gained, thus breaking down the fears that can grow later concerning travel on public transport.

As the child gets older the nature of the parental support may become more specific. The parents may be actively working with and under the direction of the specialist, working every day with the child so that skills may be reinforced. This is certainly relevant to the specialist who cannot see a particular child every day due to a heavy case load. Further support that could be given by the parent is when the child may need to learn a route or a specific skill, such as road crossing. This is particularly true of the adolescent child who may have work experience, a college placing or a mainstream school to attend. The route may take on all aspects of independent travel or may be a simple one.

Assessment of vision

There are considerations the specialist may have to take before embarking on a mobility programme with a partially sighted child. Perhaps the first consideration is assessment of functional vision. Although the specialist will have records on the child's eye condition and visual acuity it is often wise to have an assessment procedure specific to the needs of mobility, for example, the mobility teacher may have to consider if the child can see better on a cloudy day, what effect does the position of the sun have on his vision, how does the child react to car headlights at night and what experiences does the child have when having to accommodate from light to dark or vice versa, and how much functional vision the child has at night. In addition to this list the mobility teacher may also have to consider if the child recognizes movement or colour, if he has a restricted field of vision that is peripheral vision only, or tunnel vision or if he is restricted to certain areas of vision. Also it may be a requirement to determine the distance vision of the child, and whether he can determine depth. The partially sighted child may have a method of scanning, maybe eye and head scanning, and the mobility teacher may have to determine by observation if the child has an organized pattern of scanning.

There is an assessment produced by the National Mobility Centre which deals with low vision mobility and can be referred to as 'Walk and Talk' assessment (Appendix I). The child and the teacher walk together and the teacher asks the child some questions in order to assess what details the child can see inside and outside, what is seen as static and what is seen as mobile, what colours and detail are seen, and to assess distance and night vision. It is also important for the assessment of functional vision to be on-going – especially when dealing with a child who has a degenerative condition. Regular assessments of functional vision are required as the programme progresses.

Planning the programme

The next consideration for the specialist is to know at what point to start a programme of training. This will depend on the personal attributes, past experiences and learning of the child. The chronological age of the child is also an important consideration, since it is unfair amd unrealistic to expect the partially sighted five-year-old to perform skills that would not be considered for his fully sighted peers, just because he is visually impaired.

There are also many accompanying handicaps with partial sight. Experience has shown children who have partial sight may also suffer epilepsy or diabetes, partial hearing, hydrocephalus and cerebral palsy. With such children the techniques that are standard mobility techniques may need to be adapted to fit the individual child's needs. Certainly with the diabetic child vision may fluctuate from being good functional vision to being almost blind.

The mobility officer, therefore, bases a programme on the individual needs and skills of the child. However, for the specialist based in a school there is a need to organize a mobility programme efficiently so that general principles and an individual approach can be offered to the children.

The organization may also take into account working with other professionals, parents and family, and the social services. It is general practice for the child to be removed from lessons for between 30 minutes and one hour on a one-to-one basis with the specialist. The ideal situation is for the child to receive a lesson every day of the school week so that a constant reinforcement of the skills is possible. However, this is not always possible within the school timetable.

The specialist may need to be selective and first consider those with the greatest need or those who are likely to succeed quickly. Whichever way the specialist organizes a school programme it is true to say that he will enjoy a unique relationship with most of the students which is based on trust and mutual respect.

One approach the specialist may take is to organize mobility into two sections. That is mobility for the younger child and mobility for the older child, as it is common for the specialist to teach children from the nursery to the secondary age range. This approach is not written as the definitive way to teach mobility but rather as a flexible framework (see Figures 3 and 4). Some of these areas overlap and have been mentioned earlier as general factors for successful mobility, therefore, consideration will now be given to the other areas of skill.

Mobility training for the younger child

Broad base of skills

The diagram represents a broad base of work that may be covered to establish a foundation for future mobility skills. At this stage we are dealing with broad skills for the younger child to learn. However, it must be stated that a mobility teacher may be presented with an older child who lacks some of the skills and areas in this section, therefore these skills are relevant to the older child as well as the infant.

Figure 3:Broad base of skills

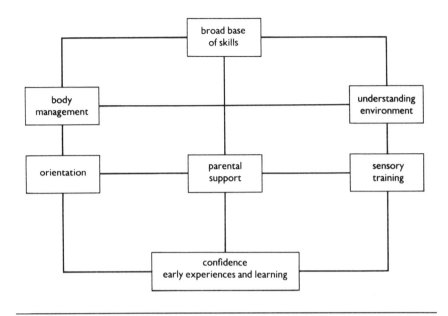

Figure 4:Individually based skills

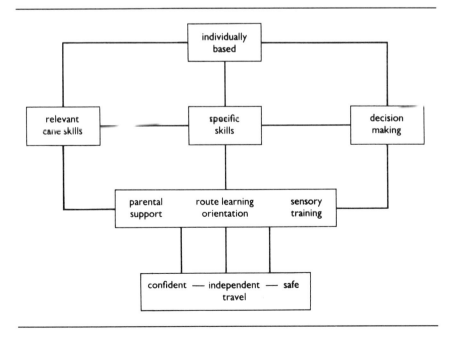

The approach is flexible and the skills at this stage may be taught on a one-to-one basis with parent and child, mobility teacher and child, or in group activities with the teacher and a group of children.

Body management

Body management means understanding your body and how it moves. The development of body awareness is extremely important to the visually impaired child. It is true to say that a child must know about and feel confident about his own body and how it works before he can learn about the world outside. This is true of fully sighted children and partially sighted children, however the child with impaired vision may need help in fully understanding how the body moves. What we are trying to establish is confidence in moving, whether it is running, jumping, rolling or just walking and not cautiously shuffling, unsure of making the next step. Also to encourage coordination of movement with good balance which are important when dealing with the more specific skills of later training.

At this stage experience in and knowledge of all the elements of body awareness must be encouraged. These are: how different body parts move; how to move in different ways; the position of the body at a given time; where objects are in relation to the body; and how to influence the outside world by using the body.

In the school situation one approach is to include such skills of mobility training into the class PE sessions. This not only enables the children to learn from one another but it also enables the development of such skills to be fun and pleasurable. For such group activity a clear space must be provided, an area where the children know there are no obstacles is essential to gain confidence to run and jump freely. A hall or gymnasium are ideal places. Also very useful is a soft play area where the child can play 'rough and tumble' without getting hurt. One school for the blind has two such 'soft play' areas consisting of rooms filled with soft cushions (up on the walls too!).

Moving and identifying parts of the body

Playing games where the child has to stretch high, wide or curl up into a ball are useful ways for the child to understand body position. Games such as 'Simon Says' are useful ways of teaching children to identify different parts of the body and a warm-up session at the beginning of a PE lesson is a good time to use this. Balance games will also help the child to understand body position, by forcing them to think of which particular parts of the body they can balance upon.

The above ways of moving and identifying parts of the body all try to encourage the child to locate objects and to move in accordance with that object, whether through visual or audible means, or both, and then to act upon that object whether it is a football in a game, a pedestrian walking along the street or an obstacle to be avoided. In a group situation there are two excellent games to aid in the evolution of these skills. The first of these games described below is 'End to End', the second merely an adapted version of 'non-stop cricket'. These games can be played either in groups at special or mainstream schools, or can be easily adapted to play at home with family or friends.

'End to End' is played with a ball, which can be audible or brightly coloured or both and about the size of a plastic football. There are two teams at either end of a court or a small hall and each team protects their goal, which can be a wall, or a line, or a bench turned face in. Each team must be kneeling and the way to score is for a member of one team to roll the ball or throw the ball under arm towards the opposing team's goal. Each member of the team has a turn at throwing the ball, the defending team can dive and stop the ball from crossing the line. This game again is great fun but it also encourages the child to follow the ball, be it visually or audibly and to move the body to stop the movement of the ball. The child is aware that the goal is behind them. They also have to move to roll or throw the ball and must be aware of the direction in which to roll it even though in many cases the goal cannot be seen.

Understanding environment

Both teacher and parents can help the child understand the environment and how it works. By identifying objects through the senses the child can build up a mental picture of the world in which it lives. There are items of road furniture that can assist in building up a picture of the way the outside environment works such as lamp-posts, street signs, bus stops, telephone boxes and post boxes. Amongst these items of road furniture there are also items that assist road crossing, such as zebra crossings, pelican crossings, traffic light crossings and island crossings. It is good practice to explain to the child what these items are used for. However, it must be stated that at this stage understanding of such apparatus should be explained, but that crossing roads at such controlled crossings may be left until later on when the child is mature enough to take on the skill of crossing roads. The younger child and teacher may cross the road together to experience the skill.

Giving the child early experiences in the use of public transport is also beneficial. Explanation of the function of bus stops and the different kinds, as well as exploration of a stationary bus is very useful. The mobility teacher may ask the local bus garage to use a bus for this purpose. The mobility officer at one school for the blind hires a bus for the day so that the children there may explore the stationary bus, both inside and outside. Early experience in all forms of public transport should be pleasurable so that many of the potential barriers may be broken down.

Confidence building, early experiences and learning

In using all the components in this section on mobility training it is hoped that foundations for future skills have been established in the young child's behaviour, thereby achieving a state of motivation and confidence in the child to do more mobility training.

Mobility training for the older child

Individually based approach

If the child has had plenty of useful past experiences then the approach may be more specific and advanced, for example learning a route from home to school. It then depends on the child's abilities as to where to begin the training. This is a decision that can be worked out by both the mobility teacher and the child. In some cases the older child in the school situation may request mobility training himself – this may take the form of a route from home to school or learning how to use public transport. There may also be the necessity of learning how to get to a work experience placement or to a college.

The final goal or the degree of independent travel the child eventually achieves is an individual one, and may be linked to intellectual ability, motivation, personality and the degree of visual impairment. In a school for partially sighted children there may be a general goal for the children in the senior class to be able to travel to school from home and to home from school.

Relevant cane skills

A white cane is used as a mobility aid. It is used as a 'bumper' and a 'probe', that is it can bump against obstacles and can give information to the traveller of different surface textures, or potential dangers underfoot and obstacles that cannot be seen, thereby making travel safer to the individual using it. There are three basic kinds of cane: the long cane, the guide cane and the symbol cane. They can all be obtained from the local authority or the RNIB, and each of these canes requires a different technique.

THE LONG CANE

Although generally issued to blind persons, partially sighted children who suffer from night blindness or who have to travel in adverse lighting conditions may find it useful. The length of the cane is individual to each person, depending on their height. When held upright the cane should reach from the floor to the chest. Intensive training precedes the issue of the long cane in Great Britain for safety reasons. The individual uses a sweeping action with the cane when walking, scanning from left to right.

THE GUIDE CANE

This is a sturdy folding cane. It is shorter than the long cane and is more limited in its use. A person can be issued with a guide cane regardless of training. However, it is usual practice for the mobility teacher to show the individual the best way to use it. The position of the cane can run diagonally across the individual's body to protect the user from obstacles, such as goods displayed outside shops or parked cars. It can also be held in the middle of the body maintaining contact with the ground constantly.

THE SYMBOL CANE

This is a light cane which can be folded and is carried as a symbol of visual impairment. Like the guide cane they come in various sizes. There is no set technique for symbol cane use and it needs no specialist training. Many partially sighted children and adults do not like using a came of any sort as it is a sign of being handicapped. The symbol cane and sometimes the guide cane can be used as a compromise when the individual has difficulty crossing roads. The partially sighted person can get out the folding guide or symbol cane either to attract help to cross a busy road or to show the traffic that he intends to cross the road at a controlled road crossing such as a zebra crossing or a pelican crossing. Having crossed the road the user can then fold the cane away and get it out again when it is needed next. This general principle can also be used when travelling by public transport, for example the individual who cannot read bus numbers may use the cane to gain assistance from the general public. However, the white cane is not a magic wand that can stop traffic or lead the individual to his destination safely. It is an aid to be used correctly in relation to the individual's needs. The techniques used can be adapted to fit the individual's abilities and limitations.

Specific skills

ROAD CROSSING

When introducing road crossing the mobility teacher should use a quiet area on a straight road. The child then locates the down kerb. This can be done visually or with the use of the cane. Having established this position the child then waits for a 'lull' in auditory and visual clues. At first the mobility teacher may tell the child when it is safe to cross. Then the child crosses the road locating the 'up kerb' on the other side and stepping up on to the pavement. The partially sighted pedestrian also has to deal with controlled crossing such as pelican crossings, zebra crossings and traffic light crossings. In these cases the mobility teacher should point out to the child that controlled crossings are the only crossings where the partially sighted child crosses the road when the traffic has stopped for them to do so. The child may locate the pelican crossing by visual means either by the colour or general shape of the traffic lights. The child may also locate the crossing by auditory skills.

The individual then locates the kerb at which to cross, having done this he then finds the traffic light post so that he can use the 'button box'. He then relocates himself at the correct place to cross and waits for the bleeping sound. The partially sighted road user may well be able to see and use the visual clues present. For example, he may indeed see the colours change from red to green, or see the wait light as an extra clue on the 'button box'. Of course, not all traffic light crossings are accompanied by the bleeping sound of the pelican crossing and so the visual clues that are present become more important to the partially sighted individual who has useful vision.

ZEBRA CROSSINGS

In the case of zebra crossings the mobility teacher may point out to the partially sighted child that not all traffic will stop automatically for someone to cross the road and that when traffic has stopped the individual must make sure that both sides have stopped.

Having located the zebra crossing the individual places himself so that the post is between him and the nearest traffic floor. If there is no traffic the child crosses. Those who use a cane make sure the cane can be seen as they wait to cross. If there is traffic the individual then waits for one side to stop and then the other and then crosses. The mobility teacher may point out that the child should take his clues from stationary traffic and not traffic which is slowing down.

Public transport

BUS TRAVEL

The partially sighted traveller needs to locate the bus stop before he can travel by bus. Again, this can be done by visual clues, cane skills or auditory clues or a combination of all of these. If the child cannot see detail he may need to ask a member of the public to inform him of the number of the bus, or if there are no other people at the bus stop, the child may need to ask the bus driver (on one-man buses) or the bus conductor, the number and destination of the bus. The mobility teacher may need to point out the different kinds of buses to the child, such as the two-manned back loader buses. The partially sighted child may well be able to distinguish between the two kinds of bus by use of his vision. Again there is a system for getting on the bus which relates to blind techniques. This, as with all the specific skills, can be adapted to meet the needs and abilities of the partially sighted. (It is usual practice for the mobility teacher to let the individual go through the system on a stationary bus before getting on a moving bus).

The child is encouraged to sit where he can be easily seen in the driver's rear view mirror or by the conductor. This may help the driver or the conductor to remember that the child has asked to be put off at a certain stop. Once at the stop the child gets off the bus; this technique may be introduced on a stationary bus.

TRAIN TRAVEL

Again, the partially sighted child needs to locate the train. The same principles apply to train travel as with bus travel. The mobility teacher may advise the visually impaired person to stand at the furthest point away from the edge of the platform to avoid being pushed from behind by the public. The mobility teacher may also point out that people are usually very helpful.

Skill development

For the visually impaired individual to reach this stage there is a basic principle from which the mobility teacher works and is relevant to specific skills like bus travel and route training. As an example, look at a specific skill such as crossing the road at a pelican crossing and the principal system the mobility teacher may apply is the gradual withdrawal of his support and teaching and the building up of the visually impaired person's independence and learning. In the initial stages of the skill of pelican crossing the mobility teacher will be either making contact with the visually impaired person through sighted guide (see Glossary) or by walking with the visually impaired person. The mobility teacher teaches the techniques in easy to learn stages so that success is maintained by the visually impaired person. There is a great deal of repetition and reinforcement on the part of the mobility teacher. As experience and learning progress the mobility teacher may begin to withdraw gradually from certain aspects of the overall task such as locating the walk box – this task is done independently by the visually impaired person, whilst crossing to the other side may still be done together. In the later stages the support is almost totally withdrawn so that the visually impaired person performs the whole task and on the recognition of certain clues makes his decision as to the next appropriate action. In the case of crossing the road at a pelican crossing, the traveller decides to cross the road when the bleeper starts and the traffic has stopped.

When travelling a route, the visually impaired individual has to make many decisions based on landmarks and clues as to what direction to take. There are many examples in the experiences of mobility teachers of visually impaired people making an incorrect decision at a landmark. Here there is a dilemma for the mobility teacher, he has to decide when and if to step in and help the individual. The usual rule is to wait for the individual to realize and decide to retrace his steps, for it is certainly more satisfying for the visually impaired person to correct himself than to be stopped and told that a decision was a poor one. When making decisions the visually impaired individual is involved in problem solving. This is apparent when the person has several alternatives and has to choose one based on past experience.

The partially sighted person who is using blind techniques and long cane work for night travel is an example. The situation may be that the partially sighted individual is walking along the pavement at night using the long cane, he knows there are houses on his inner shoreline and grass verge on the outer shoreline, if he keeps to this position then he is travelling in the correct direction. The problem may be that he then discovers that the grass verge is now in front of him. The next stage may be to decide what action to take. Here the mobility teacher may have previously given the visually impaired person a system by which to solve such a problem or he may wait until the problem arises. There may be different reasons for the grass being in front of the visually impaired individual, he could have veered towards the grass, or the pavement may have curved, so that the grass verge is now in front of him.

What action can be taken to decide on the situation and the next form of action. The procedure may be for the individual to 'sweep' with the cane to locate the path. If the path is located, the individual can then decide whether to follow the road round or to cross, depending on his route direction. The individual chooses what direction to take based on the information given. He then considers the situation and decides on the solution and action.

Confident, independent and safe travel

To be able to assess the visually impaired individual's final achievement is especially relevant to the partially sighted pupil. This is particularly so if the individual's sight fluctuates or is unreliable. The skills that may need to be assessed thoroughly are cane skills, such that the individual can use the cane almost unconsciously whilst attending to clues and landmarks present on a journey. This is often compared to driving a car where the driver unconsciously uses the gears whilst attending to the road ahead. Also the efficient use of the senses may need to be checked, such as vision or hearing, especially when orientating a route or crossing a road. The individual may need to have mastered all the aspects of low vision mobility training so that he can travel under different lighting conditions and changes in the environment.

The individual programme for the partially sighted is based on thorough assessment of the individual's vision and on other techniques necessary where vision cannot be used. It is essential that when a mobility programme for a partially sighted person reaches its end, the individual can perform the different tasks involved by sight or by other means.

In conclusion, the following case study shows how a combination of specialist training, parental support, specific and cane skills, route learning and orientation can lead to independent travel.

Case study

A 16-year-old girl, with cataracts and nystagmus, had a place at a mainstream sixth form college to do a vocational course in secretarial skills. She had attended a school for the partially sighted for most of her school life. She travelled to the school for partially sighted children by school bus and did very little travelling. She had no friends in her home area. The sixth form college was near her home and involved a long walk or a short bus ride.

It was decided that although she was going to a new school she would have the full support of the staff and specialized equipment of her previous school for the partially sighted. This entailed mobility training inside the sixth form college and the route from home to school and from school to home.

She was shy and unremarkable in physical appearance. She was intelligent and had a good sense of humour, a very strong character and was highly motivated. It was decided by the girl and her mobility officer that it would be good to go into the school building during the school holidays to learn to orientate her inside the school. The mobility teacher assessed her functional vision and found that she had some functional vision and could recognize landmarks visually, usually those which had extreme colour contrast. However, obstacles that were not so distinguishable were not recognized. She had poor depth perception as well as poor distance vision, she could see movement but had difficulty recognizing facial expressions. In addition she was affected by poor illumination. However, she had a good field of vision. From this point the girl and the mobility teacher decided that a cane would be needed when she was travelling to and from school. In addition to that, the mobility teacher visited the parents to explain what was going to be done and to ask for their help with explanation of some techniques that were going to be used.

In the school building the first task was to familiarize the girl with the entrance hall of the school. In the initial stages the mobility teacher described the shape of the entrance hall pointing out and emphasizing visual clues as well as tactile clues such as surface changes underfoot! As she began to know the entrance hall the mobility teacher gradually withdrew support so that after several days she knew the hall for herself. From this, the rest of the interior of the school was learnt in the same way, taking in the rooms that were to be used everyday and under the direction of the mobility teacher the mother began to help her with the route to the school which was a long walk. First, she observed the mobility teacher do the whole route with her daughter, commenting on different landmarks and use of cane. Then the route was broken down into numbered sections, each section being approximately five basic points and clues to remember. The method was for the mother initially to give a lot of support to the girl on doing the first section, asking the girl to locate visual, tactile and audible clues as well as some quiet road crossings. It was not long before the first section of the journey was being completed independently. At this stage the mobility teacher came back and did the second section and the same approach was used. This method was used until the girl was walking along the route independently; it was also used for the route going back home from the school.

The basic method in learning a route for the visually impaired is by 'chunking' that is, the breaking down of a route into chunks. In this case there were five. In each of these chunks there may be several things to remember giving a clearly defined task so that the individual can attend better to the task. These different elements in a chunk may be visual clues such as grass verges or white posts, or audible clues such as sounds from a quiet residential area to a busy main road, or tactile clues such as different surface textures felt through the cane, all of which were relevant to the girl's route to school. In this way the route becomes less confusing and with the stringing of these chunks gives meaning to the route.

Having mastered the routes and the orientation tasks the girl could then attend to her studies more readily having already learnt these necessary skills. As a point of interest she progressed to doing the short bus journey to and from the school gaining confidence and self-esteem and has since become more socially skilled with fully sighted people.

Having successfully completed her studies she has obtained a job, travels independently to work and continues to enjoy a full and purposeful life.

6   Talking and Listening

This chapter is closely linked to Chapter 7, and many similar points arise in both. Talking and touching are the vital communication channels for the partially sighted although perhaps less so than for the blind. Partially sighted children do touch and feel things more than their fully sighted peers and they get into things with their fingers to explore them. This is all to the good except that the breakage rate of delicate equipment can be high!

Talking

It is very tempting to keep children quiet and there are of course times when they have to be so, but for children with loss of sensory input through a major channel such as vision, they have to learn about the world and other people's ideas and feelings in other ways than by just being able to look. They also have to learn to be good verbal communicators of their own inner states. The auditory environment for these children must be a rich one to fill in information which is not quickly available by use of the eyes. The optimal learning environment for a partially sighted child must, therefore, be one in which there is a lot of talking and active listening. A very practical point here is that within a mainstream classroom the partially sighted child should ideally sit next to a thoughtful and talkative child who can fill in some of the missing visual detail. A very intelligent but severely partially sighted seven-year-old girl, for example, asked 'Can a monkey fly?'. This was an intensely interesting question for she had recognized the picture of a monkey but had not learned incidentally that a creature needs wings in order to be able to fly. Perhaps she had only seen one or two pictures of monkeys and had not been able to see them on a visit to the zoo, so could not see how they spring from tree to tree, using their tails and arms; or maybe she had seen this activity very approximately and it resembled flying. Her question was a form of orientating and checking and needed an answer from someone who would be in a position to be accurate and maybe elaborate on her understanding of a monkey.

If questions such as that go unanswered or if the situation is such that the child does not feel able to ask the question at all the partially sighted child will continue to have some very strange categories and undifferentiated members of those categories. Each question is important and gives a glimpse of the child's internal lexicon as it builds up and becomes more refined. Obviously, once a child can read, books are a huge source of information but reading is a slow and tiring process and fluency not acquired perhaps until eight or nine years of age so there are many years before then for developing through verbal communication.

For partially sighted children it also seems likely that unlike fully sighted children they will learn words and perhaps even sentence structures through reading and not the other way round, for by the age of five their language skills are not complete. Both structure and vocabulary have to go on growing at an age when fully sighted children are more advanced. The philosophy of teaching reading which is based on prediction and assumes that reading arises solely from a language base which is already complete is not appropriate for these children and it seems from detailed work with them that their vocabularies have to go on growing throughout their primary years in a way which is not so for fully sighted children.

Another child of seven or eight asked 'Is a butterfly as big as a bird?' This question revealed one of the more perplexing issues with which partially sighted children have to grapple – namely the relative size of objects. In tasks in which they have to look at pictures these children will often call a dog a horse and a sheep a bull at the age of seven or eight when fully sighted children can pick up subtle clues from the shape of the dog or the texture of the sheep's coat. This gives the picture a context. Partially sighted children have to be taught to look for those small clues and to talk aloud as they do their looking so that the listener can hear what they are seeing.

A seven-year-old partially sighted child was looking at a picture of an ostrich. She had five seconds in which to look and as she did so she said, 'it has the face of a horse then it goes along, then there's a C at the back and two legs – it's an ostrich.' Looking at a line drawing of a peanut she described it as having a 3 underneath, but did not guess it was a peanut, to do so she needed more information.

Size is always a clue to what the object is – deprived of that information many errors are made on the basis of the objects having a similar shape – a picture of a vase was labelled as an egg cup, a mouse was seen as a rabbit, a butterfly was named a kite.

Other mistaken verbal labels also give clues to the way the child is categorizing objects: clothes reveal whether a sketchy picture of a person is male or female and whilst it is unlikely that a person wearing a skirt is a man, a person wearing trousers is harder to differentiate. Length of hair is another clue, and size – is this a girl or a woman, a boy or a man? Many errors in naming pictures are made in this sphere and the only way of hearing the kind of clues which help the child to identify what he is looking at is to listen and talk. Once having entered into dialogue it is then possible to expand the child's concepts, point out important details in identification and distinguishing between, say, different types of dog, or between dogs and horses. It is the articulation and awareness of small detail which refines the internal lexicon.

All children ask questions and it is suspicious if they do not, particularly if they feel silly doing so or feel foolish, or if the adults do not appreciate the questions as turning and learning points but would prefer the child to be quiet. Mostly partially sighted children have a tendency to be too quiet and so their internal world remains partially differentiated just as their visual images are.

A partially sighted seven-year-old was reading a book about different types of dog, and came across a passage about wolves. She said, 'I've never seen a wolf so I don't know whether to believe in them or not'. This is a philosophical question of some magnitude but at one level it again opens a window on to the perplexing sorting out that has to go on between what is real and what is fantasy. This is true for all children and of course fairy tales enshrine myths and fantasies and feelings which children can experience and own up to in story form before they meet such a situation in real life. They can experience other people's experiences and feel feelings through those other people's tales. But for the child who cannot see properly and for whom the world is blurred and unclear many things can be frightening which for other children are not – the swimming pool, for example, or food which has a strange texture.

On the other hand, not being able to see far can have its good side. Many partially sighted children seem very able to stand on a stage and sing or read or act without being able to see their audience and therefore without too much stage fright.

However, the issue of what to believe is real and what is made up and not true is taxing. One answer is to read and listen only to true stories and factual accounts of events or lives or what people have really done. Much feeling is carried in the voice, and it is important to realize that if partially sighted children and adults both have difficulty in interpreting facial expressions and body language, they are likely to rely on clues from the voice concerning feeling and underlying messages. They learn to listen well – it is not an inborn skill but it is something which is learned – others use it in different settings in life and refer to it as active listening. By the same token the partially sighted child has to learn to have the confidence to speak his own mind and to state his presence through talking. The non-verbal skills of eye contact, body language, being noticed and seeing people from afar are not available to them, so others have to be learned in their place to enable them to be assertive and state their identity.

Listening

At another level partially sighted children derive considerable fun and pleasure from using tape recorders and personal stereos and from listening to taped material and to their own recordings of themselves and their friends. The one danger of over-use of tape-recorded stories is that it is much easier to listen to a tape-recorded story than learn to read for oneself and although enjoyable and educational for the child in mainstream school it could be a factor to watch out for – the partially sighted child who spends too much time listening to tapes at the expense of learning to read fluently.

Because talking and listening are so important for the partially sighted child, it is important that the context is one which encourages them. This means ideally that the adult:child ratio is favourable. This is often not for the reason which seems obvious to those who provide resources – the need for adult time for the partially sighed child is often not to help with the purely physical tasks of moving around, threading needles, learning to magnify print to the best advantage and avoid physical hazards but rather to develop this invisible part of the child – the internal lexicon – made up of images and words. The facility which most differentiates fully sighted and partially sighted children is that of being able to name pictures accurately. It is for this vocabulary development that partially sighted children need additional adult help and explanation at an age when their peers have acquired the words and concepts.

A further point is important here and in the context of talking and listening. If a child's visual horizon is limited in some way, there is a restriction in what they can talk about, so the world becomes very circumscribed and inward looking. However, listening to stories and to the radio can overcome this and can give material from which interesting questions arise – interesting words too – such as bivouac. A child has only to ask what bivouac means for a whole conversation to open up in the group about camping and the outdoors, which sparks off the imagination and extends the range of words the child knows. So, as we said before, for these children books will lead them to words which were not previously in their repertoire and will lead them to think of matters which are not at that time within their reach – but could be. They love to listen to stories being read to them at an age when other children would think it 'babyish'; they also love to have good explanations or descriptions. For example, if they know you have been to the airport they want to know all about it and it is an injustice to the child with poor vision to give them brief and empty replies – they want detail and colour and size and shape in order to fill out their own impressions and experience.

This is one aspect of the issue of integration which is spelt out in more detail here. Integration if it is to be properly undertaken will take into account this need for enhanced verbal communication. It is difficult to achieve in a large group of children and although children talking to each other can enhance their own verbal skills, it is likely that for the partially sighted child this will not be enough. It will lead to the persistence of false ideas and misconceptions and to underachievement at school and then later in life. The language lag has been established to exist at pre-school age through the work of Dr Joan Reynell and a large group of blind and partially sighted children. The lag does not just disappear – it has to be met and made up for by enhanced input. In special schools and units this is achieved by having small groups of children and a high child:teacher ratio – often in addition to speech therapy services. The same end can be achieved for many partially sighted children but the need has to be noticed right from the outset and the adults made conscious of it. Having two adults in the room can be very advantageous, for then the child can hear and be part of conversations rather than just hearing the one adult – but even with one adult it is important that this key aspect of development does not go unnoticed and unattended.

Useful materials

At whatever age the child is, a good starting point for testing breadth and extent of vocabulary could be a home-made test consisting of pictures in the books in your classroom – whatever they are. The partially sighted child will need pictures which are as realistic or clear in outline as possible. See which pictures the fully sighted children can name without difficulty and then see how the partially sighted child does by comparison – that will give you a starting point for vocabulary building.

A further source of materials are those published by LDA Learning Development Aids. Because partially sighted children have to pay particular attention to looking and to vocabulary building, the LDA materials which make use of individually opening flip-flaps or windows are useful. So, too, are the 'Learning to Look' set of pictures and 'Picture Clues'. Early picture books such as the Usborne 'Find It' board books are excellent, for these are just pictures with no words and the child has to find the dog or the puppy or the bird on each page. Picture dominoes aid visual matching and are also a stimulus to talking. Surprisingly with even very young partially sighted children teachers have found that use of the computer has also provoked a lot of conversation, both with the teacher and amongst the children. Tape recorded sounds taken when out on a walk are also a good talking point on return from the park or the adventure playground. Indeed the tape recorder has a variety of uses in easily promoting analysis of everyday sounds and in developing careful listening. It is evident that there has to be stimulation and something to talk about to promote the skilled communication which has been the consideration of this chapter. It is a skill which is vital to the partially sighted child at school and later in life.

7 Pictures and Illustrations

Pictorial material presents particular difficulties for the partially sighted child. In this chapter the problems will be outlined, helpful materials will be suggested, and ways of structuring a task will be put forward, together with some suggestions for useful classroom activities.

The problems with existing materials

If a severely visually impaired child opens a reading book, it is often quite noticeable that the pictures are of not interest at all. It is the text which is attended to. If pictures are inspected, they are sometimes regarded at a strange angle – perhaps tilted or held close to the eye or sideways. This does not matter in the least for the child is gaining the best image possible and will learn from feedback how to do so. The child will often reveal verbally what is seen and it is from comments overheard that the sighted adult will learn whether the child is understanding what is portrayed in the picture.

Some of the difficulties with pictures in children's books are that they are two-dimensional and assume a knowledge of three-dimensionality which comes from experience based on full use of vision. Often the paper is glossy and gives off a reflection. Any kind of magnification aid will distort the wholeness of the page layout, context will be diminished and in many workbooks figure and ground are difficult to separate out. The materials used include pictures of everyday objects, silhouettes, pictures of objects at unusual angles and pictures of different facial expressions. As mentioned in Chapter 6, many LDA materials are very valuable particularly the 'Learning to Look' sets of pictures, best viewed through flip-flaps – opening windows which reveal part of the pictures at a time. To help children search and scan a picture the books without words in the Usborne series, 'Find The Kitten', 'Find The Puppy' and 'Find The Bird' are excellent.

Useful activities in the classroom

It is equally useful to use books already in the class and test the naming capabilities of the fully sighted children and of the partially sighted child amongst them. Careful analysis of their verbal responses will reveal whether your pupil has difficulty with pictures or not. Photographs taken in class of known people or familiar places will also be a good way of seeing directly what the children recognize and can name. It must be remembered that in many families in which there is a family history of partial sight, the family will not have nor use a camera, so the whole process of taking photographs may well be novel. Prints should be made on matt not glossy paper. The children can act feelings and scenes such as 'being proud of having won a prize', or 'puzzled about something', or 'angry that someone broke the toy'

– these little scenes can be discussed, acted, photographed and then inspected and identified.

The partially sighted child is likely to have difficulty in seeing well enough to see facial expressions, so use and interpretation of body language is important – learning to mime and act are immensely valuable, particularly at a young age, for then the children can unselfconsciously learn to express feeling visually and also learn to watch others for visual clues to their mood.

Maps and diagrams

For older children the problems with picture materials may arise in quite different subjects such as in Biology, Physics or in Geography. The layout and print contrast of some secondary text books is unsuitable for a partially sighted student and secondary teachers of such a child would need to look critically at the texts presented to even an academically able child with impaired vision. It is essential that the partially sighted child has access to the same full range of curricular choice as the fully sighted child, even where there is considerable map or diagram work.

For viewing detailed maps with symbols, contour lines and varying scales a colour CCTV monitor will be required to enlarge the material to a suitable level. It is possible to make slides and project them on to a wall, but for the quantity of material required for examination subjects as well as at a younger age a colour CCTV reading aid is needed. Too much of the meaning of a map or a picture is lost by having only black on white or white on black that colour viewing is nearly essential. It is a common misperception that partially sighted children are all colour blind. This is obviously not the case and they do need and appreciate the richness of colour to enliven the material and to derive meaning and differences conveyed through and by colour symbolism. The Large Print London Underground map is a good example of where having colour helps the viewer and traveller understand the map.

As far as understanding diagrams and maps in general there is no real difference in principle about how abstract two-dimensional symbols come to be understood by partially sighted and fully sighted alike. The path to understanding is the same – it is built up through considerable practical work with models viewed from different angles, from constructional toys, models and toys made out of wood themselves, and later by following plan. Understanding how a model can be made from a plan and vice versa is a process which gradually builds up and is enhanced through such different spheres as mobility training and sport. For here routes have to be learned, directions understood, memorized or worked out and internalized. Practical work should never be skimped or rushed with a partially sighted child and it is fair to say that the partially sighted child will need more work for longer than the fully sighted child – that is where the difference lies.

This is likely to be an unwelcome message, for it becomes harder and harder to provide appropriate practical experience when other children are already learning from books. However, it could well be argued that it would benefit the fully sighted also to lay the foundations of science, maths and geography more firmly than time often allows at present in extensive practical understanding of the ideas and principles behind maps and diagrams.

Drawing and painting

There is no reason why partially sighted children should not become very good at drawing and painting just because they need to learn to look, feel and inspect objects in great detail. This may, however, come later in life, as school days are possibly too soon for this to develop. Those with myopia may be excellent at still life drawing particularly if they are allowed to go up and feel and inspect the subject matter to be drawn or painted. There is a danger of not allowing the child to touch sufficiently, for touching does often lead to breakage or mess or damage of some kind, yet it is only by touch and search that their experience of the visual world can be filled out.

Young children can find writing and drawing unrewarding, but this is not true of all partially sighted children and sorting out different shades of colour is a good exercise in learning. Children want to use their sight, and a child who is technically blind revealed this by searching through the crayons and then going over to the window to inspect a colour saying, 'I want to see brown' – this at the age of three! So, it is important not to make assumptions and to realize the areas where there may be difficulties. But they are not always there and they are not always the ones which are expected. Above all, the children want to do things for themselves and be independent – so they need to learn how to do things and operate equipment at an early age.

Structuring the task

The younger partially sighted child has to learn to look methodically, and in order for him to have time to do this it is best if the looking or studying of the picture is unaccompanied by talking. However, it is useful to prepare the way by limiting the range of objects which the picture might represent. The child then has some advance idea of which categories to search. For example, if a partially sighted child is given a selection of eight line drawings and is asked to name them, without any help as to what they might be, the response might be far from the original though quite understandable – thus a man's hat may be seen as a cake on a plate, a dog is likely to be seen as a horse, and a book as a box. However, when the same child is asked to point to a man's hat, a dog or a book, no errors are made because the options have been greatly reduced at the outset. Once again this highlights the need for a high teacher:child ratio if the partially sighted child is to learn from pictorial material rather than be confused by it, or learn just to ignore it.

8   Reading

This chapter describes the early stages of reading, covering children aged from five to nine years old. The chapter is not intended to be in any way a review or comment on general methods nor approaches to reading. It is a description of one way of teaching partially sighted children to read successfully. It is a practical, rather than a theoretical description, but nonetheless there is a sound theoretical basis to what is written. The main message is that partially sighted children learn to read and write on a par with their fully sighted peers if the correct equipment and teaching method are used. Their capacity to do this must neither be underestimated nor lower levels of attainment expected of them than of other children.

The chapter contains a short section on the starting point, then a description of a tried and tested approach, a brief section on theory with some typical reading levels, finally some typical miscues made by partially sighted children and the strategies used by the teacher to bring success. But first, there will be a distinction made between the miscues and style of a reader with specific reading difficulties and a partially sighted reader.

Specific learning difficulties as distinct from impaired eyesight

Both groups need to be individually and very thoroughly taught to read. However, partially sighted children will tend to have difficulty in the early stage of initial word acquisition. This stage will be rather long and laborious and gaining the overall shapes of words, often enlarged to quite a size in the Visualtek, is difficult. Their visual channel is the weaker one. For the child with the commonest type of specific reading difficulty, the visual channel is often the stronger one and they manage the early stages of reading with fair success, building up a small store of sight words. The partially sighted child is taught to use the slower phonological route with very thorough phonic teaching because this is thought to be the strongest, most intact channel of input to the lexicon. However, for the children with specific learning difficulties it is this route which is often problematic so that they have great difficulty in acquiring the alphabetic principle. They are taught the phonic rules for a different reason. It is because it is often at this stage that they get stuck – strategies of prediction and whole word attack are obviously used but they need some phonic principles to be able to see the regularities of the language. It is these regularities which elude them and so the economy of the rules is not easily theirs. They are likely to spell or to read regular and irregular words alike whereas the partially sighted child is likely to read regular words with more ease.

At the later stage where the irregularities of the written language occur the partially sighed child again has trouble, for whereas the child has built up some fluency through use of phonic strategies, he now has to slow down in reading pace and take another look at the words which have foreign origins to see the detail of the spelling. The child with specific learning difficulties will take much longer to reach this stage in all probability but is not likely to have more difficulty with this stage than with the preceding one, for it is mostly the phonological analysis of words which causes the problem rather than the visual appearance.

It is worth mentioning that if a partially sighted child has even a mild hearing loss then he is likely to have major difficulties in learning to read which will be overcome, but only with time, for in this case both the direct visual route and indirect phonological one are problematic from the information processing point of view. For this reason a section is added in Chapter 9 concerning the awareness of word and letter sounds and short tests which can be used with partially sighed children at an early stage to ensure that they are developing good prephonic skills. These are not novel, but consist in the main of tasks such as rhyming, which young children do for fun and spontaneously when they discover that new words can be made in this way and old ones rediscovered.

Where to begin

The starting point, as with all beginner readers, must be an appraisal or assessment of the point the child has reached in the reading process, together with an appraisal of your teaching approach. For the partially sighted child, in addition, there must be a consideration of whether your approach is the appropriate one to tap his strengths, there must also be a consideration of the aids, equipment and any special lighting the child may need. Further details about this are in the chapter on the subject. The child may not need any special books, the scheme used by the school may be appropriate, but whether it is or not should be in your mind as you read on. When you are reading, bear in mind that when print is enlarged with an illuminated enlarging machine the least mark on the page is magnified as well as the print, so the books have to be kept in good order or extraneous marks on the page distract the child. Another point to recall as you consider equipment is that when print is enlarged some long words hardly fit on the screen and that the child has difficulty in looking ahead, in scanning a line and in seeing the punctuation some way ahead.

Next, review the seating within the class and the position of this child in particular. Think not only of the lighting but of the child's position in relation to the teacher and to the blackboard, if you use one. Ideally the partially sighted child should sit beside a bright talkative child, not a quiet child, and not a pupil with special needs of another kind. The reason for this rather severe statement is that verbal descriptions and explanations are vitally important to the child who cannot see things clearly, and although there is a danger of the partially sighted child relying too much on a neighbour, it is essential that either a child or an adult or both is able to be readily at hand to modify the child's perceptions of what is only part seen. Further clarification on the language needs of partially sighted children is included in the chapter on that subject. It has to be stressed that partial sight can and usually does have an impact on the child's language development. It is misleading to think that the partially sighted child's difficulties are solely located in the sphere of vision, for this is not so. The tasks which most differentiate the fully sighted and the partially sighted are not reading and writing but they are tasks which rely on speed, naming tasks, and those which require the child to match shapes or to recognize visual illusions.

Which teaching approach should be used?

The time has now come to consider the teaching approach. The child with impaired vision must be taught principally by a structured phonic method. A look-and-say approach is not appropriate, and a language-based approach which capitalizes on linguistic prediction followed by a visual check is also not advised for the reasons set out in Chapter 6. The successful approach will be a very thorough working through the letter sound correspondences, beginning with learning the names and sounds of the letters, then moving on to letter clusters, encouraging the child to sound out words phonically, discouraging guessing. Learning the letters may need to be with the help of felt or magnetic letters. It is important that the child knows the names and sounds thoroughly for the teacher will depend on this knowledge in later instruction. Some upper or lower case letters look very similar and have to be carefully distinguished – p and q or a and o, for example, are particularly difficult for the partially sighted child to distinguish between.

With this broad phonic principle in mind, many reading schemes will be suitable: the Ginn 360 Reading Scheme and the Magic Circle Readers which accompany the main scheme are known to be so. Whichever reading scheme is used, there must be many regular words in the early stages. Schemes which make use of small cards with individual words on them are likely to be unsuitable for the child with poor vision, the cards will fall on the floor and will not easily be found. They will be difficult to fit into and retrieve from a folder by a child whose hand-eye coordination is not good, and they will not be easy to magnify, if this is necessary. So an ordinary book-based scheme is the starting point. The issue of pictures and illustrations is the subject of a separate chapter. Here it is enough to stress that the content must be of high level because the pictures will often be only partly seen.

What is the theoretical basis for this approach?

The theoretical base for this approach is that the direct visual route to word recognition is impaired, and because this impairment is likely to have resulted in the early years in some restriction in vocabulary range and the detailed understanding of words, it is essential to make full use of the phonological route. This means the child translates the letters or letter cluster into their component sounds and assembles a word from those sounds. This is a slower route to take and there are, of course, those who feel this is an artificial way of learning to read: the skilled, fluent reader does not read like this and English contains many irregular words which cannot easily be broken down in this way. Both these lines of thinking are true of learner readers in general. Phonics are considered to be old-fashioned. However, for the partially sighted child, this is the teaching approach which will be successful.

It is worth reading Chapter 9 on spelling for the comments about phoneme awareness and reading 'Children's Reading Problems' by Bryant and Bradley (1985) for a fuller description of a total approach.

In Chapter 2 you will recall that in the early years of the development of special classes for partially sighted children the view then of Dr James Kerr – one of the initiators – was that the attainments of partially sighted children should not be compared with that of their contemporaries and there was the supposition behind this comment that the comparison would reveal that the children in the special class would have lower attainments. At the time that may have been true because of the regime which was felt necessary in order to save sight. In his research with a large group of partially sighted children completed in 1973, however, Richard Lansdown found that in terms of reading accuracy, comprehension and in spelling, partially sighted children performed on a par with their matched fully sighted peers. They were slightly better at spelling but they had a slower reading speed. This is worth remembering as you look at the reading levels quoted for eleven children taught by the method described and using the Ginn 360 Reading Scheme. Obviously the children are of different ability levels – they range from below to above average. One child who was slow to begin to read had an additional hearing loss as well as vision loss. One child had good

Table 2: Reading levels achieved by 11 partially sighted children tested over a year on the Salford Reading Scale on forms A, B and C

Pupil no.	Chrono-logical age years:months	Form A	Chrono-logical age years:months	Form B	Chrono-logical age years:months	Form C
1	5:9	no score	6:7	below 6	7:0	6:7
2	6:0	6:9	6:8	7:1	7:2	7:11
3	6:2	below 6	6:11	6:6	7:4	6:10
4	6:2	no score	6:11	6:2	7:4	7:2
5	7:1	6:1	7:7	6:9	8:0	8:5
6	7:9	8:3	8:5	9:10	8:11	9:8
7	7:11	no score	8:8	no score	9:1	no score
8	8:2	7:9	8:11	8:10	9:6	9:0
9	8:3	8:2	9:0	8:3	9:6	8:7
10	8:3	no score	9:1	6:2	9:6	6:6
11	8:9	9:3	9:6	9:4	10:0	9:10

hearing but had difficulty in analysing sounds – the phonological awareness tests revealed this and she was slower than expected in making a start with reading. Other prompts were needed to capitalize on her language strengths. Table 2 shows the reading levels which have been achieved over a year by ll partially sighted children.

Typical reading difficulties displayed by the partially sighted child and the strategies used by the teacher

1. If the child has not learned the names and sounds of the letters fully, these should be taught in upper and lower case, if necessary using felt or magnetic letters in order to utilize the sense of touch.

2. If some letters and words are easily confused visually, e.g. look and took, cup and cap, b and d as in bed and deb, then the child should be encouraged to spell each word out letter by letter looking at the fine detail. New words should be spelled out when they are first met so that the child attends to each part of the word and also learns to use this strategy.

3. If the print is fuzzy under the Visualtek CCTV, the child should be encouraged to take time to reach the best picture or print resolution possible. He should also experiment with different contrast polarities – white on black or black on white. Some computers offer a wide range of possibilities.

4. If the light of the Visualtek is too bright or too dull, the child should be encouraged to vary it until the optimum is reached. This may need altering during the session.

5. If the child tires because reading is slow and difficult, it is important for him to rest occasionally. This must not be interpreted as laziness in the case of the partially sighted reader, because it may be quite the opposite.

6. If the child misses a line or loses his place in the text, it is worth considering the use of the typeoscope obtainable from the Partially Sighted Society. The Visualtek has line markers which can be used to isolate one line of text at a time.

7. If the punctuation marks cannot be seen, so that the child misses the meaning and reads with the wrong intonation, the older ones should be taught individually about punctuation marks and their function. They will then learn to look for them and will learn to distinguish real punctuation marks from random marks on the page. It is worth noting that it can be quite alarming for a partially sighted child, particularly one with a degenerative condition to see a blank page, for the child is expecting print and in the absence of it, may be shocked into thinking he is nearly blind.

8. If the child misses the ends off the line of print or off words, or puts the wrong ending on the word – 'pressted' for 'pressed' for example – then he is reading too quickly and should be urged not to do so. It

is useful to teach the older ones grammatical rules as they read. They should also be urged to slow down and read meaningfully.

9. If having to decipher each word, letter by letter, the child cannot predict or scan a line of print, indeed is urged not to do so because of the errors it generates, then instead he should be taught to look at the words within words, and the possibilities for breaking words down into sections, often meaningful ones. He should also be urged to use phonic attack in order to avoid passivity.

10. If, as is inevitably the case, many words are irregular and cannot readily be decoded by phonic rules, the child should be taught systematically the common digraphs and trigraphs of the language and the foreign roots so that the more complex orthography can gradually be mastered.

11. If the child constantly sees only parts of words, he should be encouraged to use semantic clues. For example, if 'Jill' is repeatedly read as 'Jip', he could be prompted to 'think of that girl's name'.

12. If, without central vision, the child has to use peripheral vision and so has to learn to focus on a word other than the one to be read at the time, it is important to allow time for this slow process, to give rest pauses and not to be too worried about head posture – providing, of course, that all the appropriate medical personnel are involved.

13. If the child fails to use the phonic attack skills which would bring success, then he should be praised whenever he is successful, and the child and teacher should read together to reinforce the flow and feeling of independent reading.

14. If long words are magnified to such an extent by the Visualtek that they do not fit on to the screen as a whole, the child should be given ample time to move the book on the x-y trolley backwards and forwards until the whole thing has been seen and read.

15. If some text is supposed to be read with the aid of the accompanying pictures in the reading scheme, but the partially sighted child cannot interpret the pictures, it is worth considering a different scheme.

9 Writing and Spelling

Where to begin

It is important to underline the point made in Chapter 8, that if a partially sighted child is not making progress in literacy skills, the reason is not because the child has poor vision, for we know that if the right approach is used and if the right equipment is available to the child and used, then partially sighted children can attain on a par with their fully sighted peers. They may be slower in doing the tasks, and their rate of acquiring the skills in question may differ from those of their peers, but there should be no question in the teacher's mind about what the child can achieve. It is important to keep this standard in mind.

As with reading, the starting point for the teacher with a partially sighted pupil is to review the materials and approach in use for the other children in the class. At pre-school level, activities such as drawing and colouring may be less enjoyable than for a fully sighted child. The feedback from paper is not necessarily rewarding, and at nursery the partially sighted child may not readily choose paper and pencil tasks and so may, in a free choice environment, avoid pre-writing activities. For this reason drawing, and later, writing, should be specifically taught – actively and intentionally. They will not be picked up unless they are taught. This is important, for the adult has to have targets and goals on behalf of the child. It is not sufficient to wait until the child is ready or interested. Moreover, early drawings may well look very immature and colouring-in very ragged until they have been practised. Use ordinary classroom drawing paper but avoid shiny paper and make sure the colour contrasts are bold. When the child begins to write, use paper which is heavily lined and a bold black pencil. Examples of handwriting are shown at the end of the chapter.

Writing will follow the usual stages of tracing over, then copying. This stage is a long and laborious one and cannot be left to choice or chance. The partially sighted child has to practise every day, both drawing and writing. It is easy to judge a child by the quality of his writing. The partially sighted child is likely to have very untidy and awkward writing, because it is such a difficult task. Table 3 shows the spelling levels of 11 partially sighted children. Their spelling levels were measured twice over the period of 15 months and they are designed to show typical levels reached at different age levels, and typical progress made over a period of time, given daily phonic teaching on an individual basis. Compare the partially sighted pupil in your class with the one nearest in age in the table below, noticing the variation in attainment between pupils of similar age.

It has been noted from the 'Daniels and Diack Graded Spelling Test' that there is very little evidence that the spelling levels of a partially sighted child are any different from those of his fully sighted peers. The words on which

Table 3: Spelling levels reached by 11 partially sighted children tested twice on the Daniels and Diack Graded Spelling Test

Pupil no.	Age years: months	Test score years: months	Words correct	Age years: months	Test score years: months	Words correct
1	5:9	no score	0	7:1	6:4	13
2	6:0	6:5	14	7:2	7:5	22
3	6:2	5:3	2	7:4	7:0	18
4	6:2	no score	0	7:5	7:2	20
5	7:1	5:5	4	8:1	8:7	31
6	7:9	8:7	31	8:11	9:2	33
7	7:11	no score	0	9:5	5:5	4
8	8:2	8:1	31	9:5	9:5	34
9	8:3	7:1	19	9:6	8:2	28
10	8:3	5:2	1	9:6	6:3	12
11	8:9	8:1	27	10:0	9:0	32

errors were made and the types of errors were found to be very similar between fully and partially sighted children. However, in part because of the phonic teaching method used, some partially sighted children persist in over-using phonic rules unmodified by full mastery of orthographic features of the language.

As with reading, the letter names and sounds have to be learned and over-learned. This can be done with the use of felt or magnetic letters, if necessary. There are often confusions between letters which look alike, 'a' and 'o' for example, 'p' and 'q', 'n' and 'h', or 't' and 'l'. Because of the markedly phonic approach to reading and spelling, partially sighted children tend to persist for too long in using phonically regular spelling rules for orthographically irregular words. They over-learn the rules and then find it difficult to go back to very close visual inspection of irregular words to see their irregularities. These observations often come from wide and extensive reading which is difficult for the child with impaired vision to achieve. There are some interesting features to observe in Table 3, one of which is that three children seem to have rested for a while at about the same level. This is the stage at which they have to begin to be able to write words like 'any', 'sure' and 'beautiful' all of which defy phonic rules.

It is worth remembering that both reading and writing are a slow and painstaking task for the child who may not see the whole word all at once or for whom the image may be blurred or imperfect, even with correct lighting and magnification as needed. Written output may be quite small. It will be slowly and reluctantly produced at first. It is tiring for some children to focus for long and the end product may not always be a rewarding sight.

It has already been mentioned that the partially sighted child's handwriting may be uneven and look ungainly and ill-formed. It is also noteworthy that their own and others' handwriting cause enormous difficulty for a very long time. That is why older children often complain that they cannot read the various teachers' writing when they move into mainstream school, whereas they can read print very well by then. The visual impact of handwriting provides a very imperfect and uneven image from which to decipher the sound code. Wherever possible material for the partially sighted child should be typed and most partially sighted children themselves learn to type at a young age for the sake of clarity. At the end of the chapter there are some samples of handwriting of partially sighted pupils aged seven and eight. The comments underneath each sample draws attention to the salient points about each one.

Frith (1985) has suggested that there are three main phases in the mastery of the English reading and writing system, these can then be sub-divided again into two sections each and in the developmental sequence the normal progression would be from one to the next – the first is the logographic stage, the second the alphabetic stage and the third the orthographic stage.

At first, spelling lags behind reading, for it is logically almost impossible to conceive being able to produce the written form of a word if the word is not first instantly recognizable to read. However, at the second stage spelling can lead the way, for it is possible with a small set of known letters to create new regular words which have possibly not been read before. At the orthographic stage reading once again goes ahead of spelling.

Partially sighted children have most difficulty at the logographic and then at the orthographic stages for it is then that most reliance is placed on vision and the visual detail contained first in the whole word formation and then in the meaning components of the words. Markedly phonic teaching will lead to an over-reliance on phonic rules but by the same token it is not possible to read and write solely by reliance on sounds, for in order to be able to use the sounds, the visual form of the print has to be transformed into sounds and vice versa, so partially sighted children do make use of visual information and may indeed make use of the direct visual reading route rather than the slower phonological one despite the teaching they receive. Before moving on from here it is useful to recall that Frith distinguished the three named stages of literacy in this way – the logographic phase is very dependent on the instant visual recognition of a word shape as an entity. At the alphabetic stage the process is based on an analysis of sounds in sequence. The orthographic phase is different from both the others in that it is not a visual whole word based phase and not a phoneme-grapheme based alphabetic phase but rather it is based on syllables, on morphemes and the deeper language units which carry long-standing word roots, and meanings.

Children with specific reading difficulties experience great trouble in mastering the alphabetic phase and because of this and the relative neglect of phonic teaching in recent years Bryant and Bradley (1985) among others, turned attention again to phonological skills in young children at nursery school. They found that teaching and planned training in awareness of sounds carried out with four-year-olds yielded demonstrable dividends later when sounds were needed for reading and writing. Of course, there are many rhymes, jingles and sound games played at that age, but what is a game to the child is of extreme seriousness to the adult. If a child at that age cannot segment sounds and cannot hear the rhymes or produce them it is a warning sign to be acted upon. There are obvious steps to take, such as having the child's hearing tested or instituting speech therapy assessment if it is necessary, but apart from that there are children whose hearing and speech development is judged to be in order and do not have articulatory defects but nonetheless have not grasped the nature of sound segmentation nor the fun of making up words like 'music-pusic'. Some children can hardly stop themselves making up rhymes if they think that is what the adult wants.

This is the sphere of the educator and tuition is important here to reduce the potential backward readers of eight or nine years of age. It will also serve to identify those children with specific learning difficulties who will require individualized tuition early in their school life. All children will benefit from attention to the listening and sound assessment proposed. For the partially sighted child, it is vital that this channel is as well trained as possible ready for the time when formal reading and writing begin. The music of speech sounds has to be audible and reproducible. If the capacity to segment sounds is one which is difficult, the child can be taught to listen and tune in better. For some children when it comes to formal tuition in literacy then tangible letters, whether felt or magnetic ones, are necessary to help make the intangible sounds and feel of the letters more real.

There is a set of ten phonological tasks which could be used as a starting point. They were devised by Stanovich, Cunningham and Cramer (1984) for the six-year-olds they were working with. These together were predictive of reading progress a year later. They have been used with partially sighted children over a wider age range and again, correlate as a set, with reading and writing competence. In other words they can be used diagnostically to pinpoint an area of difficulty for the child and then teach to remediate, but they can also be used predictively to highlight any children who are in need of particular listening tuition if they are to receive very markedly phonic tuition later, or indeed if they are to be reliant on good phonological awareness.

Each test takes only a few minutes to administer and each one can be prepared individually for the child you know, using words from that child's own repertoire. When you have detected an area of difficulty then devise materials so that the child can learn what to do to be successful at that task. In the work quoted the easiest of the ten tasks for the six-year-olds were the three rhyming tasks and the hardest was the one which required removal of the first letter to make a new word. The others were intermediate in difficulty. Take a tape recording of the child as he completes the tasks so that there is a sound record to study later for any areas of difficulty. First of all on each task practice with the child to make sure he knows what is required, because often the child thinks the adult wants a rhyme when this is not what is wanted, so three to five practice tries should ensure that the instructions are understood.

Stanovich, Cunningham and Cramer (1984) found that at the end of their kindergarten or middle infant year, the skilled readers could complete several of these tasks perfectly whilst the less skilled readers were barely getting half of the items correct. This is a starting point for young partially sighted

Task 1:Rhyme supply
The adult says a word and the child provides one which rhymes with it
(e.g. house and mouse). This is done with ten words.

Task 2:Rhyme choice
The child is given one word as the target and then a set of three. Out
of the three, one rhymes with the target (e.g. star: hat, pig, car). This is
done ten times.

Task 3:Initial consonant same
The child is given a target word and told to listen carefully to the first
letter. Then the child is given a set of three and has to select the one
which begins with the same letter as the target (e.g. coat: apple, comb,
book). This is done ten times.

Task 4:Final consonant same
As above but this time the child has to listen to the final letter and is
instructed to do so. The child is also given a picture of the target object
(e.g. man: pen, door, deck). In both tasks 3 and 4 the child is asked to
say the target word aloud.

Task 5:Strip initial consonant
The child is given a word and then asked to delete the first sound
and say the word which is left (e.g. pink, ink). As before there are ten
words in this set.

Task 6:Substitute initial consonant
Here the child is asked to take away the first sound and put another in
its place to make a different word (e.g. bell: fell or sell). Again there are
ten target words for this task.

Task 7:Initial consonant different
The adult reads out four words to the child and the child is asked to
listen for the one where the initial letter is different from the others. The
child has to say all four words and pick out the one which is different at
the beginning (e.g. witch, window, table, well).

Task 8
This is like *Task 7* but the instructions are phrased differently. Here the
child has to say the target word and then three more words. This time he
has to say which word does not have the same initial sound as the target,
i.e. 'not the same' as opposed to 'different', (e.g. king: kite, key, shop).

Task 9
The child is asked to say aloud four words which the adult has just said,
listen closely to the end sounds and select the word with a different final
sound (e.g. dress, cake, pass, moss).

Task 10
The child is given ten pairs of words and asked to see what sound has
been left off the beginning to make the second word of each pair (e.g.
land – and 'l'; pair – air 'p').

children of four upwards – those who cannot do the tasks should embark on a learning programme devised by the teacher to help them learn to listen to discrete sounds. This will help them in many spheres and it could well be linked to music and singing as well as to nursery rhymes and songs or listening to tapes if need be.

When considering the handwriting of partially sighted children it is worth bearing in mind the underlying processes in writing a word from memory. As with reading, where a visual code goes through a phonological translation process, in writing the output reflects phonic rules principally, but the later spelling check for orthographic irregularities is slower to follow.

While the early logographic stage is hard to master, the alphabetic rule stage is the main focus for teaching, and the orthographic stage once again results in some plateauing until extensive reading and dictionary use leads to the mastery of the irregularities of the English spelling system.

The following are examples of the handwriting of seven- and eight-year-old girls and boys with impaired eyesight. All are averagely able pupils. The points listed below should be noted as characteristics of the handwriting of partially sighted children (Figure 5).

1. the difficulty experienced in writing on the line;
2. in one case, clear difficulty with pencil control;
3. evidence of phonic teaching and miscues, 'wen, bak, ofen';
4. a word and spelling which has been partly seen and absorbed, e.g. 'contry' for 'country'.

Figure 5: Some examples of the handwriting of partially sighted children

A bright ten-year-old who has difficulty in seeing clearly what he has written and could not really see the pencil unless shown.

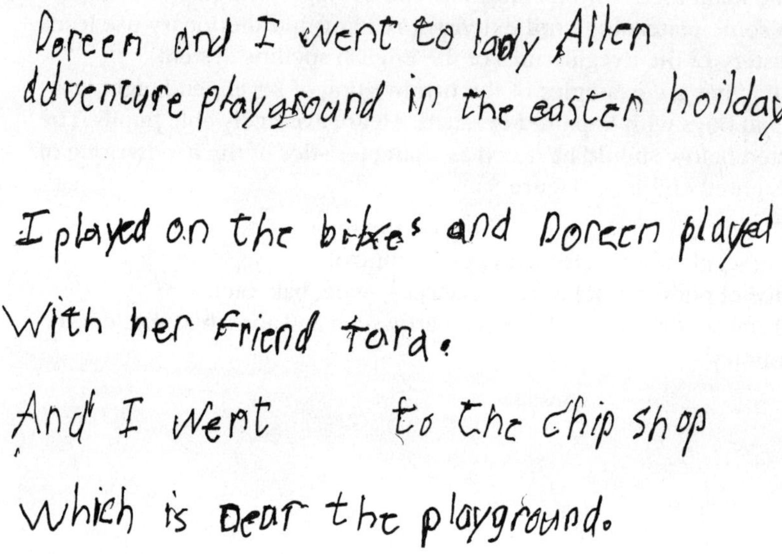

Doreen and I went to lady Allen
ddventure playground in the easter hoildays:

I played on the bikes and Doreen played

With her friend tara.

And I went   to the chip shop

Which is near the playground.

A bright ten-year-old who sees the line well and has clear, well formed writing. Nonetheless there are many written errors – some phonic – attributable in part to the difficulty of checking and scanning quickly to detect misspellings.

I am trying to make a
car with some lego.
It will run of there
baturys it will have foar
wheels.
I am Making it my self

A hard working ten-year-old who has wide ranging learning difficulties and still has problems in writing on the line.

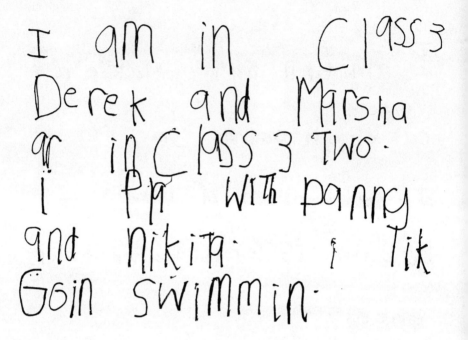

I am in Class 3
Derek and Marsha
ar in Class 3 Two.
i pa with panry
and nikita. i lik
Goin swimmin.

10 Mathematics

This chapter begins by introducing general points concerning the teaching of mathematics to partially sighted pupils and then touches on some specific topics to generate teaching ideas.

It is often stated as an accepted fact that partially sighted children have particular difficulty with mathematics, and yet the nature and origins of this difficulty are less frequently spelled out, and the statement itself may not be based on fact.

The basic principle at any age, but particularly in the early years, is that for the partially sighted child mathematics must always be very practical and investigative for longer than is the case for the fully sighted child.

The roots of mathematical thinking lie in real experience of the three-dimensional world and in language – and it is possibly the restrictions imposed by impaired vision in both these spheres which give rise to greater difficulty than is normal in mastering mathematical ideas – if that is a genuine difficulty. We know that the partially sighted child takes longer to gain concepts which involve eyesight, and that it is therefore a longer task to assemble a filing system or a system of sets or categories. So even at secondary level when this becomes more difficult to achieve, the partially sighted child needs more practical experience for longer than the fully sighted child. There also needs to be considerable teacher–pupil talking through of ideas and concepts – not a communication based on telling but the use of subtle questioning to elicit and elucidate the idea or concept in the teacher's mind. The partially sighted child has to learn to go and look, not just wait to be told, for passivity is the danger to watch for, and thoughtful activity and discovery the goal. If the teacher is clear about which concept the child is striving to understand next and has a clear idea of what the next learning step is, then the provision of the setting and materials for the partially sighted child will be relatively straightforward. It is difficult to think each time how to bring a particular experience within the grasp of a pupil with impaired eyesight with creativity and imagination.

Learning from experience

The major principle is that real experiences of a nursery type must be provided for longer for the young partially sighted child and that skimping this essential basis results in a very shaky foundation for the future. If the basic ideas are well grasped, then when it comes to more abstract work, the major problem lies in presenting it in legible well printed form. The layout of some school workbooks is too cramped and visually confusing for the partially sighted pupil.

There is always a danger of the visually impaired child being mistakenly shielded from some physical stress and practical learning – coming to school by bus instead of walking, for example – but to gain an experience of steep, the best way is to climb a steep hill; to gain an experience of distance, go on a long walk or on a cycle ride; to gain an experience of fatigue, stretch the body physically. The challenge is to provide real experiences of a relevant kind for long enough. Providing the proper safety measures are observed, there is no reason to shield the partially sighted child from these.

Published schemes

For the Junior school teacher the first specific practical point to be made at the outset is that the 'Ginn Mathematics Scheme', which is widely used in regular schools, has been found to be as good as any available for partially sighted children too, in terms of approach, workbook layout and large display materials.

If you teach secondary school children, the main point at the outset is that it is important that the partially sighted youngster can be as numerate as all others and not debarred from later professions or occupations through lack of mathematical qualifications. Algebra, geometry and simple trigonometry are all taught as well as basic arithmetic. In public examinations a time allowance of up to as much as 25 per cent additional time is allowed to partially sighted candidates who may also have their examination papers enlarged, if necessary, with the usual cautions about the pitfalls of inadvertently altering scale drawings and maps. Such allowances always need to be checked with the Examining Boards well in advance of the examination. The six GCSE Examining Groups have now issued comprehensive guidance notes for pupils whose disability is likely to handicap them in the GCSE examinations. A book covering all these regulations (Bostock, 1987) is listed in the Bibliography.

Equipment

The RNIB catalogue is a good source book for special equipment, though for the partially sighted pupil little may be needed. There is, for example, a Talking Calculator. Larger protractors make the measurement of degrees easier and allow for the inaccuracies which may develop when using a thicker pen. Keeler Low Vision Aids, Windsor, have a device for measuring which fits into their prescribed hand-held magnifier. Other equipment is in use in regular schools, such as selecting a ruler in which the inches are calibrated alternately in red and natural. One advantage of this kind of ruler for the partially sighted child, apart from the clearly demarcated measures, is that there is no extra piece of ruler at the end which does not count in the measurement. The conventional rulers with the extra extensions at each end are just an additional hazard for the young partially sighted mathematician. At a later age conventional transparent rulers are in order. Other equipment can be easily adapted or just carefully selected. For example, an ordinary surveyor's measuring tape can be marked specially to show clearly specific distances. For younger children, clear plastic containers are preferable to ones which are opaque for pouring liquids and for seeing the levels alter in the process.

Early stages

The development of partially sighted children will follow the normal course but for them certain processes will require extra emphasis. They have to learn to look, for example. So the normal tasks and activities expected of other children should be expected of them too, but they may need more verbal guidance and explanation, as described in Chapter 6, Talking and Listening.

Young children learn to pick up one object at a time, instead of a handful, and here tasks such as threading and pegboards are used. The children learn about one object, here the peg, going into one hole, and they learn to make lines and patterns with them. Beads are also used to make patterns and strings. Gradually, as they learn to crack the alphabetic code, so they learn to crack the number code. This means learning to group individual items in various storage systems according to their properties and attributes – size, shape, weight, colour and other differentiating features. Then they can match, sort and group unique individual items into sets which teaches that ten units make one ten and that ten tens make one hundred and so on. There is a pattern to counting which they can grasp. It seems difficult for partially sighted children to attain these vision-related concepts of the properties of objects, and the real danger is that they will rush too quickly into abstract arithmetic before some of the basic experiences have been properly grasped. Chapter 3, on integration issues will put forward the ideas that extended time at nursery or infant level is advisable in some cases to avoid this precipitate move to abstractions.

Colour, weight and size

Partially sighted children learn their colours in the same way as other children. Some do have considerable difficulty in seeing shades and in distinguishing colours, for example, selecting crayons when only a small area of colour is showing. However, unless the child is colour blind, even one with severely impaired eyesight can learn the colours. Similarly with concepts of weight, the children learn to weigh and balance themselves and other objects. Weight ideas are gained by handling and carrying items of different weight and by weighing them. By using weights made of different substances such as brass and plastic, they can observe the different size of the weight depending on the material. Sweets can be weighed out and real life comparisons made, such as weighing 450 grams of jam and 450 grams of flour.

Size is more difficult, for we learn the size of objects very much by using eyesight and not just by handling objects. Questions about size and errors of size are often made by partially sighted children. So a child looking at a picture of a butterfly thinks it is a kite, or another asks if a butterfly is as big as a bird. The partially sighted child cannot climb a tree or a hill or a church tower and look down or back to see that the people and cars all look like toys, nor can he go to the zoo and see at a glance the difference in size between a tiger and a cat, an elephant and a dog, and so this property of objects gives rise to endless identification confusions.

Distance, length, height, shape and volume

In estimating size and distance, the self is used as a standard gauge – self reference is important. 'How tall am I?' 'How tall are you?' 'Are the children smaller or taller than the adults?' 'How long is my foot or how wide is my hand span?' 'How long is my pace?' 'How many paces is it to walk from the medical room to the classroom?' Estimate first, then measure the correct answer. This basic principle underlies the modern approach to mathematics and is common to both fully and partially sighted children.

The concept of length, as above, is also gained by self reference – the length of a pace. 'How many paces from here to the other side of the classroom?' 'How long is the corridor in paces?' 'How wide is the desk?' The difference between a child's pace and an adult's pace can be gained by comparison and questioning and discovery. The child must discover some of the discrepancies and answers for himself, otherwise there is a danger of the child being the passive recipient of facts rather than an active explorer and discoverer. This is a particular danger for the partially sighted child.

As the child grows he can learn about height and the altered length of a pace. He can learn to approximate and estimate. At an older age very small measurements can be illuminated in the CCTV enlarger and the child will learn that a tiny length exists and is a millimetre, even though he cannot see anything so small.

It seems likely that it is with shapes that the partially sighted are in greatest difficulty. When learning about triangles, for example, they may only discover the points at first. There always has to be considerable talking as the child is feeling a new shape – 'what do you notice about it?' He then has to 'discover' the sides of the triangle. Then there are triangles with equal sides – 'what do you notice about this?' The right angle has to be discovered, too, by practical experience and discovery. Do not be afraid to urge the partially sighted child to go out and look at nature, for example. Look for any straight lines in nature, look at leaves and trees and weeds and tree trunks. Only man makes straight lines and eventually these stop and an angle is formed.

When it comes to categorizing, it is difficult for the partially sighted child to see small differences, but once again, he has to learn to look and has to have real experience to draw on. Some objects look so similar in picture form that they cause problems – a picture of a balloon, for example, can look like an orange though the child would be able to distinguish between them perfectly well if the real objects were used rather than pictures. So there is a real danger of some errors being created by drawing on peripheral processing of two-dimensional information, instead of providing three-dimensional, real objects.

With volume, much experimentation is done using clear plastic containers of different shapes and coloured liquids. The child can see sufficiently well to learn about volume by looking carefully at levels and by comparing quantities. The partially sighted child may seem clumsy and inaccurate in pouring liquid into a container but that does not mean that he is any the less able to grasp the concept. Nor does it mean that he should be prevented from the necessary experimentation and any ensuing spillage that there may be.

There are some concepts which it is harder for the partially sighted child to acquire. It is known that reaching out to find objects out of sight and out of reach, and looking in the direction of a dropped object, is a landmark in the development of a child without sight and the same is true to a lesser extent of a child who is partially sighted. The child has to turn to look for and find hidden objects, and has to learn that if a ball rolls behind a box, and if it is unobstructed and follows its flight path, it will come out at a predictable place. Early threading tasks are based on this principle. So the movement of objects in space has to be learned and experienced – partially sighted children learn to ride tricycles, to climb on climbing frames, to slide down slides, to push trolleys, and later to take part in other sports, but there is not much jumping off things into the visual unknown, nor are there many ball games involving the accurate judgement by sight, of flight path, speed, height and velocity. The children themselves are, of course, objects moving in space. They run and skip and swim certain lengths of the baths. They have to learn whether they can squeeze through a space or not – whether a chair will fit in a corner or under a table. There is inevitably a lot of bumping into things in the early years, a great deal of falling over, dropping things and spilling, but without all these the child is protected from learning and denied the basis for later growth. It is worth pondering on the consequences for this in terms of teacher time in a mainstream school and more has been documented on this subject in Chapter 3, on integration issues.

Conservation

There comes a time for the fully sighted child when the messages coming to the eye are in fact illusory – these stages are well charted out in some work on the conservation of size, volume and weight (Piaget and Inhelder, 1941). As partially sighted children can see less well, it could be argued that they would be less prone to visual confusions and illusions and deceptions. Tobin (1972) reported on work with blind and partially sighted children looking into the conservation of substance. The children were aged from five to 17 years of age. For the purposes of looking at how partially sighted children managed on the tasks set, only one of his groups is of significance here and that was the first group who could see and count the experimenters' fingers at their own chosen distance. The children were first given balls of plasticine and told that two were of the same weight. When they had felt those two, the others were removed and one of the balls was rolled out to a different shape. The child then had to say again, having helped to make the sausage shape, whether there was still the same amount of plasticine in it as in the other ball. The same increase with age in correct responses was found with the blind and partially sighted as with the fully sighted, and the best of the visually impaired attained conservation responses at the same age as fully sighted children – i.e. at six or seven years of age. However, amongst the visually impaired there was a much bigger spread with some still not having the idea until nine or ten. For group one – the nearest visually to partially sighted – the big jump when a lot of children began to understand this idea, was between seven and eight. Tobin's study was not able to show a lag which was directly attributable to degree of vision. Nonetheless there certainly was a lag in grasping the idea that shape can alter, but that to be longer does not mean it is bigger or smaller or of a different weight than before.

Mastering the monetary system rests on the conservation of number, the children learn that one coin is worth ten, 20 or 50 pence. So what may seem small or less may in fact be more or a greater amount. This is an illusion or a problem to be solved and the child has to reason the answer out despite visual appearances. Parents are often very much involved at this stage in helping the child learn the value of coins when out shopping. Children also have to learn the symbols for the numbers of objects they have experienced and for the four operations, they have to learn the relationship between adding and subtracting, multiplying and dividing. If they have grasped the ideas behind these symbols, then any errors which arise stem from materials designed and printed for fully sighted children which are difficult in printed form for the children to see clearly and with too little space in which to put their answer.

Perspective

It has already been noted that partially sighted children experience difficulty in judging relative size correctly – the same is true of perspective in pictures. If a child has sight in only one eye, this affects the judgement of size and distance. If an object is close, it will look bigger, if it is far away it will subtend a smaller angle on to the retina and so will look smaller. Only experience and sense tells the viewer that objects remain constant in size and that if a picture of a man looks tiny, it is because he is a very long way off, or if one hand of a person looks bigger, it is because it is nearer the viewer.

This form of optical illusion has received considerable attention and has been the subject of experimental studies with children. There are various classic designs or figures which are used because of their particular propensity for creating illusions. Generally for the best known, there is a decrease in the magnitude of illusion with age. In the case of partially sighted children it is still questionable as to the extent to which they are susceptible to optical illusions. Lansdown (1973) found that it was the responses to a horizontal illusion figure which illuminated clearly the difference between fully and partially sighted children aged six to ten years of age, with the partially sighted being more susceptible to the illusion than the fully sighted.

Much perspective is learned by experience of seeing things at a distance, of oneself moving through the built environment, or of looking along a corridor and seeing a friend in the distance. The viewer knows the friend is not so tiny and so the brain corrects what the eye sees. However, if the eye is faulty and gives blurred or distorted images to the brain, this particular lesson is harder to learn. Verbal explanations are probably essential to elaborate and learn from what is actually seen.

So the basic foundations of mathematical principles are put in place through considerable real, practical experience with a great deal of verbal explanation and thinking. Everything is a problem to be solved – a puzzle for the child which should be fun. For the partially sighted child there can probably never be too much practical experience in the infant and junior years, and when it comes to formal maths and more advanced concepts they are then fully understood.

By secondary level the pupil will be able gradually to move into algebra and geometry and elementary trigonometry. Allowances do have to be made for the tidiness of diagrams and drawings and for degree of accuracy in measuring. If a fully sighted child is allowed one degree or one millimetre measurement error then it is reasonable to allow a partially sighted child five degrees or five millimetres error. The important point is that they have the correct concept and can estimate whether their answer is in the correct direction rather than being very accurate at measuring and not having grasped the concept.

Some practical applications

For partially sighted students who learn rowing and canoeing as their sport, it is interesting and practical to combine these with maths and study navigation. There are other practical applications such as woodwork or technical drawing, model-making or geography fieldwork. Many partially sighted pupils will be very competent at computer subjects and a thorough grounding in mathematics, together with an interest and confidence in number work, will be essential for them. The myth has therefore to be exploded that mathematics is a particularly difficult subject for the partially sighted pupil. This is not the case. Just as they have demonstrated that they are on a par with their peers in literacy skills, provided they have the right reading aids, so in maths they can compare favourably with sighted children if well taught. The only horizons are those of the teacher. For the pupil's future employment prospects, mathematics is a priority.

11 Sport and Leisure Pursuits

This chapter is concerned with sport and leisure for the partially sighted child not only in a specialist school but also in integrated mainstream settings. If the right sports are available, they can be carried on into adult life. Traditional as well as adapted sports and games will be mentioned in which partially sighted pupils can be actively involved. Sport has many dimensions – there is the physical side, the social side and there is the personal challenge and health aspect. Some form of physical activity is essential for partially sighted youngsters wherever they are at school.

The starting point for a teacher, before undertaking any sporting activity or school journey with a partially sighted child, must be to consult the child's ophthalmologist, for some children are forbidden to dive or to jump off the side of the swimming pool. Others are not allowed to jump from heights even on firm ground, nor to head a football. It is essential to know who is allowed to do what.

Rowing

There are some sports which have been long established as activities which can be enjoyed to the full by the partially sighted child. This is true of rowing. It may well be the case that the partially sighted have to spend more time learning to feel comfortable in the boat and learning about the shape of it and of the blades. They have to be trained rigorously to do things the correct way. Carrying the blades, for example, if not done properly, vertically, can be dangerous for everyone else. So the partially sighted have to learn these courtesies and cautions of each sport particularly carefully if they are to be participating on equal terms. Rowing, if mastered, is a wonderful team activity in which the partially sighted can compete with the fully sighted, but the cox at least has to be able to see well enough to navigate.

There are two more sports which are ones that partially sighted pupils can take up at school and enjoy for the whole of their lives – these are sailing and cycling. Both depend on having access to the right facilities – a lake and a cycle track – and on having a teacher with the enthusiasm, confidence and skill to bring these sports within the sphere of these youngsters.

Sailing

To begin with sailing, the pupils have to learn both about the boat and about the elements and navigation. They learn through extensive inspection of the boat and the equipment, and by handling the sails and the ropes and the rudder. The safety rules and the capsize drill have to be rigorously learned and practised. So, too, have the correct ways of doing things. This, like so many other skills, will perhaps take longer for the partially sighted pupil and will need considerable talking through, for it cannot be learned just by watching as with the fully sighted, it has to be accompanied by good verbal explanation.

The first sailing lessons cover the boat generally and the direction of the wind, which way it is blowing that day and at that time. The pupils learn about changes of wind and finding the wind in order to work out where to sail to with the wind behind them, or on either side of the boat. They learn to aim for a distant point and to do this there has to be at least one person in the boat who can see the distant landmark towards which they are sailing – initially this is likely to be the adult but later, when more competent and confident, a small group of partially sighted pupils can sail alone with good safety precautions built in.

Cycling

Cycling for the older pupils begins on a cycle track. One advantage of this sport over and above the advantages mentioned for other sports such as fitness, stretching the body physically, learning about fatigue and rest, the outdoors, working in a team and setting individual goals, is that cycling involves balance – which, once mastered and for those whose sight is good enough, also has a practical usefulness.

Partially sighted pupils use standard solo bicycles and they take the regular cycle tests for safety, skill and endurance. Later they are able to cycle on quiet roads and those whose sight is too reduced for solo cycling can ride on tandem cycles with a sighted person. Endurance is stretched by cycling as far as London to Brighton – on quiet roads and with a large number of accompanying adults to ensure a high level of safety, naturally.

The advantages of cycling are far reaching. It enables city children to get out into the country and experience travelling at speed. It gives a real experience of uphill and downhill in a way which it is impossible to gain through travel in a bus or a car. If the children are accompanied by fit, knowledgeable and talkative cyclists they are able to learn about different terrain or areas of built-up environments other than their own home area.

In all these ways partially sighted pupils are provided with opportunities to be outside and to have real and exciting experiences – like finding thin ice on the lake and hearing the different sounds as it cracks, or hearing the slight echo made by ice bounding off ice.

Swimming

One major consideration, if there is a choice, is which sport the person is likely to be most successful at and able to continue later in life. In nearly all cases swimming is a good selection for a partially sighted pupil. This has long been a sport which has been encouraged for visually impaired children. The swimming pool is a controlled environment and the techniques for swimming are the same for the partially sighted as for the fully sighted child. It is a sport at which the partially sighted child can be on a par with his fully sighted friend.

The younger partially sighted child will probably require considerable adult support for longer until he is fully confident in the water. In one sense a swimming pool is excellent for the partially sighted because it is an enclosed space and the design of most swimming pools is similar, so that once the layout of one is familiar, learning about a new one is not so difficult. For a child with very poor vision it may be necessary for an adult to be with the child in the water for a while, and the adult should constantly say the child's name if at any distance so that although the child may not see the adults clearly, he knows that he is seen and under supervision. This is an ideal sport for the partially sighted child in a mainstream school. In the water the partially sighted child can compete on an equal basis with the fully sighted. Once the strokes are mastered the other aspects of the sport do not depend on visual clues in the same way as a fast ball game does.

Sports centres for the fully and partially sighted

Sporting and leisure pursuits can bring together the fully sighted and the partially sighted, for example, in outdoor activities such as canoeing, rock climbing and abseiling which both groups of children or youngsters can do together, helping each other as necessary. There are two centres where visually impaired youngsters can try out a wide variety of outdoor pursuits which may not all be readily accessible in their home area. The Bowles Centre for Outdoor Pursuits and *Insight, an eye to Adventure* which is run by 'Adventure Unlimited'.

The Inner City link course run at the Bowles Centre is for pupils over the age of 14 from the inner cities and is designed specifically to bring together the fully sighted and the partially sighted to learn some unusual physical activities for five days. There is a choice amongst canoeing, dry-skiing, overnight camping, rock climbing, abseiling, assault courses, team games and night walks. The aims and approaches on the course are educational, using experience of adventure activities to help personal development for both fully sighted and partially sighted children. In taking part in the activities, the children find they can do things they never thought they could. Also there are times when the fully sighted and the partially sighted children are dependent on each other, for example in rock climbing. This can encourage a real sense of responsibility. In addition, living and working together away from home leads to a great awareness of others' needs. The children usually thoroughly enjoy themselves and hopefully carry with them an idea of the enjoyment of outdoor pursuits long after they have left school.

Coupled with this they learn about the safety requirements needed to undertake certain sports. To be able to take up canoeing, for example, the person concerned has to be able to swim 50 yards or at least feel comfortable in the water and able to roll the canoe over when it overturns, as it inevitably will. The underlying importance of this is that in some sports the terms are the same for the fully sighted and the partially sighted.

The second successful course mentioned earlier for partially sighted pupils is run by 'Adventure Unlimited', called *Insight, an eye to Adventure*. The course is residential and usually involves camping. The same activities as for the Inner City Link Course are available in a relaxed atmosphere so that the pupils can try them out when they feel ready to do so. Two additional activities on this course are drama and orienteering, both used in such a way as to bring together the fully and the partially sighted.

Both these organizations are registered charities working with children and adults. The tuition at both is excellent and thorough, with emphasis on gentle persuasion. All the activities are within the capabilities of the visually impaired and very popular with partially sighted youngsters.

PE lessons

In a mainstream school PE lesson, when a partially sighted pupil is present in the class, there is a lot of responsibility placed on the teacher to make the experience a success, not only for the partially sighted child but for the whole class. The teacher must think carefully about the nature of the sporting activity: certainly ball games present the partially sighted pupil with far greater difficulty than other sports. The teacher may find that the partially sighted child takes longer to master the skills of the game but it is not impossible to do so. The difficulty may come when the game speeds up and the initial stages have passed, because the partially sighted child is at a disadvantage in not being able to read the whole game as the fully sighted child learns to do so. When learning to pass the ball in football or hockey, the partially sighted child may have to attend to the ball at his feet. To use this skill in a game which is ever changing, there are almost bound to be difficulties in picking up visual clues quickly enough. Nonetheless, it is much better for the partially sighted child to take part in some way rather than just be left out. The following illustration shows how fully sighted children used the skills and assets of a partially sighted child when playing a game of netball.

Netball

Having successfully learned all the skills related to netball, it was time to put these into a game. As the game progressed, it was evident that the partially sighted child was being bypassed by the speed of the game and the ever changing situations and strategies of it. Because the partially sighted pupil was tall – in fact the tallest in the class – she was given the role of goal defence by the other members of her team. When the opposition were attacking, the members of her own team would shout out to her to put up her arms and block the shot. Although this might not be full participation in the game, the partially sighted child enjoyed being a proper member of the team and the others in her class were pleased to be using her asset – her height.

It seems likely that joint sporting activities that are not subject to visual cues and varying situations and improvization are the ones which are most likely to be successful. Certainly, as mentioned previously, swimming is a very good example, for all the strokes are closed skills and neither subject to variation nor dependent on visual cues. To a certain extent the same is true of some forms of athletics. Partially sighted pupils are quite able to do a sprint or a jump, though running over a longer distance and gauging position on the track and overtaking moments are likely to present them with difficulty. In all that has been written, the PE teacher may need to take account of the fact that the partially sighted pupil may need longer to master the skill and may need more explanation than the fully sighted, but given those there will be a sport that the pupil can and should do, unless advised not to by the ophthalmologist.

There is a temptation to think that because a partially sighted child cannot see well that sport should be avoided – this is, of course, a fallacy. Both the games and the equipment can be adapted for partially sighted children whichever schools they attend. Footballs and netballs, for example, can be made audible, or a good colour contrast can be provided. Audible balls are available from the RNIB. It is also possible to make an audible ball from an ordinary plastic football, as described in the RNIB leaflet. The nylon valve is removed by screwing a size 8 woodscrew into the valve and then pulling the screw and valve out with pliers. Alternatively the valve can be pushed back into the ball. If the valve is metal, it can be removed by using its own screw-in metal adaptor. With the valve removed, ball bearings are inserted. A new valve, purchased from a sports shop, is then put back in place. This is then available for use in a host of games apart from football and netball.

These games, together with cricket and rounders, can only be played between teams of common visual ability for the obvious reason that they are so visual that if there were not this balance, then the teams would be too unequal to play an even game. Apart from adapting the equipment and the rules, it is also possible sometimes to reduce the area of play. This means that the players can all maintain audible and visual information as the game develops.

Conclusion

It is important to note that the visually impaired sportsman is as competitive as the fully sighted one and that the strategies of coping with defeat or victory are relevant to both equally. For the partially sighted child, sport and leisure pursuits bring challenges, fitness, targets to strive for and a sense of achievement. These all contribute to greater self-esteem, which is essential for success in other spheres of life.

The interested reader should turn to the RNIB leaflets listed in Appendix III which give details of the ways in which games can be adapted for visually impaired people.

12 Future Prospects – Employment, Training and Careers–

Writing about employment is always difficult because opportunities open to young men and women reflect the areas in which they live and the cultural norms as well as the expectations of time.

For the partially sighted, recent advances in technology have opened up new possibilities. Modern electronic or battery run typewriters, CCTV, print enlargers, photocopiers, commercial and home computers, all of which are mentioned in Chapter 4, on equipment, have revolutionized the world of employment; so, too, though not so dramatically have the greater availability of good quality and easily portable tape recorders. The twin problems of lighting and transport remain. Once again, it has to be stressed at the outset that each partially sighted person has individual needs in all these areas and inevitably in this chapter there will be generalizations which do not fit the individual person.

Most partially sighted pupils nowadays continue their education beyond the statutory leaving age of 16. Many who have enjoyed specialist provision until then enter mainstream colleges. Others remain successfully within the mainstream or, at that point, enter a specialist college. There are five such colleges at present, and the reader is advised to turn to the addresses in Appendix III and make contact with each one for an up-to-date brochure and information.

A key person to consult about post-16 education and training is the specialist careers officer. It may also be time to seek advice from the ophthalmologist. Each person's eyesight is different and in some work settings there are requirements which it is essential to be able to meet. Some jobs, for example, require the employee to be able to drive, others need employees who can see colours without difficulty. There are sometimes reservations about a partially sighted person having oversight of young children but it is important to have exact information about the individual's sight for it might be easily sufficient for the task and the employer's fears can be allayed by information from the eye specialist. There are some eye conditions where it is unwise to lift or carry heavy weights and the advice of the ophthalmologist is essential. For those going to university or polytechnic the Partially Sighted Society publication 'Higher Education Preview' could be helpful as a guide to facilities for partially sighted students in the UK.

What follows consists of a short glance backwards and then a review of the kinds of employment being taken by young people now. In 1911 Dr Harman's suggestion made after the census that year was that the definition of a partially sighted person was an adult who would be unable to earn his living by ordinary sighted means. What partially sighted people have achieved in the sphere of employment since he suggested that would undoubtedly have thrilled and amazed him as the following paragraphs will reveal.

In the 'Report of the Committee of Enquiry into the Problems Relating to Partially Sighted Children', (Board of Education, 1934) the terms of reference were 'To enquire into and report upon the medical, educational and social aspects of the problems affecting partially blind children.' This was the first report specifically looking at the needs of this group. The first point was that there was no official definition yet of partial blindness. There were two main drawbacks: the first was that it meant that official returns of census forms were inaccurate and the second was that there was still no guarantee of finance educationally, for in the Education Act of 1921 the definition of blind was still 'too blind to be able to read the ordinary school books used by children'. It was Dr Harman who, following the census of 1911, asked that the word 'totally' should be inserted before blind and said that in future it would be helpful if the two terms blind and partially blind were used. His suggested definitions were that a blind person was a person who was not able to see his way about, whilst a partially blind person would be an adult who was unable to earn his living by doing ordinary sighted work.

It is interesting to note that he used the work criterion as a way of defining part sight whilst by the 1921 Education Act there were three groups of blind children categorized, two of which we would call partially sighted. The three groups were:

(a) those who, having no perception of light or having extremely defective vision, cannot be taught by methods involving the use of sight;
(b) those who, on account of having defective vision, cannot follow the ordinary school curriculum but can see well enough to be taught by special methods involving the use of sight;
(c) those who are suffering from conditions such as myopia, which may be aggravated by following the ordinary school curriculum.

By 1934 the committee stated categorically that in their view those children in categories (b) and (c) were partially blind rather than totally blind and the emphasis of this book has been focused on children from category (b).

Finally, in the Report of 1934, apart from attempts to collect data comparing the academic results of segregated versus special schools and partially sighted children in special schools as opposed to partially sighted children in ordinary schools, there were lists of the occupations followed after school by partially sighted pupils – all this in an attempt to gather and provide hitherto unavailable information, but also to try to find measures of the success or otherwise of special schools and classes.

With regard to the collection of data on attainments more has been covered elsewhere, suffice it to say that numbers were too small to provide conclusive results. There was also the difficulty of classifying all partially sighted children under one heading for clearly they were and are a very heterogeneous group. However, a survey of LCC schools for the partially sighted saw that,

of those pupils who left school in 1924 the vast majority of those whose occupation was known fell into the following three categories:
1. shopkeepers, porters, messengers, assistants, etc.;
2. factory and warehouse workers, packers, vanboys, etc.; and,
3. domestic and allied occupations.

The survey revealed an absence of mention of professional occupations; it is perhaps a reflection of the philosophy of sight saving which had prevailed and of the lack of magnifying equipment and good lighting that it must have been virtually impossible to study sufficiently for employment which required study and reading at that time, although the skilled trades are mentioned.

A review of a similar group now, i.e. those partially sighted pupils leaving a special school in the same area, would take three areas into account:
1.   direct or indirect entry into employment, Youth Opportunity (YOP) and Youth Training Schemes (YTS);
2.   continuation of education and study at the sixth form of a mainstream school, in a Sixth Form College, Further Education College or Tertiary College or at a specialist college for the partially sighted;

Table 4: Possible careers for partially sighted people

Visually impaired men and women are known to have succeeded in the following occupations. The categories are very broad and obviously include many other possibilities.

1. *Direct entry – unskilled/semi-skilled:*

(a)   Gardening. Local Authorities either nursery or outdoor; private parks and gardens, e.g. country houses, commercial nurseries.
(b)   Manual work. Local Authorities; agriculture; building; public works; constructing.
(c)   Factory work. Packing; checking; inspection; capstan lathe.
(d)   Retail trade. Shop assistants.
(e)   Domestic work. Hotels; Local Authorities; private.

2. *Direct entry with an element of training:*

(a)   Public Service. Civil Service departments; many departments of the Hospital Service; Local Government, the public corporations.
(b)   Nursing. State Enrolled Nurses (as opposed to State Registered Nurses).
(c)   Social work. Some categories of Social Worker; Social Work Assistants.

3. *Entry through full-time study/training:*

Physiotherapy; Teaching; Social Work; Speech Therapy; Occupational Therapy and Commerce, etc.; Computers, University Lecturer; Telephony; Audio Typing; General clerical; Appeals; Sales; Barwork; Tourism.

(Reproduced with permission from 'Good News for the Partially Sighted' by Geraldine Holloway. A Partially Sighted Society publication).

3.   the first two points followed by entry to University or Polytechnic at a later age.

In all cases the specialist careers officers for the area is a key person to consult at an early stage.

The most popular choice of occupation of school leavers over a number of years was marriage and parenthood. Most partially sighted children now leave school at 16 or 17 and then go on to further study or training, very few go straight into employment.

Table 4 shows categories of careers which are possible for partially sighted men and women, taken from Geraldine Holloway's book, 'Good News for the Partially Sighted', (Holloway, 1985).

Appendix I
'Walk and Talk' Assessment

National Mobility Centre – Low Vision Mobility

Assessment and functional vision training

Indoor vision – static viewing
Can the person see?
Daylight /windows
Electric lights

Gross details /colours /hues
The walls
Curtains
Floor
Ceiling
Recognize colours
'Best' colour identification
Shadows
Sunlight on wall, floor, etc.

Fine detail
Window frame cross-members
Picture frame on wall
Newspaper on floor
Wall ends
Doorways/frames
Furniture: bed, table, work surface, carpet
Stairs: risers and tread, hand rails
View through window: garden (grass, hedge, wall, etc.)
Seeing people: outline, male, female
A white football on floor
Recognition of faces
Reading print
Watching television

Outside vision (static)
Type of daylight – bright sunshine or overcast
Can the person see?
 the sky
 the skyline
 the 'dip' above the street
 pavement
 wall
 kerb edge
 grass verge
 down kerb
 end of block building line
 entrances, gates, posts
 houses
 street/road markings – white lines or yellow lines
 street furniture – lamp posts, street signs or letter boxes

pedestrians
vehicles – parked, moving; colours; chromium/shining parts; signal indicators

At night – as above
car lights – side, head and rear
street lights
window lights

Outside vision (mobile)
Can the person walk straight along the pavement?
Walk around the block?
Cross a street – indent method; parallel method; zebra crossing; pelican crossing, or
traffic light crossing
Can the person find:
Home
A shop
Bus-stop (enter and sit in a bus)
Can the person obtain:
help in crossing roads
information from the public
Can the person:
read signs – streets
read timetables /maps, etc.
cross wide entrances – petrol stations, etc.

Useful exercises for trainee instructors who can travel adequately under blindfold in busy
residential areas. Use simulation goggles in the following tasks:

1.   Walking along a quiet pavement.
2.   Road crossing (indent and parallel).
3.   Travelling a complex unfamiliar route.
4.   Shopping area – find a shop, ask one's way and make a purchase – e.g. chocolate in a
       supermarket and from a shop assistant in a specialist shop – a specific item.
5.   Public transport.
6.   Take refreshment and sustenance at a restaurant or pub with a menu.

(Reproduced with the permission of The National Mobility Centre)

Appendix II
Identification Checklist

These are some signs a teacher might notice of some impairment or deterioration of eyesight, not previously noted at a school medical examination. Any of the following signs warrants further investigation.

1. The child complains of headaches or painful eyes, or keeps rubbing his eyes.

2. The child has watery, itchy or inflamed eyes.

3. The child complains of discomfort in bright light, or of suddenly not being able to see at night.

4. The child makes frequent errors when copying from the board and generally fails to make the expected progress.

5. The child bumps into things, spills water or accidentally knocks things over.

6. The child peers at reading matter, places books abnormally far from or close to his eyes or tilts his head when reading.

7. The child goes over to the window to get a better light for reading.

8. The child cannot distinguish pictures in books which the rest of the class can distinguish.

9. The child's handwriting is off the line or difficult to read.

10. The child walks up to the blackboard to read what is on it.

11. The child fails to see signs and notices on the board.

12. The child fails to see expressions on a person's face or does not recognize a familiar person.

13. A child seems to recognize people more by their clothes than by their facial appearance.

14. The needlework teacher comments that the child avoids needlework.

15. The art teacher comments that the child's paintings are all greyish in colour.

16. The young child is reluctant to draw or write.

17. The child cannot see to read something written in pencil.

18. The older child cannot read the teachers' or other children's handwriting.

19. The child complains that the photocopied worksheets are too faint or that the lines on lined paper cannot be seen.

20. At football or hockey, although competent when he has the ball, the child cannot receive it well, when it is hit or kicked from across the field.

21. The child complains of blurred or double vision.

22. The child squints and frowns when writing.

Appendix III
List of Addresses

1. Adventure Unlimited, 20 Stanmer Villas, Brighton, East Sussex BN1 7HP. Tel: 0273 565602.
2. Alphavision Ltd, Seymore House, Copyground Lane, High Wycombe, Bucks HP12 3HE. Tel: 0494 30555.
3. Bowles Centre for Outdoor Pursuits, Eridge, Tunbridge Wells, Kent. Tel: 08926 4127.
4. Disabled Living Foundation, 380–4 Harrow Road, London W9 2HU. Tel: 01 289 6111.
5. Distance Learning Course for Teachers of the Visually Handicapped, Faculty of Education, PO Box 363, University of Birmingham, Birmingham B15 2TT. Tel: 021 472 1301 Ext 2217 or 2290.
6. Dorton House School, Further Education Department, Seal, Sevenoaks, Kent TN15 0ED. Tel: 0732 61477. (Direct entry 16+ FE Department in conjunction with the local mainstream FE colleges).
7. FOCUS, CCTV Reading Aids for the Partially Sighted. John Heathcoat and Company Limited, Focus Division, Tiverton, Devon EX16 5LL. Tel: 0884 254949.
8. Hethersett College, 32 Gatton Road, Wray Common, Reigate, Surrey.Tel: 07372 45555.
9. Learning Development Aids, Duke Street, Wisbech, Cambs PE13 2AE.
10. Keeler Instruments, 38 Margaret Street, Cavendish Square, London W1A 4NS. Tel: 01 935 8512.
11. Keeler Low Vision Aids, C. Davis Keeler Limited, Dispensing Opticians, Clewer Hill Road, Windsor, Berks SL4 4AA. Tel: 0753 857177.
12. Library Services Trust, The Library Association, 7 Ridgmount Street, London WC1E 7AE. Tel: 01 636 7543.
13. London Regional Transport Unit for Disabled Passengers. Tel: 01 222 5600.
14. Microwriter, Foundation for Communication for the Disabled, 25 High Street, Woking, Surrey GU21 1BW. Tel: 04862 27844.
15. National Mobility Centre, 1 The Square, 111 Broad Street, Edgbaston, Birmingham B15 1AF. (Tel: 021 643 9912). Also 55 Eton Avenue, London NW3 3ET (Tel: 01 722 9703) and Headingly Castle, Headingly Lane, Leeds LS6 2BQ (Tel: 0532 752666).
16. Partially Sighted Society, National Low Vision Advice Centre, 3 Colleton Crescent, Exeter, Devon EX2 4DG. Tel: 0392 210656. (Advice on all issues to do with partial sight and low vision functional assessments.)
17. Partially Sighted Society, Queen's Road, Doncaster, DN1 2NX. Tel: 0302 68998. (Administration, mail orders and large print.)
18. Partially Sighted Society, 206 Great Portland Street, London W1N 6AA. Tel: 01 387 8840. (Information on all matters concerning partial sight.)
19. OCULUS, The Magazine of the Partially Sighted Society, The Editor, The Partially Sighted Society, Queen's Road, Doncaster DN1 2NX. Tel: 0302 68998.
20. Queen Alexandra College, The Birmingham Royal Institution for the Blind, Court Oak Road, Harborne, Birmingham B17 9TG. Tel: 021 427 4577.
21. Research Centre for the Education of the Visually Handicapped, Department of Special Education, University of Birmingham, Birmingham B15 2TT. Tel: 021 471 1303.
22. Royal National College and Academy of Music for the Blind, College Road, Hereford HR1 1EB. Tel: 0432 265725.
23. Royal National Institute for the Blind, 224 Great Portland Street, London W1N 6AA. Tel: 01 388 1266.

24. RNIB Commercial Training College, 5/6 Pembridge Place, London W2 4XB. Tel: 01 229 6673 and 01 221 0048. From 1989 onwards: RNIB and Loughborough Technical College, Loughborough, Leics.

25. RNIB North London School of Physiotherapy for the Visually Handicapped, 10 Highgate Hill, London N19 5ND. Tel: 01 272 1659.

26. RNIB Reference Library, Braille House, 338/346 Goswell Road, London EC1V 7JE. Tel: 01 837 9921 or 01 278 9611.

27. Viewscan Text Systems VTS, Wormald International Sensory Aids Limited, 7 Musters Road, West Bridgford, Nottingham NG2 7PP. Tel: 0602 820600 or RNIB.

28. Visual Impairment North East (VINE), Simulation Spectacles from F. Hodson, Peary House, Preston Park, North Shields, NE29 9JR.

29. West of England School Further Education Department, Countess Wear, Exeter EX2 6HA. Tel: 0392 413333.

A new vocational college for blind and partially sighted adults is due to be completed in 1989 on a site in Loughborough next to the Technical College. This will replace the London based Commercial College. There will be courses in audio and shorthand typing, word processing, telephony, computer programming and business studies, together with access to all the Technical College courses.

It is possible that in the near future a training course will be introduced, enabling students to qualify as teachers of the visually impaired, which will be held at The Institute of Education, University of London, 20 Bedford Way, London WC1H 0AL.

Appendix IV
Reading List

1.   Access Guide. Advice to Stores, Banks, Offices and Transport Systems on Meeting the Needs of Visually Disabled People. Published by the Partially Sighted Society.

2.   COLBORNE BROWNE, M. and TOBIN, M. (1982 and 1983). *Integration of the Educationally Blind*. The New Beacon.

3.   DUGUID, I. and BERRY, A. (1978). *Ophthalmology*. Sevenoaks: Hodder and Stoughton Unibooks.

4.   ELLIS, A.W. (1984). *Reading, Writing and Dyslexia. A Cognitive Analysis*. London: Lawrence Erlbaum.

5.   EVANS, S.C. (1984). Prevention of Blindness in England. Details available from 271 Oulton Road, Oulton, Suffolk.

6.   FORD, M. and HESCHEL, T. (1987). *In Touch*. London: BBC Books.

7.   HOPKINSON, R.G. (1973). 'Lighting in Schools for the Visually Handicapped'. In: *Light, Lighting and Environmental Design*, pp. 262–5.

8.   HORNE, P.W. (1986). History of Clapham Park School. Unpublished account.

9.   JAMIESON, M., PARLETT, M. and POCKLINGTON, K. (1977). *Towards Integration*. Slough: NFER.

10.   Library Services Trust (1987). *Can't See to Read*. Resources for Visually Handicapped People: 4th edition.

11.   Partially Sighted Society publications: Brochure and Catalogue; Higher Education Preview; Lighting and Low Vision. Available from the Partially Sighted Society.

12.   RNIB Booklets: One Step at a Time; Please Help Me – For parents of children with impaired vision. Available from the RNIB.

13.   TOOZE, F.H.G., CHAPMAN, E.K., MOSS, S.C., and TOBIN, M.J. (1977). *Look and Think*. Available from the Schools' Council.

References

ATRILL, C. (1986). *Sports for Visually Handicapped People – 2 Perspectives.* A booklet available from the RNIB.

BOARD OF EDUCATION (1934). *Report of a Committee of Enquiry into the Education of the Partially Sighted.* London:HMSO.

BOSTOCK, A. (1987). *Examination Provision for Candidates with Specific Learning Difficulties.* GCSE Edition. London:ILEA DCLD.

BRYANT, P. and BRADLEY, L. (1985). *Children's Reading Problems.* Oxford:Blackwell.

BUULTJENS, M. (1986). 'Parental perceptions of special educational provision for the visually impaired', *British Journal of Visual Impairment*, IV, 2, pp.65–8.

COLLINS, J. (1987). 'The evaluation of light source for near vision tasks', *Oculus*, July/August, pp.67–71.

FRITH, U. (1985). 'Beneath the surface of developmental dyslexia'. In: MARSHALL, J.C., PATTERSON, K. and COLTHEART, M. (Eds). *Surface Dyslexia.* London:Routledge and Kegan Paul.

GINN READING 360 and GINN MATHEMATICS PROGRAMME (1983). Details available from Ginn and Co. Limited, Prebendal House, Parson's Fee, Aylesbury, Bucks HP20 2QZ.

GREAT BRITAIN. DEPARTMENT OF EDUCATION AND SCIENCE (1893). *Elementary Education (Blind and Deaf Children) Act.* London:HMSO.

HARMAN, B.N. (1910). 'The education of high myopes', *British Medical Journal*, Vol ii, p.1320.

HARMAN, B. N. (1912). 'The education of high myopes. Proceedings of the Royal Society of Medicine', *British Medical Journal*, Ophthalmology section, pp.146–63.

HINDS, R. (1986). *Games for Blind Children.* Booklet available from RNIB.

HOLLOWAY, G. (1985). *Good News for the Partially Sighted.* 3rd edition, London:Partially Sighted Society.

KERR, J. (1916). *Newsholme's School Hygiene.* 14th edition. London:George Allen and Unwin.

KERR, J. (1926). *The Fundamentals of School Health.* London:George Allen and Unwin.

KLEMZ, A. (1977). *Blindness and Partial Sight.* Cambridge: Woodhead-Faulkner.

LANSDOWNE, R.G. (1973). A study of the effects of severe visual handicap on the development of some aspects of visual perception and their relationship to reading and spelling in children in special schools for the partially sighted. Unpublished PhD thesis,

OREGON PROJECT (1977–8). Revised Edition for Visually Impaired and Blind Pre-school Children. Details available from Jackson Education Service District, 101 North Grape Street, Medford, Oregon 97501, USA.

PIAGET, J. and INHELDER, B. (1941). *Le developpement des quantités chez l'enfant.* Neuchâtel: Delachaux et Niestlé.

REYNELL, J. and ZINKIN, P. (1975). 'New procedures for the developmental assessment of young children with severe visual handicaps', *Child: care, health and development*, Vol. I, pp.61–5.

REYNELL, J. (1978). 'Developmental patterns of visually handicapped children', *Child: care, health and development*, Vol. 4, pp.291–303.

SPENCER, C. (1986). *Football.* Booklet available from the RNIB.

STANOVICH, K.E., CUNNINGHAM, A.E., CRAMER, B.B. (1984). 'Assessing phonological awareness in kindergarten children: issues of task comparability', *Journal of Experimental Child Psychology*, Vol. 38, pp.175–90.

TOBIN, M.J. (1972). 'Conservation of substance in the blind and partially sighted', *British Journal of Educational Psychology*, Vol. 42,(2), pp.192–7.

WHITE, M. and CAMERON, R.J. (1987). *Portage Early Education Programme.* Windsor:NFER-NELSON.